The Life and Comics of Howard Cruse

Critical Graphics

Series Editor: Frederick Luis Aldama, Arts and Humanities Distinguished Professor, The Ohio State University

Volumes in the Critical Graphics series bring scholarly insight to single authors and their creator-owned graphic fiction and nonfiction works. Books in the series provide context and critical insight into a given creator's work, with an especial interest in social and political issues. Each book is organized as a series of reader-friendly scholarly chapters that precede the reprinting of short graphic fiction or nonfictional works—or excerpts of longer works. The critical insight and commentary alongside the creative works provide a gateway for lay-readers, students, and specialists to understand a given creator's work and life within larger social and political contexts as well as within comics history. Authors of these books situate the work of their subject within the creator's larger body of work and within the history of comics; and bring an engaged perspective to their analysis, drawing on a variety of disciplines, including medical humanities, environmental studies, disability studies, critical race studies, and women's, gender, and sexuality studies.

Recent titles in the Critical Graphics series:

Andrew J. Kunka, *The Life and Comics of Howard Cruse: Taking Risks in the Service of Truth*

Jan Baetens, *Rebuilding Story Worlds: "The Obscure Cities" by Schuiten and Peeters*

The Life and Comics of Howard Cruse

• • • • • • • • • • • • • • • • • •

Taking Risks in the Service of Truth

ANDREW J. KUNKA

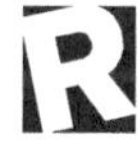

Rutgers University Press

New Brunswick, Camden, and Newark, New Jersey, and London

Library of Congress Control Number: 2021946905

A British Cataloging-in-Publication record for this book is available from the British Library.

∞ The paper used in this publication meets the requirements of the American National Standard for Information Sciences—Permanence of Paper for Printed Library Materials, ANSI Z39.48-1992.

www.rutgersuniversitypress.org

Manufactured in the United States of America

For Howard: Thanks for taking the risks

Contents

Preface

Howard Cruse died on November 26, 2019, after a short battle with cancer. Howard was an enthusiastic supporter of this book. He was generous with his time and his work. When I approached him with the idea of putting this book together, he immediately offered high-resolution scans of his art and volunteered to do an interview. He saw it as a complement to the twenty-fifth anniversary reissue of *Stuck Rubber Baby* from First Second, which will be out by the time this book sees print. He also saw it as a work that would help secure his legacy as a cartoonist for a new generation of readers who may never have been exposed to these groundbreaking shorter comics. I feel an enormous obligation to that legacy by making this the best celebration of Howard's work and enormous influence.

While I was in the preliminary stages of researching this book, soon after the proposal was "enthusiastically accepted" by Rutgers University Press in late August 2019, Howard informed me that he had recently been diagnosed with cancer (though "non-life-threatening," as he put it) and would be beginning chemotherapy treatments the following week. He wanted to let me know that, during this treatment, he would likely not feel up to doing the interview that we planned on for this book, though he offered to help in whatever way he could. "I'm happy to say that prospects look good for a complete recovery by this fall when all of this difficulty should be behind me," he wrote. We decided to push the planned interview to January, when his recovery would be in effect.

We kept in touch, and he would offer me occasional anecdotes and suggestions for the book. I was hesitant, though, to ask for too much at this time, since his recovery was more important than this project.

Then, on Sunday, November 24, Howard sent me an update on his cancer treatment: "While alternative chemotherapy strategies are being [tried] and may well restore me to blooming health, there's a real possibility that I won't be alive in January, which is when I seem to remember you were planning to interview me for the Rutgers book.... Depending on how important you feel it is to fold whatever that turns out to be into your analysis, you may want to see if there's a way to juggle your schedule to work in an earlier date for our conversation." I quickly responded with an accelerated plan for the book, including options depending on his level of energy and the amount of time he felt that he could devote to the project in light of what would obviously be more pressing and important concerns.

I never got a response, and, despite his guarded optimism, Howard passed away two days later. I regret that I wasn't able to work more quickly on this book, to be far enough along over the summer to complete the career-spanning interview that was to be the final chapter. I also regret that he never got to see the finished product, to see if it did his work justice. This would be a very different book if I had Howard's input and guidance throughout the process.

I got the chance to meet Howard once, when he was a guest at the 2016 International Comic Arts Forum in Columbia, South Carolina. He sat down next to me during a panel, and I immediately pulled out a stack of his books that I had brought with me for him to sign: the Vertigo/DC edition of *Stuck Rubber Baby*, *The Best of Comix Book* collection that had just come out, individual issues of *Comix Book*, and other assorted undergrounds containing his short works. I told him that I remember reading his "Loose Cruse" column in *Comics Scene*, which exposed me to underground comix that I would then seek out while still in my early teens, including his work. I got to ask him about the story behind "Jerry Mack." All the while, he was gracious and forthcoming. Toward the end of the conversation, I said, "I hope you don't regret sitting next to me, since I've been plying you with questions." He replied that he enjoyed talking about his work, and he was glad that I had given it attention. Later in the conference, he invited me to join him and a group of attendees for dinner. Unfortunately, I had other plans. I regret not breaking those plans.

I cannot express how important reading Howard Cruse's work was to me, from the time I was a teenager first experiencing underground comix to today. As a comics reader, it kept me interested in the medium, carrying me from the superhero comics of my adolescence into mature work that showed me the true potential for comics, both formally and emotionally. Stories like "Jerry Mack," "Billy Goes Out," and "I Always Cry at Movies . . ." made me a better, more empathetic person. If there ever were a test to qualify for humanity, *Stuck Rubber Baby* should be required reading for it.

Once the ink had settled on the contract with Rutgers, and I began telling people that I was working on this book, the responses were all identical: "Howard is the nicest person in comics," "Howard is a hero," and so on.

I'm writing this preface on November 27, 2019, the day after Howard died, while social media is flooded with remembrances of Howard and testaments to his influence, his generosity, and his kindness. He and his husband Eddie were exemplars to the power of love. The loss to the world—not just the world of comics, but the entire world—is tremendous.

If you are coming to Howard's comics for the first time through this book, then I hope this gives you an introduction to his extraordinary work and encourages you to seek out more of it. I hope I'm not setting expectations too high by saying that you may find yourself a different, even better, person once you've finished reading Howard's comics.

This book is, of course, dedicated to Howard Cruse. I feel a tremendous responsibility to make sure that this book lives up to his significance and impact on the world. I hope I did Howard justice.

November 27, 2019

Introduction

Though history and scholarship may see *Stuck Rubber Baby* as Howard Cruse's most significant work—and deservedly so—he was also a master of short-form comics, as this collection shows. The longest story collected here runs seven pages ("Billy Goes Out"), while many others are single-page stories. Unfortunately, comics creators who work primarily in the short story mode, as was the case with most underground cartoonists, don't often get the critical attention they deserve. Creators working in other short-form literary genres, like poetry, prose short stories, and prose essays, can be easily canonized and their work studied because of its inclusion in anthologies and literature textbooks. Short comics, with some exceptions, tend not to get such treatment. In addition, short comics stories are rarely collected together, as the comics publishing industry seems to favor the long-form narratives of graphic novels. Cruse struggled to get collections of his short works published: *Dancin' Nekkid with the Angels* and *The Other Sides of Howard Cruse* did not remain in print for very long after their initial publication. Cruse even resorted to self-publishing *From Headrack to Claude* in order to keep some of his most significant comics available.

This collection, then, shows the creativity, innovation, experimentation, and humor evident in Howard Cruse's shorter works. Chapter 1 contains a critical biography of Cruse's life and career as a cartoonist, as well as coverage of the scholarly reception his work has received. It also provides the context in which Cruse's work was published, especially in terms of his place in the underground comix era and after. I was lucky to have the opportunity to research Howard Cruse's letters in his archive housed in the Rare Book and Manuscript Library at Columbia University. That library also holds the Kitchen Sink Press records, which include the letters between Cruse and Denis Kitchen that provide most of the background for the period running between Cruse's first submission of *Barefootz* comics to Kitchen in 1972 through Cruse's editing of *Gay Comix* from 1979 to 1983. This material was invaluable in offering a unique, personal view of the underground press at a time of critical transition and of the creation of *Gay Comix*. The personal letters offer an intimate portrait of a cartoonist experiencing the ups and downs of a career that had an enormous impact on the history of comics in general and of queer comics in particular.

Following the critical biography, each chapter focuses on a particular theme or genre that runs through Cruse's career: his approach to personal stories that play with conventional notions of autobiography, his use of the comics medium for political and social commentary and satire, and his parodies of characters and genres from the history of comics. The chapters are framed by a general discussion of the works included, along with background on the stories' publication, context within Cruse's life and the broader U.S. culture and history, and formal and thematic analysis. In general, this book is meant to provide starting points for further discussion, analysis, and appreciation of Howard Cruse's diverse body of work. And for those who are primarily familiar with Cruse's work through *Stuck Rubber Baby*, this collection should serve as a useful companion to that groundbreaking graphic novel.

In his comics essay "Death," a darkly funny rumination on the end of life, Howard Cruse expressed a wish for his own legacy: "After I'm gone, I like to think somebody might pick up my comic books and have a chuckle!" Though not every story in this collection is meant to be funny, I hope readers also walk away from this book with an appreciation of Howard's sharp, unbridled, and often dark sense of humor.

The Life and Comics of Howard Cruse

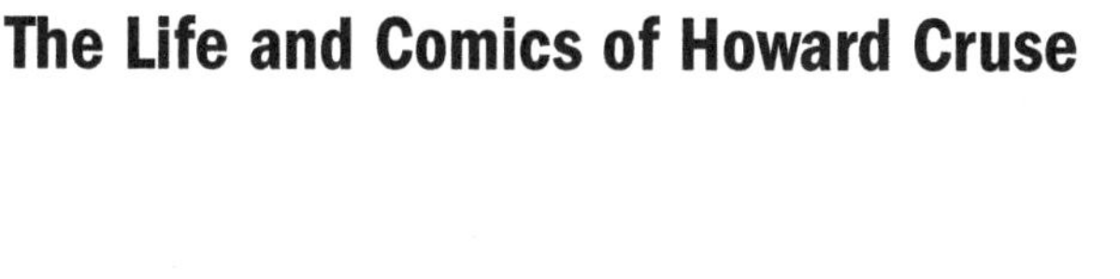

1

Critical Biography

Howard Cruse is frequently referred to as the "Godfather of Gay Comics," and for good reason. Over nearly a fifty-year career in comics, Cruse broke down barriers in the comics industry, mentored and inspired generations of cartoonists, built a community of queer cartoonists that continues to thrive, and created some of the most vital, significant, and funny comics ever made. In her introduction to the twenty-fifth anniversary edition of *Stuck Rubber Baby*—an introduction revised after Howard Cruse's death on November 26, 2019—Alison Bechdel writes, "A key part of [Howard's] legacy is something that may not withstand the test of time as well as the work itself, so I want to mention it first: Howard's personal kindness. His compassion, generosity, and lack of ego permeate his work, too. But I have run across very few artists or writers who in person are anywhere near as *nice* as this guy was" (n.p.). As Bechdel points out, the life and work of Howard Cruse are filled with these qualities, along with considerable bravery, a desire to push the boundaries of comics in both form and content, and a sharp, edgy sense of humor. Because Howard Cruse was a pioneer in queer comics, a key figure in underground comix, and a cartoonist who bridged the underground and graphic novel eras, attention to his work also involves an understanding of his life and his essential place in comics history.

Howard Cruse was born on May 2, 1944, a self-described "preacher's kid," in Birmingham, Alabama. His family moved to the small community of Springville (about thirty minutes outside of Birmingham) four and a half years later, when Cruse's father, Clyde, became a Methodist minister. However, his father had a falling out with the deacons in his church within the first year, and so he switched to the local Baptist church to become a lay minister. Meanwhile, Howard's father also earned a living as a journalist and photographer in Birmingham. Howard's upbringing in the U.S. South during the 1940s and 1950s most critically informs his major work, the graphic novel *Stuck Rubber Baby*, but it also runs through his shorter works in degrees of subtlety. At the very least, his work expresses a sense of empathy and understanding that can come from one who saw and experienced the oppressive prejudices of a culture and came out the other end with a desire to stop their perpetuation for later generations.

In the late 1940s and the 1950s, comic books were ubiquitous in U.S. culture. A 1943 market research report showed that 95 percent of elementary school kids read comic books, and monthly sales reached almost 100 million by 1954 (Tilley), when Cruse was ten years old. So, it should be no surprise that Howard Cruse's early childhood was immersed in the medium. In fact, Cruse claimed that he had drawn comics since he could remember: "When I was five or six, I was trying to imitate the comic books that we had around the house. And when I was around eight my parents told me that some people drew comics for a living. That pretty much did it!" (Ringgenberg 65). The comic books that sparked his early desire for imitation were primarily humor comics published by Dell, which, through its partnership with Western Printing and Lithographing Company, held the licenses to most animation and comic strip properties and dominated the comic book market in the 1950s.[1]

Cruse had a particular fondness for the *Little Lulu* comics of John Stanley and Irving Tripp; he even bought an annual subscription to the series. (His affection for this series can later be seen in the parody "The Nightmares of Little L*l*.") He was also an avid reader of Dell's best-selling comic books: *Walt Disney's Comics and Stories* and *Uncle Scrooge*. Like so many young readers at the time, he was fascinated by the Duck comics created by Carl Barks, featuring Donald Duck; his three nephews, Huey, Dewey, and Louie; and Uncle Scrooge. Barks, of course, was uncredited as the creator of these beloved stories, but discerning young readers could often distinguish the work of "the good duck artist," as Barks came to be known.[2]

As Cruse got older, his tastes would steer him toward the parody and humor magazine *Mad*. His fascination with *Mad* led him to scour secondhand magazine shops for back issues and to seek out the mass market paperback reprints. Eventually, he got a full education in the history of *Mad*, from the comic book version that ran for twenty-three issues under editor Harvey Kurtzman, to the magazine, where editorship transitioned from Kurtzman to Al Feldstein. Cruse reflected on the influence of *Mad* in a 1986 special issue of *Blab!* devoted to EC Comics. Foremost, *Mad* gave him a love of parody that would run throughout his career (see chapter 4). But also, artists like Will Elder, Wally Wood, Jack Davis, and Mort Drucker gave him an appreciation "for sheer craftsmanship. When Kurtzman was at the helm, both MAD's art and the ideas behind the art exemplified disciplined creators operating at peak capacity. And it was clear that they didn't reach that peak by aimless doodling. They worked. They made mistakes and learned from them. They didn't settle for the easiest solution to a given problem" (Beauchamp 58–59). This dedication to craftsmanship and work ethic is evident throughout Cruse's career. His working methods were often time-consuming, none more so than during the creation of *Stuck Rubber Baby*, and so he was never a prolific cartoonist. And in looking at Cruse's humor work, from *Barefootz* through his satires, parodies, and farces starring anthropomorphic animals and other creatures, one can discern the creative stew that formed out of these various early influences.

In addition, Cruse's father had early ambitions to be a cartoonist himself—in his college yearbook, he wrote that he wanted to be "the world's greatest cartoonist" (Willinet). Though that dream was never realized, the idea of cartooning as a professional career was evident in the Cruse household. His father also bought Howard's first rapidograph pen when he was eight, which would be his preferred drawing instrument for his comics career.

Starting at age thirteen, Howard began sending submissions to *Mad* and some of its many imitators in the late 1950s and 1960s. Those submissions were invariably rejected by *Mad*, but one was accepted by the short-lived humor magazine *Fooey* for issue 3, and he received $100 for it. (*Fooey* ran for only four issues in 1961. See figure 1.1.) Three years later, Cruse was again published by one of the more successful *Mad* knockoffs, *Sick*. Cruse's darkly comic "Suicide for the Young" appeared in issue 28 (1964) and anticipated the dark humor that would pervade his later work.[3] He had other teenage cartooning successes as well, including a strip called "Calvin" that appeared in 1959 for the *St. Clair County* (Alabama) *Register*.

Springville, a town with a population of 553 according to the 1950 census, was not a place where a child with artistic or creative interests could find much encouragement. While Cruse did have a first-grade teacher, Miss Margaret Byers, who tried to offer support to his creativity, most other teachers

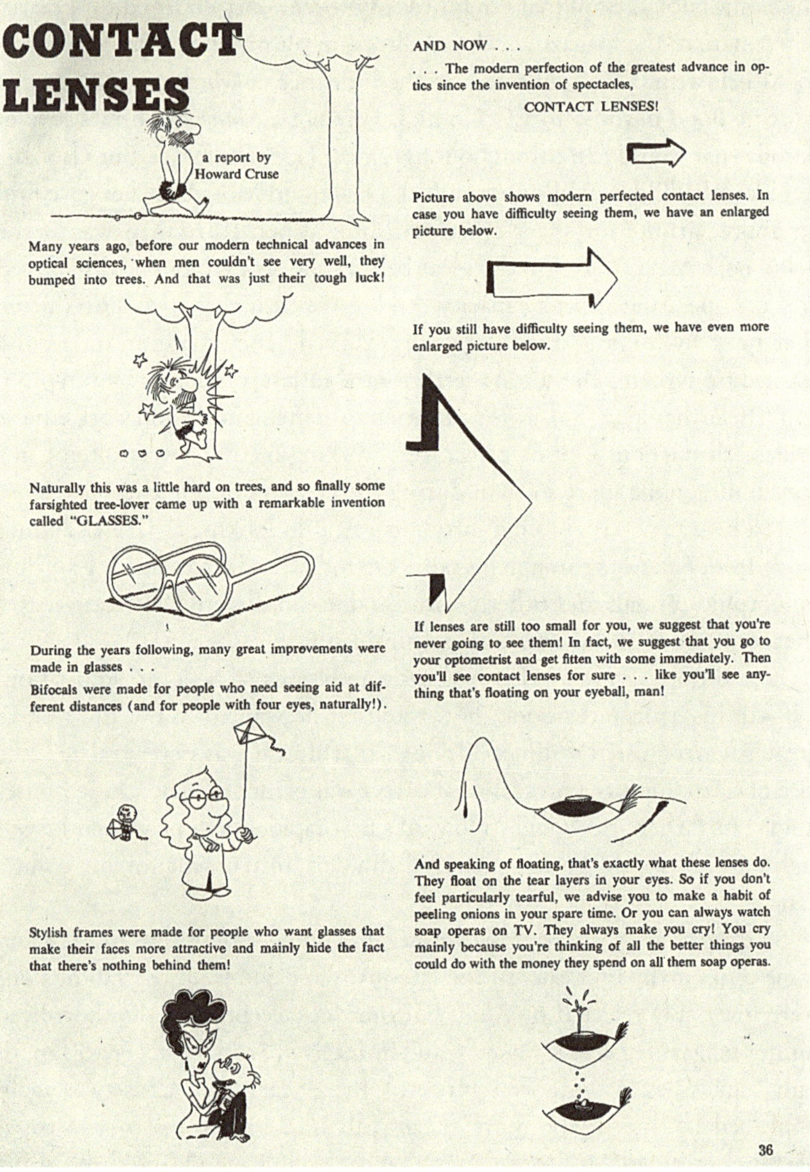

FIG. 1.1 "Contact Lenses" by seventeen-year-old Howard Cruse, from *Fooey*, issue 3 (April 1961). Image provided by Ger Apeldoorn.

and fellow students did not. Cruse claimed that, had he stayed in Springville for his entire education, he would have been stifled and depressed (LGBTCenterNYC).

His creativity flourished, though, while attending the progressive, unconventional, and experimental Indian Springs School in Indian Springs,

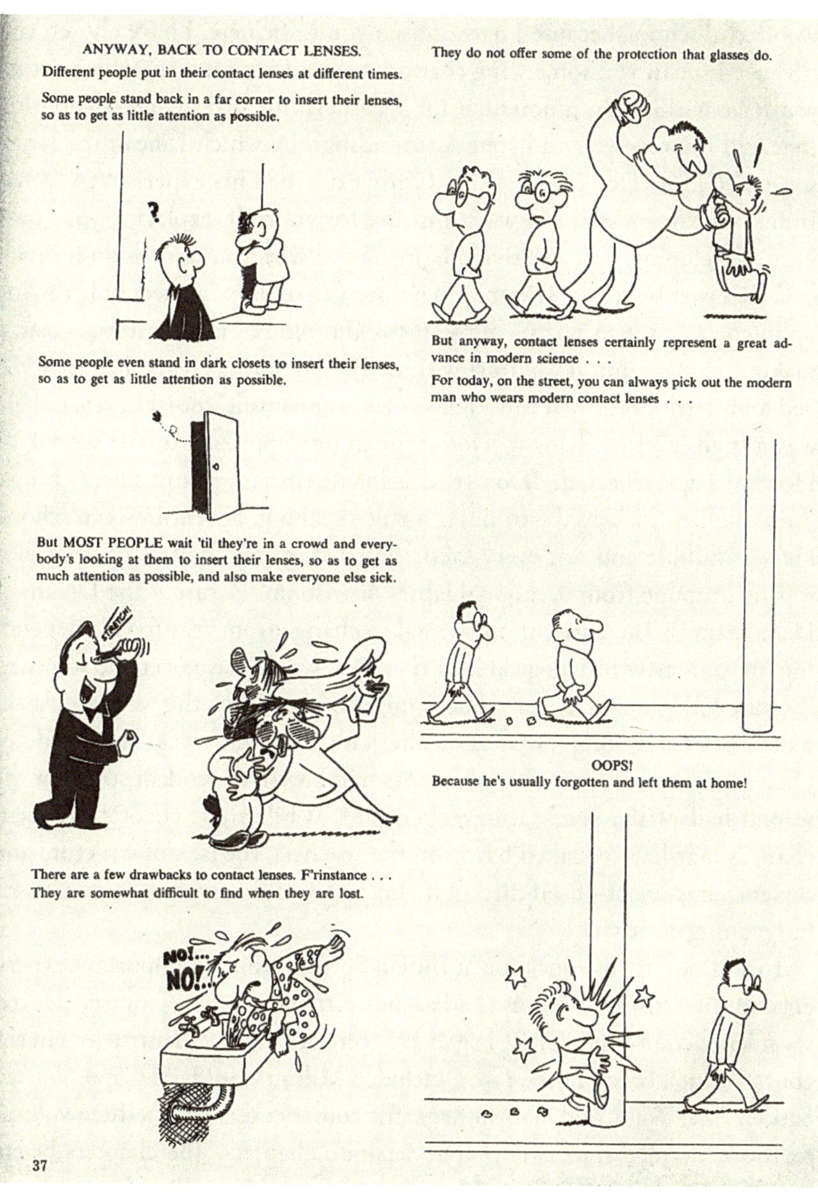

Alabama. Cruse began attending Indian Springs as a fourteen-year-old freshman in 1958 and graduated in 1962. The boys' school opened in 1952 as the brainchild of Dr. Louis E. "Doc" Armstrong, the institution's first director. Cruse's older brother Allan, who also attended Indian Springs and graduated in 1959, describes Doc's educational philosophy: "My recollection is that Doc used to take the following attitude with us: you are here, at this wonderful school, because I have chosen you to be here. I have chosen you because I see in you something that others have not yet seen, which is that you have within you a potential for greatness, for making a contribution that will improve you and your surroundings, by which I mean the larger society" ("How Doc Did It?"). As Cruse explained his experience, "What Indian Springs was about was thinking for yourself, exploring your own ideas, developing your creativity, figuring out who you were as an individual" (Ringgenberg 65).[4] This must have been an oasis for a queer kid growing up in conservative Alabama of the 1950s and 1960s: "For me it was great, a major turning point. It was during those Indian Springs years that I felt valued for myself for the first time. I didn't feel like a misfit" (66). However, there was a high level of chaos in Doc Armstrong's approach to the school, as Howard later reflected: "Doc tried a lot of things—many smart things; some slightly cock-eyed—to build a rule-breaking, adventuresome school. He was fallible and not every tactic he tried stands the test of time; nor was he immune from occasional lapses of wisdom" (Cruse, "The Dream of Democracy"). The curriculum seemed to change from year to year depending on some new pedagogical idea that Doc would have over the summer: "So one fall you'd arrive at school and he'd say: Okay, this year all classes will be two hours long and meet on alternate days. And a year later he'd say, Okay, this year the juniors and seniors will have independent study for the second half of the year" (Ringgenberg 66). While these chaotic, frequent changes may have wreaked havoc on the teachers, the lack of structure and the encouragement of self-direction and motivation served to forge Cruse's burgeoning creativity.

In addition to his education at Indian Springs, another important experience in his artistic path was the Famous Artists Cartoon Course, a correspondence course that Cruse began as a teenager in 1960.[5] Instructors in the course, which began in the 1950s, included Milton Caniff, Al Capp, Warren Sattler, Peter Wells, and many others. The course consisted of a three-volume textbook divided into twenty-four separate chapters. The chapters began with head and figure drawing, then moved to panel layout and perspective, and concluded with narrative storytelling and breakdowns of specific artists' techniques. Each chapter then wrapped up with a homework assignment. Students completed drawing assignments, usually involving some kind of scenario or visual problem to solve, that they would then mail back, at which point instructors would critique and grade the assignments. Though the instruction skewed toward 1950s newspaper strip and single-panel gag cartooning, Cruse found it extremely valuable for learning the fundamentals of cartooning (Ringgenberg 69). The influence of the course is especially notable on the character designs in *Barefootz*, which follow the models and directions found in the assignments.

Cruse became aware (or more like afraid) that he was gay around the age of eleven (Ringgenberg 67). He had a couple of formative experiences that led to this revelation. As a young comic book reader, Cruse would find back issues of *Mad* magazine at a secondhand bookstore in Birmingham. One day, while searching through a stack of magazines, he came across an issue of *Body Beautiful*, an early gay porn magazine that purported to be devoted to the art of photography and bodybuilding. He became fascinated by the magazine and soon ordered a secret subscription that he hid from his family (LGBTCenterNYC).

At Indian Springs, the boys would often smuggle in and share pornographic magazines that they had managed to obtain (though Cruse never shared his issues of *Body Beautiful*). One classmate even managed to buy a subscription to *Playboy* and have it sent to the school. Though Cruse was uninterested in the female models in the magazine, he described becoming fascinated with a feature about the daily life of Beat poet Allen Ginsberg. This, Cruse explained, was his first exposure to the idea that a public figure could be openly gay (LGBTCenterNYC).

In addition, Cruse had a close friendship with a boy who was a year older than he, and the two regularly engaged in "horseplay" that involved tying each other up (LGBTCenterNYC). As the bondage became more and more erotic, the two boys would play with progressively fewer clothes, until they were tying each other up naked. In Cruse's comics work, including "Billy Goes Out," "Jerry Mack," and *Stuck Rubber Baby*, he would often use a scene of young boys wrestling as a moment of erotic epiphany, stemming from this experience.

He later sought out research on homosexuality, but what he found in the 1950s and early 1960s treated homosexuality as, at best, a phase that young men all go through but get over, and, at worst, a mental illness. This led to denial and a desire to be straight and, therefore, "normal" (Ringgenberg 67). Yet, the education at Indian Springs taught strong critical thinking skills that caused him to question such authorities. That by no means relieved his anxiety or stopped him from attempting to find an end to this "phase," and, during his senior year of high school, he attempted suicide.

The suicide attempt led the administration at Indian Springs and his parents to recommend therapy for Cruse. However, he ended up with a homophobic therapist who claimed that Cruse's homosexual tendencies were the result of attending an all-boys school. He recommended, then, that Cruse attend a coeducational university, where he would have the opportunity to meet and date women (LGBTCenterNYC).

Cruse largely chose Birmingham-Southern College for its theater program, which he took to immediately. The Birmingham-Southern theater program was run by a dynamic, inspiring director, Dr. Arnold Powell, who would be a role model for Cruse throughout his education. Not only was Cruse quickly cast in his first production, but he also found kindred spirits in the young bohemian men and women of the theater crowd, which included some out gay members. However, the pressure to date women led him to start a romantic relationship with a fellow student and actor named Pam Walbert, with whom he shared intellectual and cultural interests. After one awkward and failed sexual encounter, Cruse revealed to Pam that he was gay. While their friendship continued, they also had spontaneous sex following a particularly stimulating academic lecture they both attended. As a result, Pam became pregnant, and the child was ultimately given up for adoption. The relationship with Pam and the unwanted pregnancy became the autobiographical core for *Stuck Rubber Baby*, where Toland Polk and Ginger Raines share a similar experience.[6]

In addition to working in the campus theater, Cruse also contributed topical single-panel cartoons to the university newspaper, under the title "The Cruse Nest." He was also able to convince the editors and faculty adviser for the campus literary magazine to publish his short comic story, "Commonest Conspiracy," which was a controversial parody of the John Birch Society.[7]

Cruse graduated from Birmingham-Southern College in 1968 with a bachelor's degree in speech and theater, and he earned a playwriting fellowship to Pennsylvania State University for their MFA program. However, after only a year in the program, he gave up his fellowship and moved to New York City, where he planned to pursue a career as a cartoonist. His time in New York was also short-lived, largely due to his inability to make a living. He returned to Birmingham, Alabama, later in 1969, where he took a job as an art director at a local television station, WBMG-TV channel 42, serving also as a puppeteer on the educational children's program, *The Sergeant Jack Show*.

Barefootz and Kitchen Sink Press

While living in Birmingham, Cruse fell in love with a budding young acting student named Don Higdon. They initially met in October 1969 at a party and bonded over their interest in psychedelic drugs. Cruse described a memorable and formative LSD trip that he took with Don while listening to a Tiny Tim record.[8] The trip started with "lingering anxieties about gender ambiguity" influenced by Tiny Tim's falsetto (*Early Barefootz* 3). Howard then focused in on Don's face, which morphed into different ages, races, and genders. Finally, Cruse explained, "I began to cry. My knot of self-doubt, buried for so long, broke loose and floated out of me, carried easily by the flood of light. I felt natural to the core, safe in the embrace of [Don's] eyes. I could see clearly that gender was irrelevant" (4). In the moment, Howard felt purged of the lingering internalized homophobia that he had been carrying for so much of his life. It was also trips like this that would inform later work in the *Barefootz* series and the short story "The Guide."

Their four-year relationship runs through Cruse's earliest successes as a cartoonist. These events seem interrelated in Cruse's life: "Looking back, I can't imagine that I'd have created *Barefootz* had Don Higdon not been in my life," Cruse later wrote (*Early Barefootz* 2). The ending of the relationship, in which Higdon decided that he needed to fulfill his ambition to be a professional actor in California, was traumatic for Cruse, and its impact on his life and work can be seen in the autobiographical strip "I Always Cry at Movies," where Cruse examines his nostalgia for the lost relationship years after it was over. In retrospect, Cruse realized that the two were heading in different directions—Don toward his acting career and Howard toward both cartooning and increased activism. That activism was sparked by Cruse's first experience with a Gay Pride march while living in Atlanta with Don (LGBTCenterNYC).

The character Barefootz began in December 1969 as a simple doodle, the pointed hair being the final characteristic that set him apart. The design was based on the geometric shape model taught in the Famous Artists Cartoon Course. Cartoonists generally refer to this as "bigfoot" style of humor drawing to describe not only the disproportionate feet that characters have, but also their abnormally large heads and eyes. Following this initial design, Cruse prepared sample *Barefootz* strips for proposals to comic strip syndicates. As originally conceived, the strip took place in an office setting, with the main character standing out because of his unconventional combination of a business suit with bare feet. These proposals did not meet with success, however.

Cruse ultimately landed a gig doing a regular one-panel gag comic called *Tops & Button* for the *Birmingham* (Alabama) *Post-Herald*, beginning on June 8, 1970, and running for two years. *Tops & Button* featured two squirrels, usually poking their heads through holes in a tree and conversing. Tops, distinguishable primarily because he pops out of the upper hole in the tree, delivers the setup to a joke, and Button, close to the ground, offers the punch line. A variety of other woodland creatures filled out the cast. The humor of the strip, therefore, was almost entirely verbal, with each vertically oriented cartoon having identical points of view on the scene. The verbal humor likely stems from Cruse's background in theater and his earlier ambition to become a playwright, and it exercised the wordplay that would also be a staple of Cruse's writing.

Like *Tops & Button*, the early *Barefootz* strips had a restricted format. *Barefootz* follows a comic strip tradition, especially seen in gag comics, where characters only appear from a couple of angles, mainly in profile. The look of the strip also resembles the "proscenium" effect of a staged play, accounted for by Cruse's background in theater, in which he was still heavily involved at the time of the strip's creation. However, this style can also be creatively limiting because it doesn't allow for varieties of angles or points of view: almost every conversation between characters is a "two-shot," to use the cinematic term. Cruse would move away from this design style with his later work, especially in *Wendel*, where he frees up angles, panel frames, and other visual elements. Later in his career, Cruse describes the "cartoony and oddly proportioned" style of *Barefootz* as potentially "disorienting" to readers who discovered his work through *Wendel* and especially *Stuck Rubber Baby* (*From Headrack* 4).

Cruse described the character as having "a tension in [his] personality between being very cosmic and very square" (Ringgenberg 88), which is evident in his look: Barefootz wears a conservative suit, but walks around in bare feet. The world of *Barefootz* is strange, though a key element of the character is that he is unphased by the strangeness. He lives in an apartment with sentient, anthropomorphic cockroaches and his roommate Glory, an unseen creature who stays under the bed and regularly shoots out frogs at anyone who looks at her (thus leading to Barefootz's catch phrase, "Don't make frogs at me, Glory!"). Glory also zaps people's minds into psychedelic experiences and performs other supernatural feats. The strip's cast includes other humans, like Barefootz's sexually frustrated friend Dolly, and Headrack, an artist who later comes out as gay in a groundbreaking story.

Though Cruse came close to publishing *Barefootz* in a Birmingham underground newspaper, that venture failed to produce an issue. He managed to land *Barefootz* in the University of Alabama's *Crimson-White* newspaper starting in June 1971, where it ran for a little over a year. In December 1972,

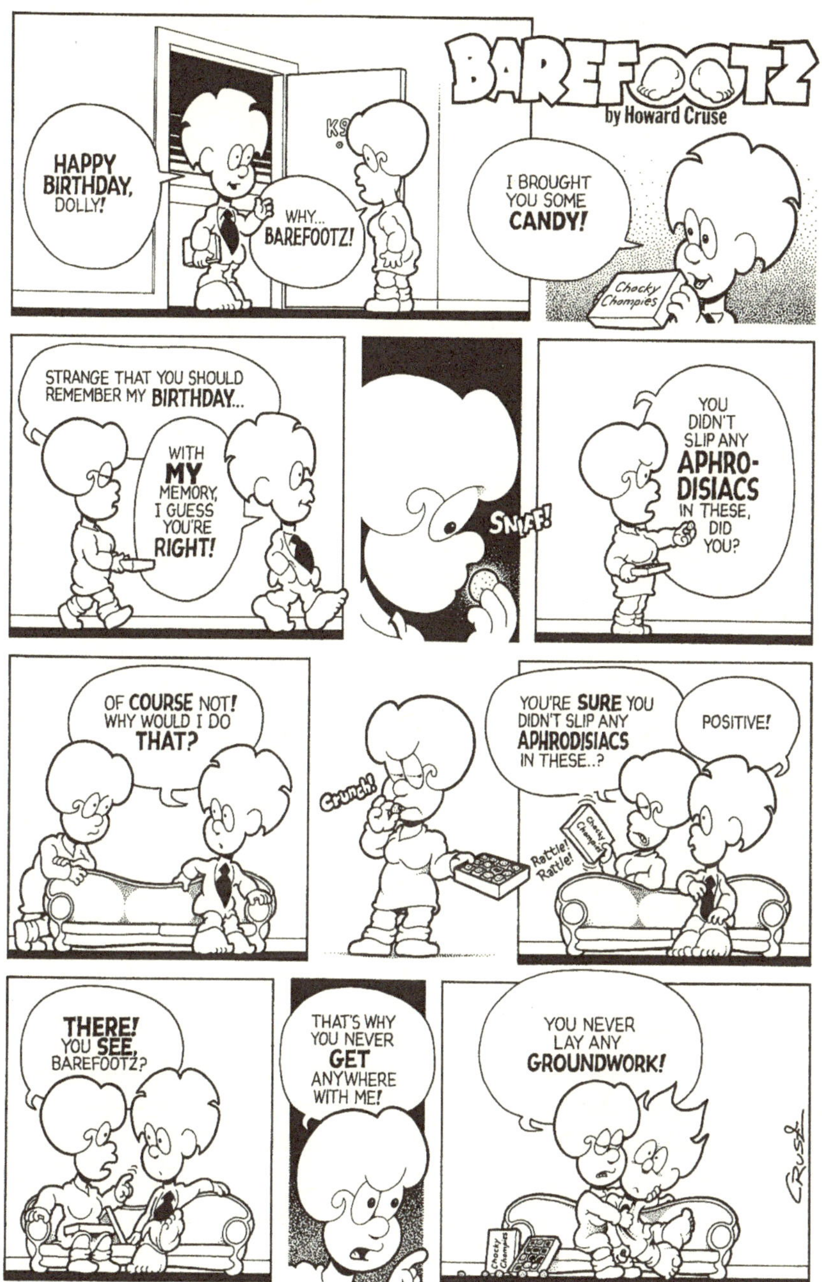

FIG. 1.2 "Happy Birthday, Dolly!" A *Barefootz* story originally published in *Bizarre Sex*, issue 3 (June 1973). Copyright the estate of Howard Cruse. Used by permission.

Cruse submitted several *Barefootz* strips to Denis Kitchen at the underground comix publisher Krupp Comic Works, which would later be known as Kitchen Sink Press. These include the nine-page story "Nuit du Tigre," along with several of the earlier strips that had already appeared in newspapers. Cruse expressed his desire to create a *Barefootz* comic book in the future, but he would also be interested in the strips being placed in one of Kitchen's anthologies. Kitchen's response was almost immediate: "I received your 'Barefootz' submissions and found them amusing. This is surprising because nearly all of the unsolicited contributions I get are miserable. I'm damned close to saying, YES! I'll publish them" (8 Dec. 1972). However, Kitchen offered a critique of the characters and relationships in the strip as the reasons for his hesitancy: more needed to be explained about the characters because these stories would be readers' first exposure to the strip. He proposed initially publishing some of the earlier strips in an anthology to establish the characters and relationships for readers, so that when they get to the longer story, they would be more familiar.

As Kitchen pointed out, such an immediate acceptance of a blind submission was nearly unheard of, and this initial exchange established a relationship between the two that would last the rest of Cruse's life. Most of Cruse's underground work would appear in various Kitchen Sink or Kitchen-edited publications, including *Snarf, Dope Comix, Commies from Mars, Bizarre Sex*, and, most important, the groundbreaking *Gay Comix* series and the Marvel-published *Comix Book*. Prior to *Gay Comix*, almost all of the Cruse material Kitchen published was in the *Barefootz* series, including three issues of *Barefootz Funnies*, which Cruse self-financed in a special relationship with the publisher.

Krupp Comic Works / Kitchen Sink Press was one of the major underground comix publishers, alongside Last Gasp, Print Mint, and Rip-Off Press, among others. Joseph Witek provides a useful definition of "underground comix": "cheaply and independently published black-and-white comics which flourished in the late 1960s and early 1970s as outlets for the graphic fantasies and social protests of the youth counterculture" (51). Because underground creators were pushing against authority and the status quo, no subject was taboo, and the comix contained plenty of sex, violence, drug use, social protest, and racial caricature. However, the underground comix industry was also dominated by white, male, heterosexual cartoonists and publishers, whose depictions of women were often misogynistic, and any references to gay sex were usually homophobic. Nonetheless, by resisting social boundaries, underground comix also opened the door for groups that were otherwise marginalized or even completely unrepresented in the comic book industry, like women, racial minorities, and queer creators. Anthologies like *Wimmen's Comix*, *Tits & Clits*, and *Twisted Sisters* provided venues for female comics creators covering various topics that were otherwise forbidden from other comics (even unexplored by other undergrounds), like abortion, birth control, masturbation, lesbianism, and menstruation. Queer creators like Mary Wings (*Come Out Comix* and *Dyke Shorts*), Lee Marrs (*The Further Fattening Adventures of Pudge, Girl Blimp*), and Roberta Gregory (*Dynamite Damsels*) also published their own solo comics, and all three would later contribute to *Gay Comix*. It was in this milieu that Howard Cruse saw a home for his own work, especially when his efforts in mainstream syndicate strips were not paying off.

The underground comix era generally began with the publication of Robert Crumb's *Zap Comix* 1 in 1968, (though works by underground cartoonists Jaxon, Frank Stack, and Gilbert Shelton predate this), with the major period of the movement ending around 1973, with the U.S. Supreme Court's *Miller vs. California* decision. At the time, underground comix were available mainly through head shops, record stores, the earliest comic shops, and mail order. Undergrounds continued well past this point, but the boom era where nearly everything the underground presses put out sold well had passed. So, Howard entered the underground just as the movement was winding down. However, by hitching his wagon to Kitchen Sink, Cruse had connected himself to one of the publishers that weathered the ups and downs of the underground market the best.

By December 1972, then, the underground bubble was bursting, and underground comix were selling a fraction of what they had been doing just a few months earlier. The downturn accelerated in 1973. Dan Mazur and Alexander Danner explain the social and cultural forces that contributed to this extreme market change: "The U.S. Supreme Court's *Miller vs. California* decision [June 1973] declared that local communities could establish their own standards for obscenity. This forced head shops, already under pressure from anti-drug forces, to discontinue offering Underground comics out of fear of prosecution. At the same time, many rebellious attitudes regarding sex, drugs, politics and dress were no longer as shocking or titillating as they had been when the Undergrounds first burst onto the scene" (40). Kitchen was blunt about this downturn in a letter to Cruse from July 10, 1973, after Cruse inquired about a late quarterly royalty payment, which would be his first one. The letter not only describes an important moment in the history of underground comix, but it also reveals Kitchen's ethical publishing practices, which would retain the loyalty of creators like Cruse through the tumultuous years to come. Specifically, Kitchen explained that creator royalties were a priority and would be paid even if the publisher had to close. He concluded on a supportive note: "The response to your work has been encouraging. You are among the new artists whose potential appears unlimited. You can, at the very least, continue to reach a growing audience" (10 July 1973). Earlier, on March 14, 1973, Kitchen had praised Cruse in a similar fashion: "I personally think you are one of the most promising new cartoonists around. Your strips display a unique style of humor. I've laughed out loud at several. And that's not a common occurrence." However, being a promising new cartoonist at what was being seen as the end of the underground comix era seems like a mixed blessing at best.

In his response letter from July 13, 1973, Cruse expressed the need for underground comix to expand its audience if it would continue to survive, and, as such, Cruse anticipated the transition from the underground to independent comics and graphic novels—a movement in which Cruse would hold an important place with his editorship of *Gay Comix* and his groundbreaking graphic novel, *Stuck Rubber Baby*, some twenty-two years later: "It seems inevitable that u-g [underground] comics must broaden its base so as not to be too dependent on the fragmenting Woodstock generation (in which I include myself). There are, and always will be, many readers who would not open an underground comic unless they were royally stoned; but you have a tremendous audience (potentially) of adults who could really appreciate the liberating humor and experimentation of your product, but who never go to head shops." Such a transition out of the near-extinct world of the head shops would happen with the advent of the direct market and comic book stores,[9] and Kitchen Sink was one of the very few underground publishers to move successfully into the direct market.

Cruse's main point is that availability is the biggest problem: the audience is there, but it doesn't have access to the material or, in most cases, doesn't even knows it exists. So, though Cruse expressed anxiety over his late arrival in underground comix, he also would ultimately participate in the very validation and expansion of the medium that he predicts.

In late 1973 and early 1974, Kitchen developed an anthology of work by underground creators for Marvel. Publisher Stan Lee had been pursuing Kitchen for a while, looking to tap into the underground audience that wasn't coming to Marvel comics otherwise. The magazine-sized series called *Comix Book* (published through Marvel's parent company, Cadence) featured such underground luminaries as Art Spiegelman, Kim Deitch, Justin Green, Trina Robbins, Skip Williamson, Sharon Rudahl, S. Clay Wilson, Bill Griffith, and

Lee Marrs, alongside creators with more mainstream credentials like Basil Wolverton and Mike Ploog. Kitchen also included *Barefootz* strips by Cruse in each issue, with prominent exposure on the full-color back covers of two issues. Cruse's inclusion in *Comix Book* not only gave him added exposure in a mainstream magazine sold through newsstands, but it also gave him a considerably higher page rate ($100) than he normally received. *Comix Book* ran for five issues between 1974 and 1976, with the first three issues published by Marvel and the final two by Kitchen Sink.

In his history of the series, James Vance details the difficulties Kitchen had navigating the demands for restraint from Marvel and the criticism from underground creators that the series was too watered-down for the mainstream audience. Cruse himself was the target of some of the latter criticism, most notably by Art Spiegelman, who "reserved particular disdain" for the cute, cartoony, "bigfoot" style of *Barefootz* (Vance 25). In a December 10, 1974, letter to Cruse, Kitchen also added *Zippy the Pinhead* creator Bill Griffith as another cartoonist who found Cruse's work, along with most other contributors to *Comix Book*, "beneath contempt." Kitchen attributed Spiegelman's and Griffith's harsh criticism to their plans for creating the rival magazine *Arcade* through Print Mint.

This was, in fact, a common criticism levied against Cruse's early work. Even when *Barefootz* was defended, as Bill Sherman did in 1980, the defense was positioned as counter to more widespread disdain for the strip: "Among comix readers, admitting that you like 'Barefootz' is about as cool as admitting that you like nose hair. Say it with a large enough crowd and you're liable to be met with withering stares suggesting that your time'd probably be better spent studying back issues of Little Dot" (Sherman 12). Sherman's praise for the strip, though, is in its content: "Cruse may Draw Cutesy, but the contrast between the cutesiness and the frantic comic desperation of his main cast is one of the strip's main tensions" (13). (He reserves his highest praise for Headrack.) Indeed, the criticism *Barefootz* received overlooks the subtler, more transgressive ideas that slip in through the strip's cartoony veneer. As Cruse responded to the criticism, "My strategy at the time was to do comics that looked innocuous, like might be found in mainstream comics pages, but had a counterculture subtext and a certain subversive quality—but I know a lot of people couldn't get past the 'nice' look. I felt there was a validity in the approach, but it was an uphill battle to get the underground people turned on to it" (qtd. in Vance 25). The initial resistance to *Barefootz* due to its cute style seemed to follow Cruse throughout his career. For example, in 1979, John Benson's overview of underground comix for the magazine *Alternative*

Media criticized Cruse's style as being too conventional and incongruous with the personal styles of other underground cartoonists. Benson complained that some later underground comix, especially those published by Denis Kitchen, tended toward "'professional' slickness [and] slight lighthearted material. Perhaps Howard Cruze's [*sic*] 'Barefoots' [*sic*] strip, with its cutesy cartoon midgets and cockroach antics is the archetypal example" (21).[10] Cruse made his case directly to Benson in a September 8, 1979, letter: "I intentionally took a different road from the more grotesque or angular styles favored by the artists commonly regarded as heavyweights because I wished to use the tension between surface and essence to examine issues which I consider to be of great importance in our world." As *Barefootz* progressed, it dealt more with issues of sex, sexuality, and larger philosophical questions about humanity's relationship with the universe, including some mind-warping psychedelic experiences. Later, Cruse would exploit this incongruity between style and content even further, using a "cute" humorous cartooning style in conjunction with edgy humor, sharp political satire, and commentary.

Kitchen also advised Cruse to take a "darker" approach to his art, which would make it stand out more to readers (28 Mar. 1974). This advice results in Cruse's adoption of Zip-a-Tone, which would become a staple of Cruse's style during this period. Zip-a-Tone was a brand name for a type of screentone that contained shading through minute dots on a clear adhesive sheet or "screen" that could be cut out and laid on a comics page. It could be used for anything from background shading to smaller shadows on figures and objects. Cruse used it mainly for the backgrounds of *Barefootz*, with a kind of wavy gradation of shading that added to the strip's trippy feeling. He later explained that this was a practical consideration for *Comix Book*, due to the fact that Stan Lee did not like the stark black-and-white imagery of the strip in its earlier appearances, plus it allowed for more texture and shading. However, in later years, he abandoned this technique because it gave his comics an artificial, manufactured quality (Ringgenberg 86). In *Stuck Rubber Baby*, Cruse achieves texture and depth through intense crosshatching and stippling while also maintaining a handmade quality that he found missing from Zip-a-Tone.

In early 1975, Cruse ramped up plans to self-finance a *Barefootz* comic through Kitchen Sink. Kitchen agreed to this, with a fee of $950 to cover the costs of 10,000 copies and a cover price of 75 cents (4 Feb. 1975). A group of investors, collectively known as Woofnwarp Productions, financed the printing of what came to be known as *Barefootz Funnies*, with a two-thirds cut of the 30-cent return on each issue. Though Cruse was able to pull together investors to back the publication of three issues of *Barefootz Funnies*, he was disappointed in the sales. Issue 1 (published in July 1975) started out well, selling around 4,700 copies of its initial 10,000 print run and earning back the initial $1,000 investment within six months.[11] While that was good enough for the investors to back a second issue, the follow-up, which came out in April 1976, was far less successful, selling only a little over 1,000 copies in its first quarter of release. Cruse wrote to Kitchen on August 9, 1976, about his disappointment in the sales of issue 2.[12] A big part of the problem, as Kitchen had explained, is that the underground comix market was driven by anthologies featuring multiple artists, rather than "solo books" collecting work by a single creator. By 1976, with the undergrounds in sharp decline for several years, the only creators who could sustain profits with solo books were Robert Crumb and Gilbert Shelton (*Fabulous Furry Freak Brothers*). For Cruse, though, the solo book was more economically and artistically viable than publishing short stories in anthologies that had infrequent publication schedules and sporadic royalty payments. Cruse was faced here with the perennial artist's dilemma between art and commerce. As he told Kitchen: "I'm losing confidence in the underground cartoonist's traditional approach of 'hanging in there' whatever happens; I'm scratching about for courses of action. If I can't do exactly what I believe in, my fallback position is doing something else well and guarding my options to return to my primary area of interest later, or 'on the side'" (9 Aug. 1976). This art/commerce debate is not unique to Howard Cruse, but it serves as a defining theme and frustration throughout much of his career, where critical acclaim and artistic success do not always translate into financial gain. Though Cruse laments the economic and creative restrictions of short-form comics in anthologies, some of his most significant work would appear in such publications, and his most important impact on comics history would come as editor of one such anthology series.

Throughout the time that it was published at Kitchen Sink through its presence in various anthologies like *Snarf* and *Comix Book* and in the *Barefootz Funnies* solo comic books, *Barefootz* evolved from a gag strip to "an extended allegory populated by a repertory troupe of players perfectly tailored for social and political satire, observations about personal relationships, and explorations of the very nature of reality" (*From Headrack* 12)—all of which were themes and concerns that dominated Cruse's work throughout his career. But toward the end of his time working on *Barefootz*,[13] Cruse began producing other comics stories, mainly still for Kitchen. Stories like "Unfinished Pictures" and "The Guide" would show the new direction that his work was headed toward.

In 1974, Cruse made some tentative steps to come out publicly as a gay artist. One was a single-panel cartoon about homosexual guilt published in the *Homosexual Counseling Journal*, an academic publication with a very narrow and specialized audience and, therefore, a safe space for an artist nervous about the impact that his open sexuality might have on his career as a cartoonist. Another, smaller step came in 1976 and involved a gag about using semen as toothpaste in the story "Big Marvy's Tips on Toothcare," which appeared in *Snarf* 6 (February 1976).

By 1976, Cruse was ready to take the bigger step of creating his first gay-themed story for *Barefootz*. "Gravy on Gay" outed the semi-regular character Headrack, a struggling artist figure and friend of Barefootz. Cruse included the story in the second issue of *Barefootz Funnies*. It shows Headrack not only coming out, but also making the decision to address gay activism directly in his art. In addition, Headrack faces insidious and violent homophobia as a result of this decision. Therefore, the story both addresses and parodies Cruse's own internal debate about bringing out gay issues in his comics.

For a variety of reasons, late 1976 and early 1977 marked significant professional and personal turning points for Cruse. One such incident seems to set up Cruse's future work on *Gay Comix*. In late 1976, Cruse contributed to a series of risqué Christmas cards that Kitchen produced. The cards proved so popular that Kitchen almost immediately initiated a series of general occasion cards in the same vein. For this set, Cruse submitted several designs, including one that contained a "gay joke." The front of the card features a smiling figure of unspecified gender, with the caption, "I don't mind your being the most beautiful, intelligent, cosmic, fun, perceptive, companionable and groovy gay person I've ever known . . ." with the inside punchline, ". . . I just <u>wish</u> you wouldn't <u>flaunt</u> it!"[14] Though Kitchen initially rejected that card as too narrowly focused, he considered the card could be an opportunity to tap the gay consumer market. In a November 29, 1976, letter, Cruse responded to Kitchen's concern that the card's joke was too narrowly focused: "I don't know what you're thinking of when you speak of an idea that would be appropriate for all gays, since there is no more common denominator between All Homosexuals than there is between All Heterosexuals—other than that they all have to put up with bullshit about not 'flaunting' (that is: being natural and open about expressing) their affections." Cruse continued, "It's a market that is uniformly ignored by the media as a consumer group. You may well be justified in your caution. Of course, such caution also insures the perpetuation of their 'invisibility' and second-class status in our culture." Kitchen was convinced by Cruse's

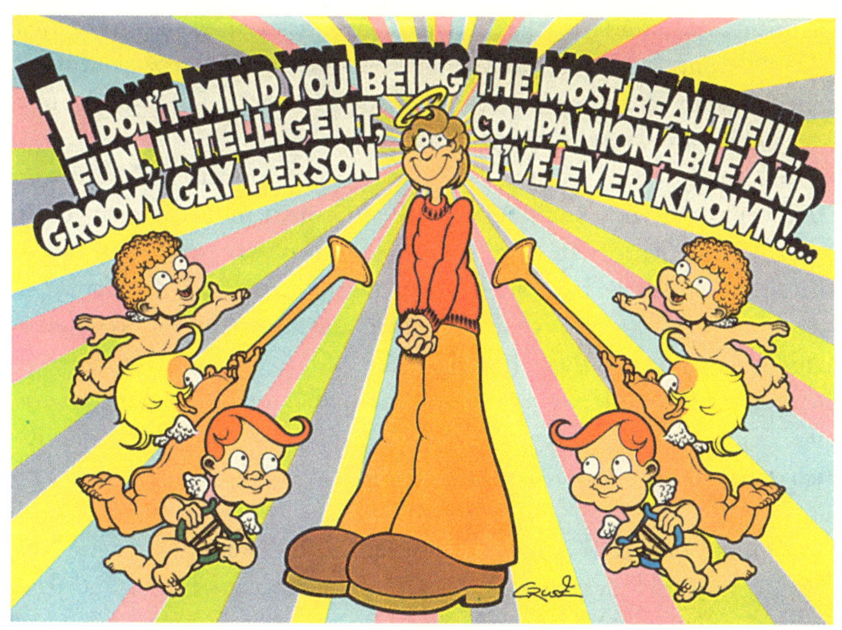

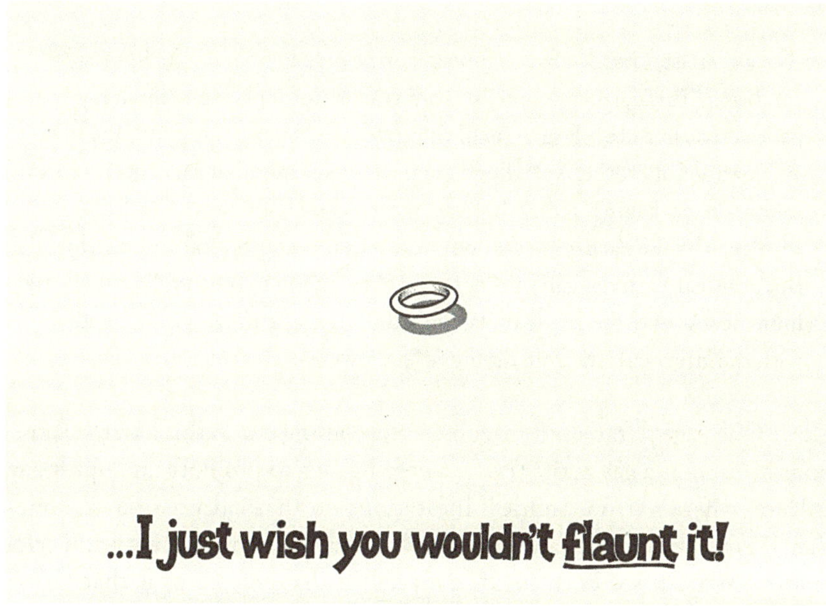

FIGS. 1.3 AND 1.4 Greeting card published by Kitchen Sink, 1976. Image provided by Denis Kitchen.

argument to go ahead with the gay card (though the word "cosmic" is removed from the front—see figure 1.3), but, more important, this impassioned and informed statement about the neglect of the gay market is one of the first steps in Howard Cruse coming out as a gay cartoonist.

The card, however, received a strenuous objection from a Washington, D.C., company called Stone Age, which specialized in distribution to gay bookstores. On January 28, 1977, Kitchen wrote that the head of Stone Age—identified here only as "Deacon," the nickname for Larry Page Maccubbin[15]—specifically rejected Cruse's card: "He said he and fellow gays he had shown it to found it offensive. I assured him the intent was not offensive and he believed me, and admitted to being very sensitive himself, but they will not carry the card." Kitchen suggested that Deacon and Cruse should communicate with each other, so Cruse reached out to the distributor with an impassioned and heartfelt letter.

In his response to Deacon, Cruse defended the joke as applying to "the virtually universal pressure experienced by gay people not to 'flaunt' their gayness" (31 Jan. 1977). More important, Cruse revealed something that had even greater significance and import:

> As a gay artist, I think I have a unique perspective to offer on the human condition. This particular greeting card is a fleeting, ephemeral bit of my perspective, but I think such small things leave a beneficial residue. The small affirmations of brother/sisterhood are the true substance of existence; politics is only the packaging. Unfortunately our lives and happiness are ruled so ruthlessly by the packaging that political action becomes vital and worthwhile. But political attitudes can smother what they intend to protect. Freeze out the humaneness of the individual's laughter and the gay culture will suffer along with the larger culture from dead-end shallowness.

Cruse's message reframes the argument: by coming out in this letter, he positions himself as a gay artist trying to use humor to promote and uplift gay culture, where narrow political limitations on that culture, like the ones that Deacon expresses, can cut out positive avenues for creativity and celebration. We can see both in the card and in his defense of it that Cruse makes some of his earliest steps in using his cartooning to explore and express gay identity. Though there may have been low risk for Cruse to come out to Deacon in this letter, the fact that he also copied Kitchen on it is significant. Kitchen, however, made no comment about Cruse's revelation in his follow-up letters.

Maccubbin responded on February 3, 1977, that his objections were misinterpreted: while he felt that the card would be positively received by gay consumers, it was part of a set that was designed for the "straight market," which might not even see the card as a joke. That is, the straight audience might send the card out of sincerity, asking the gay recipient to stop flaunting their homosexuality. The company, however, decided to distribute the card anyway, and Maccubbin even asked Cruse if he would consider designing a line of cards for the gay market. Nearly two years later, when Kitchen proposed the idea of *Gay Comix* to Cruse, this experience lingered over the discussion, where both referred to it as a reason to be hesitant about the new venture.[16]

Following the loss of his job at a Birmingham ad agency in late 1977, Cruse decided to move again to New York City so that he could be closer to the sources of work for a freelance cartoonist and designer. As he explained years later in a January 29, 1984, letter to Denis Kitchen, "I moved to New York for two very specific reasons: (1) I wanted to try and advance my career; and (2) I wanted some new kinds of stimulation for my art. I was willing to lower my standard of living considerably in my quest for these goals." After eight months of freelancing, he eventually got a full-time job as art director for Starlog, the publisher of the eponymous science fiction magazine as well as the horror magazine *Fangoria*. Later, Starlog would publish *Comics Scene* magazine, where Howard would contribute a regular series of essays under the title "Loose Cruse." For the publisher, Cruse did pasteups and other labor while also producing interstitial cartoons to run in each magazine. He even created a short-lived strip for *Fangoria*, *Count Fangor*, which ran in the first three issues of the magazine.

During the late 1970s, Cruse also found work in the "men's magazine" market, in such periodicals as *Eros*. For that magazine, Cruse created the superhero parody *Nakedlady*, which ran for three issues before *Eros* editors pulled the plug. Toward the end of the decade, Cruse contributed to "Playboy Funnies," the comics section of *Playboy*, after he was invited to submit his sample work by fellow underground cartoonist Skip Williamson (creator of Snappy Sammy Smoot), who was then working in the *Playboy* art department. For *Playboy*, Cruse produced parodies of existing comic strips like *Tumbleweeds*, *B.C.*, *Snuffy Smith*, and *Momma*, showcasing his talent at mimicking other cartoonists' styles, which we can also see in his parodies "The Nightmares of Little L*l*" and "Raising Nancies." Soon after his parodies started, however, *Playboy* got cold feet over the idea of publishing any parodies of existing properties that could result in a lawsuit after the magazine received threatening letters from comic strip syndicates.[17]

The departure from *Playboy* coincided with Cruse's decision to serve as editor of *Gay Comix* (Cruse shares news of his departure from *Playboy* in the same August 25, 1979, letter to Kitchen where he accepts the editorship of *Gay Comix*). As such, the work for *Playboy* had moved Cruse further away from the honest and personal portrayal of gay themes and issues that he had begun in "Gravy on Gay," which was becoming a stronger source of inspiration. As he later wrote of this period, "What caught me by surprise once I jettisoned my last vestiges of heterosexual privilege and began spilling my gay inner life onto paper, was the boost it can give to an artist's creativity to have a lifetime's worth of secrets and fears flushed out of his or her brain with one single jolt of honesty" (*From Headrack* 38). In hindsight, then, the transition from "Gravy on Gay" to *Gay Comix* seems natural for an artist coming into acceptance of his own identity and the creative opportunities that acceptance afforded.

Also in 1979, Cruse began his relationship with Eddie Sedarbaum, which continued for the rest of his life. The two met at a gay discussion group in New York City. Following the meeting, the group went out to dinner together, where Howard and Eddie detached themselves from the rest of the party and hit it off. At the time, Eddie was separated from his wife of ten years. Within six weeks, Howard and Eddie moved in together, with a "back-out plan" that allowed either one to move out at any time. The plan, of course, was never activated, as the couple remained together for forty years. The stability of this relationship seems to have given Cruse the solid footing to undertake *Gay Comix* for Kitchen and complete his professional coming out.

Gay Comix

The advent of *Gay Comix* serves such a critical role not only in Cruse's life, but also in the history of comics, that it deserves extensive attention. In an August 21, 1979, letter, Kitchen proposed to Cruse the idea of creating an anthology series that would provide a venue for gay and lesbian cartoonists: "Would you be interested in editing (and, presumably, contributing to) a gay-oriented comic book? It's the kind of issue comic I'm aiming more for. And I think it's a viable product." He envisions a book that might appeal to both gay and straight readers. Kitchen already established the title of the series as "Gay Comix," rejecting the alternative spelling "Gay Comics" because Marvel had previously published a comic under that title in the 1940s. Such a venture would come at considerable personal and professional risk for Cruse, since it would require that he come out publicly.

Nonetheless, Cruse almost immediately accepted the challenge in a letter from August 25. One of the primary challenges Cruse mentions right off the bat is identifying queer cartoonists who would be willing to contribute to the series. Only a few cartoonists were publicly out, like, for example, Mary Wings, the creator of *Come Out Comix* and *Dyke Shorts*, or the late Vaughn Bode. Because there were no formal networks of queer cartoonists, as there would be a decade later (see Galvan, "Making Space"), they had to tread carefully when soliciting material. Cruse lamented the fact that there were no prominent, openly gay cartoonists at the time, so no one outside of the underground had set the stage for others to follow. As Cruse wrote, "There are no role models, and it's hard to know what risks there are. Underground comix can pretty easily absorb gay artists, but UGs are a ghetto of sorts—a glorious ghetto, but a ghetto—and few cartoonists want to have their career options limited to the UG realm" (25 Aug. 1979).

It is important to contextualize just how professionally risky coming out in the comics industry was at this time. Within underground comix, the way had been paved by lesbian cartoonists Mary Wings, Roberta Gregory, and Lee Marrs in the early to mid-1970s. However, the mainstream comics industry, consisting of Marvel and DC, but also the burgeoning independent publishers, was neither open nor progressive. Andy Mangels wrote a two-part essay about queer comics, "Out of the Closet and into the Comics," which appeared in *Amazing Heroes* in 1988. In the articles, Mangels talks to a variety of queer comics creators and staff, yet all requested anonymity except Howard Cruse. As one closeted gay artist explains at the end of the second part, "The fear of losing that opportunity [to make comics] is part of the reason I don't come out. Another reason is that I don't want to be known as a 'gay artist.' I want to be known as a good artist. I don't want to be stereotyped. I don't want to be like Howard Cruse—sorry Howard—and be known as *just* the gay artist" ("Out of the Closet," II:63). This artist, then, does not see Howard as the inspirational figure that encouraged a generation of queer comics creators to come out, but instead as a cautionary tale, connecting Howard's lack of mainstream comics credits with stereotyping and a homophobic response from that part of the industry. Lee Marrs, however, had some success in mainstream comics, especially at DC, where she worked on horror titles in the 1970s and later wrote the hardcover graphic novel *Viking Glory: The Viking Prince* (1991), with painted art by Bo Hampton, and a *Zatanna* miniseries (1993), drawn by Esteban Maroto.

Despite the challenges and obstacles that Cruse foresaw, he also thought that the world was ready for such a comic book, and he almost immediately laid out a mission statement for the series: "I'd want it to be, first and foremost, honest and affirmative, not rhetorical, coming from personal experience and observation rather than generalized propaganda. I'd want to get past stereotypes and find humanness. I'd want it to be funny without apologies and without smirks. I would not want a freak show which the reader would stand apart from and feel superior to. I would like it to be well drawn, but I'd sacrifice draftsmanship quickly for honesty" (25 Aug. 1979). Cruse also wanted to avoid the overtly pornographic content that had dominated most of the earlier gay comics, like Larry Fuller's *Gay Heart Throbs*, which Cruse found disappointing. In addition, underground creators were not particularly sensitive to gay issues when addressing the subject. As Cruse explained, "Previously, most gay underground comix material had either quasi-homophobic stuff by straight cartoonists [like S. Clay Wilson's gay pirate stories and "Ruby the Dyke"] or shallow, campy stuff by gays. Actually, I'm really talking again about the gay *male* stuff. Some great lesbian stuff had been done before *Gay Comix* [Mary Wings's work, for example], and I tried to use those women in the series" (Ringgenberg 84).

The initial solicitation for contributors went out to the whole Kitchen Sink mailing list of artists, regardless of sexuality. The letter opens with a kind of call to arms for queer creators:

> Many gay artists have never included the gay facets of their lifestyle in their published work, whether from fear of ostracism on a personal level, possible negative reaction from fans, or the chance that homophobia among editors or publishers could result in long-range career damage. As a gay artist myself, I have shared those fears.
>
> However—as those of you reading this who are yourselves gay know all too well—gay people are an important and productive part of every area of human life, and our silence about ourselves has allowed myths and pointless hostilities to poison our own lives and the lives of straight people around us. It's time to take some risks in the service of truth. (Undated letter)

This inspirational rallying cry is followed by a mission statement for *Gay Comix*, detailing what Cruse expects from submissions. He places the highest value on three areas, in order of preference: "emotional honesty," humor, and "craftsmanship in drawing and storytelling." He qualifies the last item, however, as one that is potentially disposable as long as the other two elements are present. This acknowledges the reality about contributions that Cruse would ultimately see for the series: many submissions would come from relatively inexperienced and untested cartoonists who would require encouragement and mentorship, which Cruse enthusiastically provided.

In the letter, Cruse also shows concern about avoiding the pornographic focus that other gay comics had in the past. This is a delicate line to navigate because he also wants to encourage the freedom available within underground comix. So, he stresses, "if sex is presented, I'd prefer it in a context of characters and human feelings. GAY COMIX should be about people and not about genitals." He is also equally resistant to polemical screeds in the form of comics, though politics likely can't be avoided. In general, he wanted to capture the variety of voices and perspectives that could fall under the banner of "gay comix."

Another key element of Cruse's vision for the comic is reaching the widest possible audience, both gay and straight: "While its truths may be hard and may offend some, I'd like it to be informed with the larger truth that gay and straight people are more alike than different; that searches for love and struggles against oppression are not the exclusive burden of any group. Heroic as we may sometimes be, clownish as we more frequently are, we straights and gays are all, most importantly, human beings." This statement, in particular, is worth considering in light of Cruse's own contributions to the series, as can be seen in subsequent chapters where "Billy Goes Out," "Jerry Mack," and "Safe Sex" are discussed individually.

The letter is nothing short of inspirational and establishes a clear editorial vision for the series, both what it is and what it is not. The first issue of *Gay Comix* came out in September 1980, and Cruse opened it with a rousing introduction that further reinforced the rallying cry for queer comics creators: "In drawing this book, we gay cartoonists would like to affirm that we are here, and that we live lives as strewn with India inked pratfalls, flawed heroics, and surreptitious truths as the rest of the human race." The first issue featured work by Cruse, Lee Marrs, Billy Fugate, Roberta Gregory, Demian, Mary Wings, and Kurt Erichsen, among others, and sported a Rand Holmes cover, which reflects one of Cruse's main goals for the comic.[18] Of this initial lineup, the female creators had the most established careers: Mary Wings had already self-published *Come Out Comix* (1973) and *Dyke Shorts* (1978), Lee Marrs had created stories for various women's underground anthologies, and Roberta Gregory had put out *Dynamite Damsels* (1976). Additionally, all three had already dealt with homosexual content in their earlier work.[19] Future issues of the series edited by Cruse would continue to feature these creators as well as Robert Triptow, Jennifer Camper, and Jerry Mills. One particularly notable achievement during Cruse's run:

Gay Comix published the first trans comics story, "I'm Me!" by David Kotler, in issue 3 (December 1982), which shows the level of inclusivity that Cruse strove for in his tenure.

Cruse and Kitchen continued to push publicity for *Gay Comix*, recognizing that it required a different approach than Kitchen Sink's other products. Press releases and review copies went out to gay publications (like the *Advocate*, Boston's *Gay Community News*, and *Christopher Street*) as well as to gay and lesbian bookstores and distributors. They also pursued further outreach to creators, but with a new caveat that Cruse did not want each subsequent issue to be a carbon copy of the previous one. To this end, later solicitation letters contained an extensive list of possible topics, running three typed pages. The suggestions ranged from the intensely personal to the overtly political and cultural, from stories celebratory of aspects of gay culture to those critical of it (like prejudices and tensions between gay men and lesbians or racism and ageism in the gay community). Even different genres were encouraged, like nonnarrative essays or journalistic pieces. Themes included religion, parenting, drug abuse, coming out, media representation, drag, antigay violence, police brutality, and, of course, homophobia. The list, overall, seemed to encourage a wide variety of submissions so that the anthology would not get stuck in a rut of similar narratives.

Gay Comix not only proved groundbreaking for comics in general, but it also pushed Cruse into a new phase in his cartooning. The first two issues of *Gay Comix* featured two of Cruse's most significant, innovative, and creatively successful stories: "Billy Goes Out" and "Jerry Mack." In the fourth issue, Cruse took the opportunity to address the AIDS crisis through the story "Safe Sex," which also established Cruse as a comics essayist—that is, using the comics form for the nonfiction essay genre.

The impact of *Gay Comix* has reverberated throughout the history of LGBTQ representation and creative activity in the comics medium. Famously, Alison Bechdel has long cited her discovery of *Gay Comix* 1 at the Oscar Wilde Memorial Bookstore in New York City as the catalyst for her career as a cartoonist: "I'd been out as a lesbian for a couple of years, [but] the notion of cartoons about being gay had never crossed my mind. It was like, 'Oh, man! You can do cartoons about your own real life being a gay person'" (qtd. in Chute 358). In addition, Cruse and Kitchen's struggle to find queer contributors for the early issues highlighted the need for LGBTQ networks among cartoonists. Margaret Galvan discusses the importance of Cruse's editorship of *Gay Comix* in forming and influencing communities of queer cartoonists.[20] In particular, Galvan highlights the relationship between Cruse and lesbian cartoonist Jennifer Camper. Around the time that *Gay Comix* 1 was about to be released, Camper reached out to Cruse about possibly participating in the project. Camper opened her introductory letter to Cruse by mentioning a shared connection to cartoonist Trina Robbins. Here, Galvan argues, is the foundation for a network ("Making Space" 377). Additionally, Camper also mentions her work as a cartoonist for *Gay Community News* in Boston, Massachusetts. Cruse's response reveals that his interest in Camper is twofold: as a budding cartoonist who can serve as a future contributor to the anthology (fulfilling a need for more lesbian cartoonists, which Cruse struggled to find outside of early contributors like Mary Wings, Lee Marrs, and Roberta Gregory) and as someone connected to the gay community in Boston, where the series could be promoted and the first issue reviewed. Cruse's mentorship and leadership would influence Camper's work as a cartoonist and as editor of the *Juicy Mother* anthologies, for which Cruse contributed stories.[21]

Because of the relatively high profile position as editor of *Gay Comix*, Cruse also had numerous opportunities to produce topical comics for other publications, most notably the *Village Voice*. In these instances, he was given free rein by the editors to approach the chosen topic as he wanted, something he recognized as a rare freedom (*From Headrack* 74). The first strip he did for the *Voice*, "Sometimes I Get So Mad . . ." (1981), was also his first mainstream work to reveal his gay identity outside of the underground.

At the time that *Gay Comix* was starting, Cruse also had been hired for some notable freelance work. Len Brown at Topps hired Cruse in 1980 to revamp the Bazooka Joe comics that came with Bazooka bubble gum. Cruse turned Joe and his gang into modern teenagers for a few dozen strips. He later returned to Topps in 1985 when Brown, Art Spiegelman, and Mark Newgarden were hiring underground artists to create the *Garbage Pail Kids* cards and comics. Meanwhile, in 1981, Cruse drew comics for a new children's magazine, *Bananas*, published by Scholastic. Many of these strips were *Mad*-style social commentaries aimed at elementary school readers. Cruse's collaborator at *Bananas*, Bob Stine, would go on to greater success and notoriety as the creator of the *Goosebumps* young adult horror series, under the pen name R. L. Stine. Though Cruse was credited for the *Bananas* comics, they and the uncredited Topps work were invisible to the underground audience that he had developed with *Barefootz* and the new readers he was gaining through *Gay Comix*. Nonetheless, these jobs brought in income that the more visible comics work did not.

Cruse's work as editor on *Gay Comix*, while personally rewarding, consumed much of his time with little monetary reward. As an editor, Cruse had to solicit submissions, communicate with artists, mentor young talent, arrange for the covers, and publicize new issues, in addition to the editing of each individual comic book. Also, by 1983, Cruse was at work creating the *Wendel* strip for the *Advocate*—a series that would take up the bulk of his time for the remainder of the decade. Therefore, after producing four issues of the series between 1980 and 1983 and bringing numerous queer cartoonists into professional publication, many for the first time, Cruse turned over the editorial reins to Robert Triptow. Triptow produced one issue for Kitchen Sink, then the series moved to publisher Bob Ross, who owned the *Bay Area Reporter*, a gay newspaper out of San Francisco. By the fifth issue, the series was no longer financially viable for Kitchen Sink. While the series sold well enough, it simply didn't sell in comic book stores and other traditional markets for Kitchen Sink books, so the company's existing distribution and publicity didn't work. Kitchen had to maintain a separate distribution and publicity system in order to keep the comic book in gay and lesbian bookstores and to advertise it where its reader base would notice. Thus, Kitchen sold the trademark to Ross in order to put the comic book in the hands of a publisher with better access to the right markets and publicity outlets.

Triptow put *Gay Comix* on a regular quarterly schedule, as opposed to the irregular, nearly annual schedule that Cruse had kept. Triptow also introduced themed issues, like the superhero-focused issue 8, as well as issues highlighting single creators, as with issue 9, devoted to Jerry Mills's *Poppers* strip. However, after a gap of three years between issues 12 and 13 (summer 1988 to summer 1991), Triptow handed the series off to editor Andy Mangels, who brought with him experience in the world of mainstream superhero comics. Following issue 14, Mangels renamed the series *Gay Comics* in order to distance it from the underground and establish mainstream credentials, which he explained in an editorial for issue 15. Mangels continued to produce issues focused on single creators, like Roberta Gregory (#21) and Alison Bechdel (#19), and another superhero issue (#20). He also tried to maintain the equal representation of gay male and lesbian creators that Cruse had informally established. In 1998, after eighteen years of publication, *Gay Comics* ended with issue 25, a giant comic containing eighty pages of one-page stories by creators from throughout the history of the title, including Cruse.

During and after its run, *Gay Comix/Comics* served as a model and inspiration for numerous queer comics anthologies and helped to form networks of LGBTQ cartoonists that continue today. As Cruse reminisced in a 2019 interview with Samantha Puc at the *Beat*, "It's been very satisfying to see the

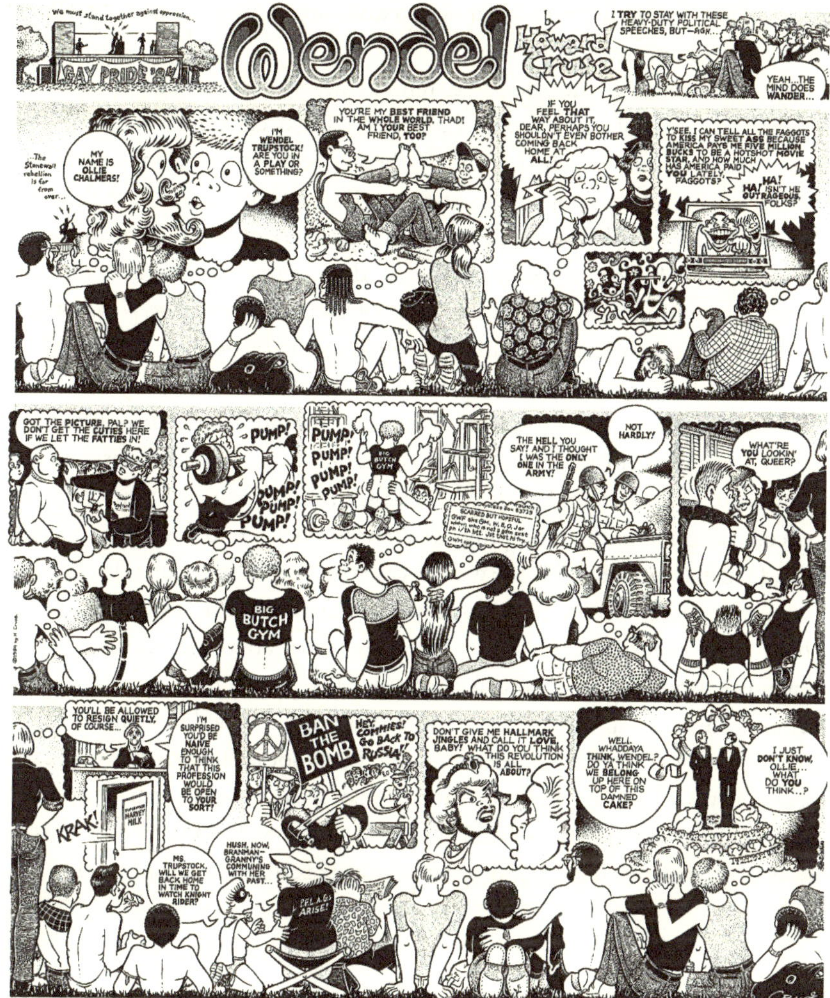

FIG. 1.5 "Gay Pride '84" from *The Complete Wendel* (54–55). Though the page is divided into three panels, this strip should be viewed as one long, panoramic panel. Copyright the estate of Howard Cruse. Used by permission.

younger generation coming along and expanding what we tried to start with *Gay Comix*. When I was doing *Gay Comix*, I was the editor you had to go to if you were a queer cartoonist who wanted to be out, but by now, I'm no longer the gatekeeper. I don't even know all of these people. . . . I feel really proud of the younger generation for taking the ball and running with it." Cruse made occasional contributions to the series under both editors, and in issue 25 he provided a final reminiscence on his own coming out as a comics creator, *Gay Comix*'s founding, and the progress that had been made since. He also continued to contribute new comics to anthologies put out by the younger generation of queer cartoonists.

Another concern, and one that remained a worry through most of his career, was a fear of being typecast as strictly a "gay cartoonist"—that is, one who was primarily occupied with gay themes and topics who would not be sought out for other projects. In an interview with Blake Bell for the book *"I Have to Live with This Guy!,"* about the partners of cartoonists, Ed Sedarbaum explained, "Sometimes he gets sick of doing gay stuff. Certainly for commercial, economic reasons, the fact that every time *The Village Voice* would call him for a comic strip or an illustration, it would be because it's something gay" (177). Even the late collection *The Other Sides of Howard Cruse* was designed to show the variety of themes Cruse addressed throughout his career—the very title implies a reader who is only familiar with Cruse as a "gay cartoonist." When Tom Spurgeon asked Cruse if the title of that collection reflected anger about stereotyping, Cruse responded, "I don't see it as an angry title, I see it as more of a 'By the way, in case you've totally begun pigeonholing me . . . [laughs] I'm more than the gay cartoonist.' I think it's useful. It's not that I feel someone's consciously neglecting me or anything, it's just that for obvious reasons the more unusual role that I've played in the comics field is bringing myself—and helping to usher other gay and lesbian cartoonists—into visibility. It's entirely understandable that's something that would catch people's eyes."[22] However, Cruse's next project, the regular comic strip *Wendel*, published in the gay periodical the *Advocate*, would take Cruse further away from the eyes of even underground comix readers for the next six years.

Wendel

Wendel ran in the *Advocate*—a nationally distributed biweekly periodical—from 1983 to 1985 and from 1986 to 1989, first as a series of one-page strips and then as two-pagers following the switch from tabloid to magazine format.[23] For that time, *Wendel* focused primarily on the romantic developments of Wendel Trupstock's relationship with the budding actor Ollie Chalmers. The series also had a rich supporting cast, including Wendel's activist parents; Ollie's unpredictable friend, Sterno; Wendel's co-worker Deb and her lover, Tina; *Gayblaze* publisher Newton Blowright; Ollie's son from an earlier marriage, Farley; and many others who would make both large and small impacts on the series. For example, Cruse devoted a twelve-episode narrative to the new relationship between Sterno and his bodybuilding lover, Duncan. "The

Romance of Sterno & Duncan" became the central story in *Howard Cruse's Wendel Comix,* which Kitchen Sink released as a single-issue comic book in 1990. Along the way, *Wendel* also became a document of gay life in the Reagan era, including the so-called Moral Majority and its oppressive homophobia couched as "family values," the AIDS crisis, and the growth of gay activism in the period. In a January 18, 1984, letter to comics writer Jan Strnad, in the midst of *Wendel*'s run, Cruse ruminated on his own relationship to Wendel and Ollie, as well as the strip's place in queer history: "I've recently begun to realize that Wendel and Ollie really are flip sides of Howard Cruse. Wendel is something of an idealization of the youth I would like to have been. My lover Eddie says Wendel is like a puppy: spontaneous, absolutely unembarrassed about seeking and giving affection. Wendel also has a naïve streak. But he's no child; he's 25 and can negotiate the practical challenges of life very well. He's what we gays call a 'post-Stonewall gay.'" By the latter term, Cruse refers to someone too young to have experienced the oppressive conditions that gay men and lesbians suffered from and fought against prior to the 1969 Stonewall Riots, which opened up a new period of gay activism.

Cruse originally proposed *Wendel* to the *Advocate* toward the end of 1982, when the editors reached out to Cruse about a regular comic strip after they had reprinted "Sometimes I Get So Mad . . ." from the *Village Voice.* Cruse pitched a variety of strips, including one featuring Clark and Luke from "Dirty Old Lovers." However, the editors settled on *Wendel.* His initial publications were sporadic and inconsistent, but positive reader response led the editors to offer a long-term contract, resulting in the strip becoming a regular feature in each issue. It first appeared in the "pink pages" of the *Advocate,* where the personal ads were located. To go along with the spirit of those ads, Cruse intended *Wendel* at first to be a sex farce and satire of gay culture, similar to Harvey Kurtzman and Will Elder's *Little Annie Fanny,* which appeared in *Playboy* (Ringgenberg 91). Like Annie, the initial version of Wendel was a kind of innocent, Candide-like figure. If one looks at the complete series, however, this approach to the strip only lasted for three episodes before Wendel is introduced to Ollie Chalmers, at which point Cruse begins to explore the developing relationship between Wendel and Ollie that would become the crux of the series. Even in those earliest strips, though, Cruse introduced several important recurring cast members, including Wendel's liberal parents and his lesbian activist co-worker, Deb. Quickly, then, *Wendel* offered Cruse the opportunity to detail the ups and downs of a gay relationship during the tumultuous period of the mid- to late 1980s. To do this, he tapped into his relatively new relationship with Eddie Sedarbaum. Like Eddie, Ollie Chambers had been married before coming out. Ollie had a son, Farley, which allowed Cruse to also explore the subject of gay parenting through Wendel, for whom it was a new experience.

When the *Advocate* switched from tabloid to magazine format in 1985, Cruse opted to end *Wendel*, finding the reduced dimensions too limiting for the one-page strip. After a year, however, the magazine negotiated *Wendel*'s return by promising Cruse two pages per issue. When the strip returned, Cruse used the new format to explore more contemporary issues and develop longer, ongoing narratives, taking advantage of the serial potential of the strip. He also began introducing even more new characters, like Wendel's uncle Luke and his lover Clark (both returning from Cruse's "Dirty Old Lovers" story) and Sawyer, Wendel's childhood friend and first lover, who had been diagnosed with AIDS.

The strip proved successful for both Cruse and the magazine, and so Cruse tried to spin off other publications to reach a larger readership. During and after the time that *Wendel* appeared in the *Advocate*, Cruse also published a collection with the Gay Presses of New York (1983), a softcover collection through St. Martin's (*Wendel on the Rebound*, 1989), and a one-shot comic book with Kitchen Sink (*Howard Cruse's Wendel Comix*, 1990). The St. Martin's volume was intended as the first collection in a series, but the publisher decided to cease publication after the first collection did not sell well enough to continue the series. Two comprehensive *Wendel* collections appeared following the strip's final publication in the *Advocate*: *Wendel All Together* (Olmstead Press, 2001) and *The Complete Wendel* (Universe, 2011), the latter also with an introduction by Alison Bechdel.

Despite these attempts to publish *Wendel* outside the *Advocate*, the strip never drew a larger audience. Cruse expressed concern in the late 1980s that, while the strip was popular with readers of the magazine, it took him away from the audience he had built with his underground and independent comics. However, immediately following the end of *Wendel* in 1989, Cruse embarked on his most ambitious project, the graphic novel *Stuck Rubber Baby*, which would take up almost all of his creative focus and further remove him from the spotlight for the next five years.

Stuck Rubber Baby

Stuck Rubber Baby is a bildungsroman about a young gay man, Toland Polk, coming of age in the U.S. South of the 1960s, against the backdrop of the civil rights movement. In the process of coming to grips with his sexual identity, Toland inadvertently fathers a child with his girlfriend, budding folk singer Ginger Raines, and the couple choose to give the child up for adoption. Meanwhile, Toland is also confronted with his own inaction and fear at publicly revealing his queer identity when his outspoken gay friend, Sammy Noone, is lynched by a homophobic gang.

Though the central plot about Toland and Ginger comes directly from Cruse's own college experience with his girlfriend Pam, and he drew some other incidents from his own life, Cruse resisted autobiographical readings of *Stuck Rubber Baby*. He described the key differences between himself and Toland: "I graduated from college, I was not a drop out. Toland gets far more into the Civil Rights movement than I ever did personally" (Rubenstein 113).

Cruse documented the origins and creation of *Stuck Rubber Baby* in great detail through several interviews and the backmatter for the twenty-fifth anniversary edition of the graphic novel, along with an online journal published on his website. The opportunity to create a graphic novel came soon after *Wendel* ended in 1989. In a conversation with his friend Martha Thomases, she recommended that Cruse look into Piranha Press, a new imprint that DC Comics was developing in order to publish prestige graphic novels that might not otherwise fit with their brand of mainstream superhero comics.[24] Cruse then had a meeting with Piranha editor Mark Nevelow about the opportunity. In this meeting, Cruse pitched an idea focused on his own experience accidentally fathering a child while in college. When Nevelow expressed interest in the idea, Cruse emphasized that the work would deal centrally with homosexuality, in case DC Comics might have reservations about such a topic. He also stressed that he would need editorial autonomy on the project—Nevelow could see an initial script, but he would not see pages until each chapter was done. Even then, the editorial notes would be treated as suggestions that Cruse could dismiss if he disagreed.

Cruse sought out assistance from Mike Friedrich, publisher of Star*Reach comics and agent for comics creators, on the proposal and, once that was accepted by DC, on the terms of the contract. The original plan was for two years for the composition of *Stuck Rubber Baby*, which would be covered by an advance on royalties.

The scripting process involved writing something like a play script, which hearkened back to Cruse's days in the theater program at Birmingham-Southern College. However, Cruse made several attempts before settling on a script format, trying out thumbnails and typed dialogue pasted into word balloons. Then, he went through multiple drafts of the script over the course of five months, before submitting the final version to DC for approval. The project was already proving to take longer than he had anticipated, and this delay predicted further delay in the creative process.

An early consideration that Cruse had to make regarded his style. The first attempts at character designs for Toland and Ginger looked closer to Cruse's *Wendel* style, which was more appropriate for a humor strip than a graphic novel dealing with sexuality, racism, and civil rights. However, after experimenting with extensive cross-hatching and stippling to give his figures depth and texture, he settled on the style that he would use for the whole graphic novel (though this style would evolve over the four years it took to complete the book, and Cruse would have to redraw some of his earlier pages to match). In order to capture all of this fine detail, Cruse's original art pages were 2.5 times the size of the final printed version. This new style is certainly a departure. More on the realistic end of the spectrum, its seeds can be seen in "Jerry Mack" and "I Always Cry at Movies . . ." Nonetheless, the change was a shock to readers who had been used to the rounder, humorous style of *Barefootz*, the other underground comix, and even his most recent work in *Wendel*.

In addition to the painstaking cross-hatching and detail in Cruse's stylistic choices, the narrative also required extensive historical research in order to get the details of Kennedy-era Alabama and the civil rights movement right. During visits to his mother in Alabama, Cruse took pictures of various houses and neighborhoods that could be used as backgrounds. He also researched 1960s-era fashion and automobiles to create an accurate atmosphere. Most significant, he talked to people involved in the civil rights movement, and he sought out sources who had known about the gay and lesbian culture in Birmingham at the time. He did not want any historical inaccuracy to pull the reader out of the story.

Up until the point in which Cruse decided to embark on *Stuck Rubber Baby*, his work had primarily appeared as short stories and strips of fewer than ten pages—even the longest *Wendel* story arc, "The Romance of Sterno & Duncan," only ran for twenty-four pages. Creating a 210-page graphic narrative, especially one requiring such intensive historical research and artistic details, would involve significant challenges for Cruse.

During the process of creating *Stuck Rubber Baby*, DC ended the Piranha Press imprint when Nevelow left the company. However, the publisher remained committed to the project and folded it into another new imprint—Paradox Press—which had a similar focus and mandate. Most of

Paradox's successes came in the crime genre, like *Road to Perdition* and *History of Violence*, both of which were made into popular, critically acclaimed films. They also picked up Scott McCloud's *Understanding Comics* from Kitchen Sink Press, and they launched the successful *Big Book* nonfiction anthology series, including *The Big Book of Conspiracies*, *The Big Book of Hoaxes*, and *The Big Book of Weirdos*. Paradox editors Andrew Helfer and Bronwyn Taggart took over duties from Nevelow.

In the end, *Stuck Rubber Baby* took Cruse four years to complete (1990–1994), twice what he originally planned, which also meant that the advance DC provided had run out halfway through the process. Cruse had to find a way to support the remainder of the project, especially because, as he explained in an interview with Anne Rubenstein on the book's publication, "about 95% of my professional energy has gone into drawing this one product" (107). With little other income from freelance cartooning, Cruse brought in some money by preselling the original art before the book was complete. Such patrons included playwright Tony Kushner (who provided an introduction for the first edition), *Teenage Mutant Ninja Turtles* creator Kevin Eastman, and Cruse's brother Allan, among others. In addition, Cruse and Eddie Sedarbaum received the $25,000 Stonewall Award from the Anderson Prize Foundation. These annual monetary prizes went to gay and lesbian activists who had made a positive impact. A variety of other efforts were undertaken to pursue grant funding and individual sponsorship of the project. Friends and fellow cartoonists rallied around Cruse to finish the graphic novel; as he described, "I think most of them saw this book as something that had some importance beyond just the career of Howard Cruse. I think they saw it as having themes that were worthwhile and deserved to be shared with the world of comics readers as well as with those people who don't normally read comics but might be encouraged to read a book that dealt with social issues of some importance" (Rubenstein 107–108).

These predictions of the book's literary and social value proved true, as *Stuck Rubber Baby* received almost immediate positive reception upon its initial publication. Cruse won a Harvey Award in 1995 and an Eisner Award for Best Graphic Novel in 1996. The *Comics Journal* devoted a long "Critical Focus" section to the book's release in its November 1995 issue (number 182). The section contained critical assessments of the work by Chris Brayshaw, Ray Mescallado, and Ho Che Anderson, alongside an interview with Cruse by Anne Rubenstein. Mescallado even praises the graphic novel as "the next *Maus*" (99). Not all of the contributors are wholly on board with this praise, however. Anderson expresses the shock that those who may have dismissed Cruse's work in the past felt when they first saw *Stuck Rubber Baby*: "The one thing that stands out about [Cruse's work] in retrospect was my being vaguely put off by the cloying sentimentality. All of his characters seemed to live in this wonderfully cushy world of greeting card sentiment where at the end of the day, despite all the strife and anarchy, the characters [*sic*] problems were mended by a hug and a few heartfelt platitudes" (104). Anderson concedes, however, that his past experience with Cruse's work was limited to borrowing a couple of books, including a *Wendel* collection, from a friend years earlier, and such a limited view of Cruse's work does not do it justice. Nonetheless, Anderson's attitude reflects the stereotype that his earlier underground critics, like Art Spiegelman and Bill Griffith, felt about *Barefootz*. After reading *Stuck Rubber Baby*, though, Anderson finds that "Cruse appears to have matured this time around and shed the sentimentality in favor of [a] more realistic, grounded approach" (105). That praise, however, is tempered by Anderson's criticism that Cruse has embraced "political correctness" instead, which seems to water down the depiction of Toland Polk in particular.

Mescallado and Anderson represent two critical poles in the spectrum of responses to *Stuck Rubber Baby*: on one end, immediate placement in the comics canon; on the other, a qualified success most notable for its technical achievements. On the latter point, Cruse receives almost universal praise for his detailed artistic style. As Ho Che Anderson colorfully wrote, "Howard Cruse draws like an absolute motherfucker" (105). With every new edition of the book, including the fifteenth anniversary edition from DC/Vertigo (2010) and the twenty-fifth anniversary edition from First Second (2020), the graphic novel receives renewed critical praise as a landmark work in both gay literature and graphic novels in general.

Most of the scholarship that addresses Howard Cruse's work focuses specifically on *Stuck Rubber Baby*.[25] This makes sense for a few reasons. First, comics studies scholarship has a "graphic novel bias" that privileges longer, book-length works over short stories or single-issue comics. Second, it is an "auteurist" work—that is, the result of a singular vision by one creator, rather than the collaborative work of writers, artists, letters, and colorists that goes into most mainstream comic books. These two biases come from comics studies origins in the humanities, where single creators or auteurs are celebrated and individual works get placed in a canon for teaching and study. Though *Stuck Rubber Baby* has gone in and out of print since its original publication, it still has been canonized within the field of comics studies by virtue of the critical attention it has received combined with its appearance on course syllabi. Therefore, it has also been the only work by Cruse that has been widely available for some time. Most important, though, are the themes of race and sexuality that *Stuck Rubber Baby* addresses, which make the graphic novel fit into common scholarly and academic concerns.

The scholarship on *Stuck Rubber Baby* tends to focus on the intersection of Black and queer civil rights that Cruse addresses, though more attention is given to the racial elements of the narrative, especially the depiction of African American characters.[26] Gary Richards places *Stuck Rubber Baby* into two southern literary traditions: what Frank Hobson calls "white southern racial conversion narratives" (qtd. 162) and the "coming out novel"—which is not indigenous to southern literature but certainly appears often, as in works by Truman Capote and Dorothy Allison (163). The former subgenre involves stories, usually autobiographical, in which white protagonists come to grips with their privilege and involvement in the white supremacist hegemony. Richards, however, is critical of Cruse's depiction of African American characters, pointing out that all of them are equally tolerant of homosexuality, thus eliding the well-documented homophobia that existed among African Americans at that time, especially as spread through many churches: "Cruse conspicuously removes all traces of black homophobia and has the black community—and he does present it as a unified, solitary one—affirm gay existence in virtually all forms. In contrast, white homophobia circulates with both great freedom and the intent to punish and seclude, as does white gay racism" (170).

Curiously, Cruse was concerned with this very issue of depicting Black homophobia when he composed *Stuck Rubber Baby*. As he explained to Anne Rubenstein:

> This book went through five drafts before I drew the first picture, and in early drafts I had Reverend Pepper exhibiting homophobia overtly and rejecting his son [Les] who was gay. But after talking to people, like a black doctor in Alabama with an activist history who was tremendously useful to me, I changed my tack. He told me stories and he introduced me to other black people who told me stories. We talked about the way that gay people were viewed in the black churches in the '60s. Obviously it would vary. All it takes is one homophobic minister to stir up homophobia in a church, white or black. But he did say it was common for there to be leadership figures in the church who were prominent—the choir director frequently, or Deacons—who everyone knew were gay. They wouldn't talk about it, but on the other hand they would bring their partners to social functions and it was just generally known. This did not

> cause them to be shunned or viewed as not welcome. I realized that I had almost stumbled into a stereotype by assuming that Reverend Pepper would be overtly homophobic. (111)

So, it is Cruse's attempt to avoid a stereotype of the homophobic Black minister that opens him up to the criticism of idealizing Black acceptance of homosexuality, even though he also based that acceptance on the research (albeit anecdotal) that he conducted for the book. Richards does acknowledge, though, that such clear and unequivocal statements about equality and prejudice serve as a valuable lesson for a "protest novel," which requires the sacrificing of a certain level of complexity (181–182).

Rachel Kunert-Graf, in her analysis of lynching iconography in *Stuck Rubber Baby* and the graphic novel *Incognegro*, builds on Richards's critique. Specifically, Kunert-Graf points out the problems with Toland seeing himself in Emmett Till's and Sammy Noone's murders. Sammy, in particular, is an outspoken gay man whose death comes about because he openly declares his sexuality and decries racism on television—something Toland is not and does not seem inclined to do. Therefore, Toland's epiphany that he could have been lynched just like Sammy does not completely ring true. Kunert-Graf calls this "problematic identification" (330)—seeing oneself in the suffering of others and thus reducing or negating the others' experience as nothing more than a vehicle for one character's insight.

Jorge Santos Jr. follows similar criticism when he describes *Stuck Rubber Baby* as "less interested in telling African Americans' history than in rendering the white societies responsible for their marginalization" (224). Santos specifically criticizes the "pat intersectional logic" that links the lynching of Emmett Till with that of Sammy Noone, a move that puts the Black civil rights movement and the gay rights movement on the same historical continuum (144). Santos challenges "the narrative strategies that Cruse employs to transfer both the agency and the traumas of the African American protagonists of the civil rights narrative onto the primarily white homosexual characters of his novel, which invariably reduces the overlap between these marginalized communities to a naively utopian fantasy" (145). That fantasy is additionally derived from the ease in which the white queer characters and their allies work together with the Black characters toward their shared goals. Richards also identifies as utopian many of the locations in *Stuck Rubber Baby* where Black and gay white characters can intermingle peacefully, like the local gay bar, the Rhombus; the Black jazz club, Alleysax; and the Melody Motel (172–175). Again, though, these locations were based on real places in Birmingham, Alabama, that Cruse both experienced in his youth and researched while creating the graphic novel. He recalled just how struck he was by the openness and acceptance he experienced at Sand Ridge, the jazz club that was the basis for Alleysax; Cruse later interviewed other patrons of Sand Ridge to confirm his experience there (Rubenstein 113).

This criticism highlights one of the major challenges that Cruse faced in creating a work that deals with such complex and enduring problems as racism and homophobia. Regardless of whether or not it was a good or bad creative decision, Cruse chose to render his message about bigotry and acceptance in a straightforward and unequivocal way in order to communicate it as clearly as possible.

Julie Buckner Armstrong directly addresses Richards's criticism of *Stuck Rubber Baby*, and her comments relate to Santos's objections as well. First, Armstrong relies on Cruse's own experience that informed his depiction of African American characters and of locations like Alleysax, the Rhombus, and the Melody Motel. Second, she conducted a personal interview with Cruse, which helps to further cement the connections between his experience and the milieu he depicted. Armstrong counters Richards by arguing that Toland genuinely risked himself by marching in solidarity with Black protesters and also by going public with his sexual identity. In this reading, Toland becomes "a fellow traveler on the political margins" with the Black characters like Shiloh, Anna Dellyne, and Reverend Harlan Pepper (123).

Armstrong also argues that Cruse resists the "consensus memory" of the civil rights movement by revealing marginalized spaces where integration could take place—gay bars, after-hours jazz clubs, and clandestine motels rather than the contested public spaces of lunch counters and city buses. Cruse does this by "queering civil rights movement history and integrating gay history" (124), since both histories separately have traditionally elided the other. Armstrong continues, "By doing so he provides a significant fictional intervention in the telling of consensus narratives, using Birmingham as a template for creating a more inclusive civil rights story" (124). This reading, then, fits *Stuck Rubber Baby* with other, later civil rights graphic novels, like Lila Quintero Weaver's *Darkroom: A Memoir in Black and White*, Ho Che Anderson's *King*, and John Lewis, Andrew Aydin, and Nate Powell's *March*, all of which also challenge consensus narratives of the civil rights movement.

Despite the strong critical reception following the publication of *Stuck Rubber Baby* in 1995, Cruse faced limited opportunities for new comics. He became a regular contributor to the short-lived humor magazine *Harpoon*, which ran for three issues in 1999 (see more on *Harpoon* in the discussion of "My Life as a TV Pundit" in chapter 3). Other rare strips include a one-page story for the *Village Voice*, "A Zoo of Our Own" (2001), regarding recent zoological studies of homosexuality among animals, and the short story "Funny Dork!" for the middle-reader anthology *Been There, Done That: School Dazed* (2016). Cruse also maintained an active and vibrant website that combined new material with an archive and commentary on earlier work, as well as an occasional blog. Most important, Cruse supported and contributed to a number of queer comics anthologies: "Auntie Moo's Typewriters" and "Bleaktown Laffs" in Jennifer Camper's *Juicy Mother* 1 (2005) and 2 (2007), respectively; "My Hypnotist" for the anthology *Young Bottoms in Love* (2007); the autobiographical story "Then There Was Claude" for the *Book of Boy Trouble, Vol. 2* (2008); the *Blondie* parody "Coming Out with the Bunksteads" in Rob Kirby's *QU33R* anthology (2014); and the one-page cartoon "The Monster Who Moved Right In!!" for the queer horror anthology *Theater of Terror: Revenge of the Queers* (2019), which is Howard's last published work.[27] That he continued to lend his name to these mostly independently published anthologies demonstrates how he remained a supporter and guiding figure in queer comics for the remainder of his career. In addition, his participation in these projects bridges a gap between the current generation of queer cartoonists and those pioneers like Cruse who were among the first to come out publicly. As such a pioneer, he is also featured in Vivian Kleiman's documentary, *No Straight Lines: The Rise of Queer Comics* (2021), which is the companion film to Justin Hall's 2012 anthology *No Straight Lines: Four Decades of Queer Comics.*

Cruse also published two collections of his short strips in later years. *From Headrack to Claude*, an anthology of his gay-themed comics, came out through the self-publishing service Lulu in 2009, with a modified and revised ebook version from Northwest Press in 2012. The title refers to Cruse's first gay character (Headrack from *Barefootz*) and his most recent one at that point, from "Then There Was Claude." Independent publisher Boom! also released *The Other Sides of Howard Cruse* (2012), collecting the cartoonist's strips on various other themes along with many of his *Barefootz* stories.

After twenty-four years living in New York City, Howard and Ed decided to move to rural North Adams, Massachusetts, in 2003. The small town appealed to them because it had fashioned itself as an artistic community. And because Massachusetts was one of the first states to legalize gay marriage, the two were wed in 2004. During the 1990s, Howard taught cartooning at the New York School of Visual Arts, and he took up teaching again in 2006 for the Fine and Performing Arts department at Massachusetts College of Liberal Arts, where he offered classes on cartooning, storytelling, and the graphic novel for the next three years. Howard officially retired in 2009 and continued work on freelance and pro bono comics and design projects, including a lot of volunteer work in the North Adams community. He also got a chance to return to the stage in local community theater productions.

From May 17 to July 6, 2019, a retrospective exhibit of Cruse's work, titled "Gay Love," ran at the Galerie Comic Art Factory in Brussels, Belgium. Around the same time, plans were made for a twenty-fifth anniversary edition of *Stuck Rubber Baby* to be published by First Second. The reissue was published posthumously in July 2020. During that same month, Howard Cruse was inducted into the Eisner Comic Industry Awards' Hall of Fame. In his acceptance speech for this posthumous honor, Ed Sedarbaum recounted a key but often hidden element of Howard's legacy: "I learned only after Howard's death from cards and emails that came to me that he had been a mentor to so many developing artists over the years. 'You don't know me,' the notes often began, 'but twenty-five years ago, I wrote to your husband for advice about a comic I was writing.' Apparently Howard enjoyed mentoring artists and getting to know artists and learning from those artists because he continued many of these relationships through the years" (Comic-Con International). Howard passed away on November 26, 2019, following treatment for lymphoma.

In a 2012 interview, Tom Spurgeon asked Howard Cruse about the legacy of the undergrounds for contemporary comics. Cruse responded:

> The important thing about the legacy from the undergrounds is that the ground was broken and that young artists take it for granted that there's nothing out of bounds for the comics medium. I think that's great. I don't have a big need to genuflect to us old-timers. . . . It's a great thing for the art form, which a lot of people became excited about in those days. They've been proven correct in that comics really can deal with grown-up things worth the attention of serious readers of literature. I think short of a major book burning, I think that's a done deal. I think that's been proven, and new graphic novels come out every year that prove this is a vital art form. Now if people could just make money from it. That's the problem these days.

Howard Cruse's work, much of it reprinted here, served as an inspiration to many young queer creators and readers who did not otherwise see a place for themselves in the world of comics. He helped to break key barriers in the industry, and he continued to serve as a mentor and influence throughout his career. Though Cruse did not want younger cartoonists "to genuflect to us old-timers," the work he did to make comics "a vital art form" that could encompass a greater diversity of perspectives and stories should not be taken for granted.

2

Autobiographical Fiction / Fictional Autobiography

Howard Cruse used autobiographical conventions in his comics throughout his career, even in works that might not traditionally be considered "autobiography." At times, he used those conventions in straightforward and traditional ways, as in stories like "That Night at the Stonewall" and "Then There Was Claude," where the reader has little reason to doubt the veracity of the autobiographical narrative. In other cases, however, Cruse challenges the reader's expectations of autobiography in creative, innovative, and playful ways. In "The Guide," for example, he lures the reader in with what looks like the straightforward personal story of Cruse's first LSD trip, but then moves into an unsettling, unexpected, and darkly humorous conclusion. With "Jerry Mack," Cruse creates a masterpiece of empathy and remorse: a story of an early romantic interest told from the perspective of a conservative minister looking back on his youthful experience with Evan Bond, a budding cartoonist. The inclusion of a young gay cartoonist, of course, automatically invites the reader to make autobiographical connections to the story, though the true story upon which it is based is much more complex.

Most of Cruse's stories identified as autobiographical feature common genre cues—most notably, having a character named Howard who looks like the cartoonist. Such an avatar triggers what Philip Lejeune refers to as the "autobiographical pact": a kind of assumed agreement between reader and text that the narrator and protagonist of a story are the same person as the author (22). Tied to this pact is also the assumption on the part of the readers that the text they are reading is "true" in some verifiable way. Of course, Lejeune applies his concept to prose autobiography, not comics. By its very nature, the comics medium challenges this concept. As Jared Gardner explains the problem with "truth" and comics, "The comics form necessarily and inevitably calls attention through its formal properties to its limitations as juridical evidence—to the compression and gaps of its narrative (represented graphically by the gutter-space between panels) and to iconic distillations of its art" ("Autography's Biography" 6). In other words, what a creator chooses to leave out between panels (and, as such, requires the reader to fill in) and the way in which an artist's unique style renders the drawings subjective make it difficult to claim that an autobiographical comic represents some kind of pure, objective truth.[1]

Beyond these basic issues with comics and autobiography, Cruse's autobiographical and semiautobiographical work is even more playful in terms of genre expectations. Cruse will give the reader a recognizable Howard avatar who often frames and narrates the story. Such a frame lends some verisimilitude to his stories, and the reader's assumption of truth-telling allows Cruse to play with the reader. As Cruse explained the decision that led to his approach to personal stories:

> I was slow to try my hand at autobiographic comics early in my career when that genre first became popular because I didn't feel that my own life would be very interesting to others. My daily existence was dominated by endless hours spent hovering over a drawing board, which would have made for sluggish plotlines. Then I realized that I was being held back by an assumption that I had an obligation to depict my life *truthfully*. Not so! By creating a cartoon alter ego unfettered by real-world constraints, I could go crazy on paper. I was a cartoonist, after all. Nobody arrests a cartoonist for exaggerating! (*Other Sides* 210)

This creation of his persona also factors into his nonfiction comics essays as well, where he can exaggerate or fictionalize his own personality and beliefs. Clearly, he embraces the freedom that comics autobiography specifically allows him.

Cruse resisted autobiographical readings of *Stuck Rubber Baby*, even though the graphic novel often gets treated as such by virtue of the fact that it is a bildungsroman about a young gay man coming of age in the U.S. South. Cruse regularly insisted that the main autobiographical element of *Stuck Rubber Baby* was that he and Toland both fathered a daughter out of wedlock, in a weak grasp at solidifying their heterosexual identities. In addition, more minor scenes in the narrative come from Cruse's life as well, like declaring his homosexuality during his draft physical. Otherwise, though, Cruse's and Toland Polk's lives are dramatically different—most notably, Toland does not have the artistic talents or ambitions that Cruse had at that age. But we can find seeds of *Stuck Rubber Baby* in the way Cruse approached autobiography earlier in his career, most obviously in "Jerry Mack," but also in the style of "I Always Cry at Movies . . ." Meanwhile, the stories in this chapter also show the playful side of Cruse's use of autobiography, in the humorous twists of "Unfinished Pictures" and "The Guide," or the dark, self-deprecating comedy of "The Basic Overview."

Late in his career, Cruse created several short, one-page autobiographical stories that appeared on his website, www.howardcruse.com. All of these comics are worth exploring, but they are represented here by "The Basic Overview." In addition, the story "Then There Was Claude" is another late example of Cruse's autobiographical comics. With both "Stonewall" and "Claude," Cruse opts for a more conventional approach to autobiography, and both deal briefly with significant events in Cruse's life.

"The Basic Overview"

This one-page strip from 2017 was originally published on Howard Cruse's website as one of the "Occasional Comix" he produced later in his career. This strip especially presents the dark humor that Cruse would often infuse in his short autobiographical work, including ruminations on his own legacy and death.

THE BASIC OVERVIEW by Howard Cruse

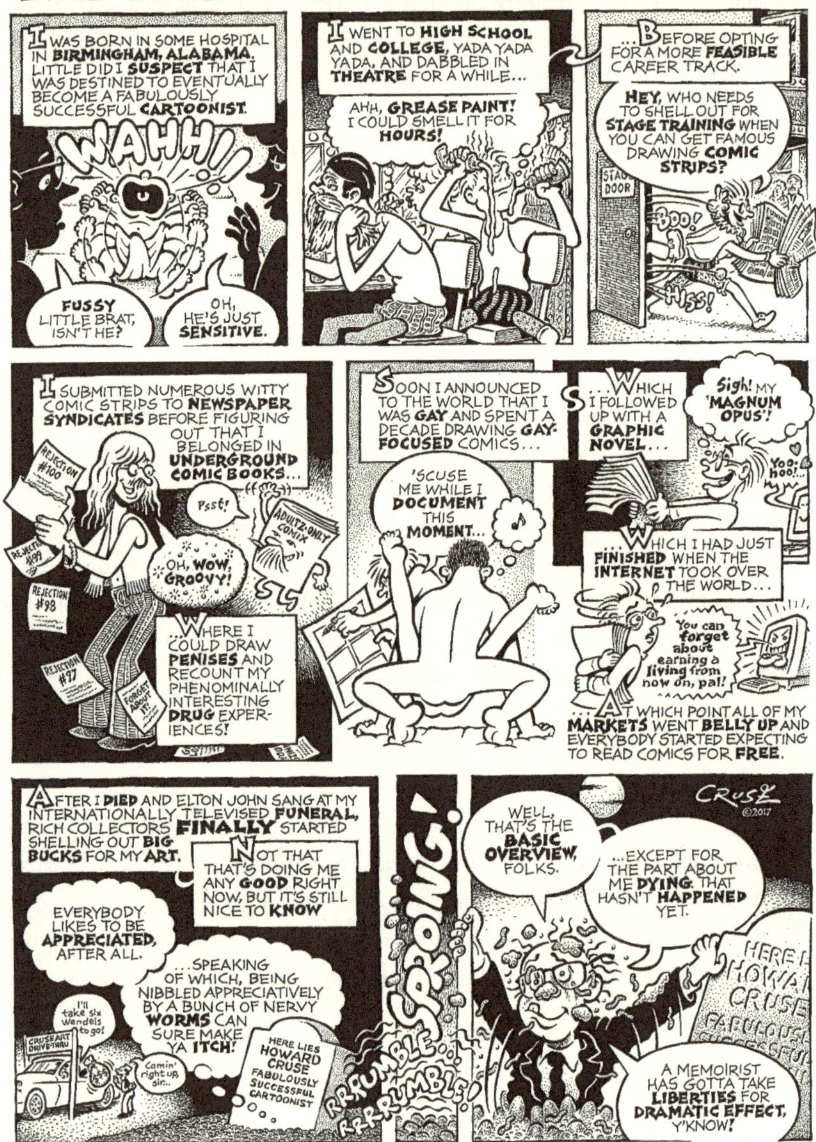

"Jerry Mack"

"Jerry Mack" is Howard Cruse's second contribution to *Gay Comix*, appearing in issue 2 (November 1981). The story lends itself to an autobiographical reading due to the inclusion of budding artist Evan Bond in Reverend Jerry Mack Wyatt's nostalgic memory trip. Seeing an article about Evan as a gay cartoonist speaking out on "gay liberation" is the madeleine that sparks Jerry's reverie.

The story is, in fact, built from an experience that Cruse had as a teenager. He takes an approach to autobiography here that he will also later utilize in *Stuck Rubber Baby*: using personal experience as a springboard for the story without strict adherence to the facts of that experience. Most of what happens in "Jerry Mack" seems to be based on a local event in Springville, Alabama, that young Howard witnessed, which ended in similar circumstances.

In addition, "Jerry Mack" is a remarkable example of life imitating art. Cruse's story appeared in November 1981; in an undated letter likely from January 1982, Cruse is contacted out of the blue by Bill, a childhood acquaintance on whom the character Jerry Mack Wyatt is based.[2] It would be an extraordinary coincidence if this letter were not connected to the publication of "Jerry Mack," though Bill makes no reference to the story or his motivation to reach out to Cruse after twenty-five years. The only indication that this is not just a random contact comes at the end of Bill's letter: "I always knew I would hear of you but had forgotten about it these many years." How he heard of Cruse, though, is unclear: if Bill had not seen "Jerry Mack," then he may have seen some publicity surrounding *Gay Comix*, in much the same way that Jerry sees the newspaper story about Evan Bond. Nonetheless, Bill also asks, "Do you have any memory of how close we used to be?" Certainly, if Bill had read "Jerry Mack," he would know of Cruse's memory, though this question may be an attempt to evade connection with the story.

Prior to sending this letter, Bill wrote to Cruse's brother, Allan. Allan's response to Bill referred specifically to an incident that resembles the climax of "Jerry Mack":

> I have continued to mull over the quite traumatic circumstances under which you left Alabama because of what the episode taught me about the people of Springville, about my parents, about the Baptist Church leaders, and about myself. It was one of the most enlightening dramas ever to unfold before me in real life, and provided a rich mine of insights about the truth and meaning of human existence. I am very proud of my father, in

> particular, for the ways in which he expressed his support and compassion for an individual in a difficult situation. I remember this whenever I am tempted to become cynical about persons who profess a commitment to Christian principles: it was one of several occasions when my father was true to his convictions in a crisis situation. So, you see, this is a gift that your life has given to mine.

Howard Cruse's response on January 5, 1982, is less blunt about specific incidences from their past, but he is open about his sexuality and critical of the "Christian Church" for spreading homophobia and other prejudices. And like Allan, Howard emphasizes how formative the experience he had with Bill was: "I've thought about you quite a few times in the last couple of decades and hoped you were faring well." Howard also includes in the letter some samples of his work, including cartoons from *Bananas*, *Fangoria*, and the *Village Voice*, as well as a column from *Comics Scene*. These all seem safe choices that would have little to offend a devout Christian like Bill, though the *Village Voice* piece is most likely "Sometimes I Get So Mad . . . ," which does address the bigotry and homophobia rampant in American society, especially among Evangelical Christians.

In his interview with Steven Palmer for the National Park Service's Stonewall Oral History Project, Cruse provides even more detail about the event with Bill that inspired "Jerry Mack." He explains that "an important member of the church congregation . . . was suddenly gone" from Springville, and Howard didn't understand what happened to him (LGBTCenterNYC). Howard's parents told him that the father of a local teenager had suspected that this person had tried to seduce his teenage son. The local preacher joined with the father to the young man's house, where the father proceeded to beat him up and demanded that he leave town immediately (LGBTCenterNYC). From this account, it seems that Howard's family was not involved, though in Allan's account, their father seemed to have some role. Regardless, it was another formative experience for young Howard—an exposure to the violence that could befall someone even suspected of being gay.

In constructing "Jerry Mack," then, Cruse inserted a semiautobiographical stand-in, even though he was much younger than Evan and not directly involved. At that time (around 1956, according to Bill's letter), Howard would have been twelve years old, while Evan in the story is sixteen. Jerry is seven years older than Evan, making him twenty-three. Jerry's first feelings of physical arousal come about while wrestling with Evan—Cruse often uses a scene of adolescent wrestling as an early development in the awareness of queer identity. The story's climactic scene draws directly from the source event: Ollie's father brutally assaults Jerry, while the local minister looks on and only comments when the father swears, but otherwise condones the violence. Jerry is then forced to leave town. Allan Cruse's letter to Bill mentions "the quite traumatic circumstances under which [Bill] left Alabama," which seems to parallel this moment in the story.

Whatever the circumstances that inspired "Jerry Mack," the story is a remarkable exercise in empathy. Cruse imagines the story not from Evan's point of view, but from Jerry's, as an attempt to envision the struggle that a repressed and closeted gay man experiences when trying to conform to an oppressive faith that requires him to pray away his true feelings. In the end, Jerry considers his own son, who is also demonstrating some artistic talent. Jerry begins to think, "If he ever told me he was a queer, I . . . I think I'd . . ." but he catches himself, asking God to forgive him "for these thoughts . . . these thoughts . . ." However, he does not spell out what he would do, nor does he specify the thoughts that are plaguing him. Are they the thoughts about his son's sexuality? Does he start to say that he would inflict the same violence on his son that he experienced, and thus seeks forgiveness for those thoughts? Or has he once again indulged fantasies of same-sex desire that he thought fully buried? However the reader fills in the blanks here depends on whether Jerry's memories have spurred some kind of moral epiphany, where he realizes that he should condemn the violent impulses he feels toward his son. Or he realizes his own shame in repressing his identity and feels guilt about wishing the same repression on his son.

In "Jerry Mack," the seeds of Cruse's later *Stuck Rubber Baby* style are also evident, though without the extensive cross-hatching. The story reveals a more realistic side of Cruse's art, which stands in sharp contrast to the contemporaneous style that he used for his humorous and satirical strips. Also evident here are the dense page layouts that would appear in *Stuck Rubber Baby*, with three tiers and as many as twelve panels per page. This density may be due to the space limitations in *Gay Comix* only allowing five pages for the story, but it fits the theme of repression that runs through the story as well. In fact, many of the panels feature images that burst through the borders, culminating in the final image of Jerry Mack covering his face in shame and regret, appearing from behind a panel and bleeding to the edge of the page.

In a February 13, 1982, letter to Richard Bruning, who was then editor and art director with the short-lived Capital Comics but would later become a creative director at DC Comics, Cruse described some storytelling choices he made for "Jerry Mack," including doing a twelve-panel grid on each page:

"I wanted a claustrophobic emotional effect, told in tiny snapshots because that's so often the way we look at our past: in snapshots piled in old boxes. And from the little fragments of reality that the snapshots contain, our imagination fills in the rest of the world. But the sense of constriction remains. It's like looking through the wrong end of a telescope."

Lost by reading this story in this collection or in one of the other Cruse anthologies is the impact that the story has within the context of its original publication in *Gay Comix* 2. Cruse envisioned an audience of both queer and straight readers for the series. He asks queer readers to empathize with the type of Evangelical Christian who has likely plagued their lives by seeing the closeted struggle beneath the surface. Straight readers get to see the complex struggle of someone in such deep denial that they might recycle their self-hatred by imposing it on their own child. And, now, we can also imagine a very specific reader, Bill, as he undeniably sees himself in the story's protagonist.

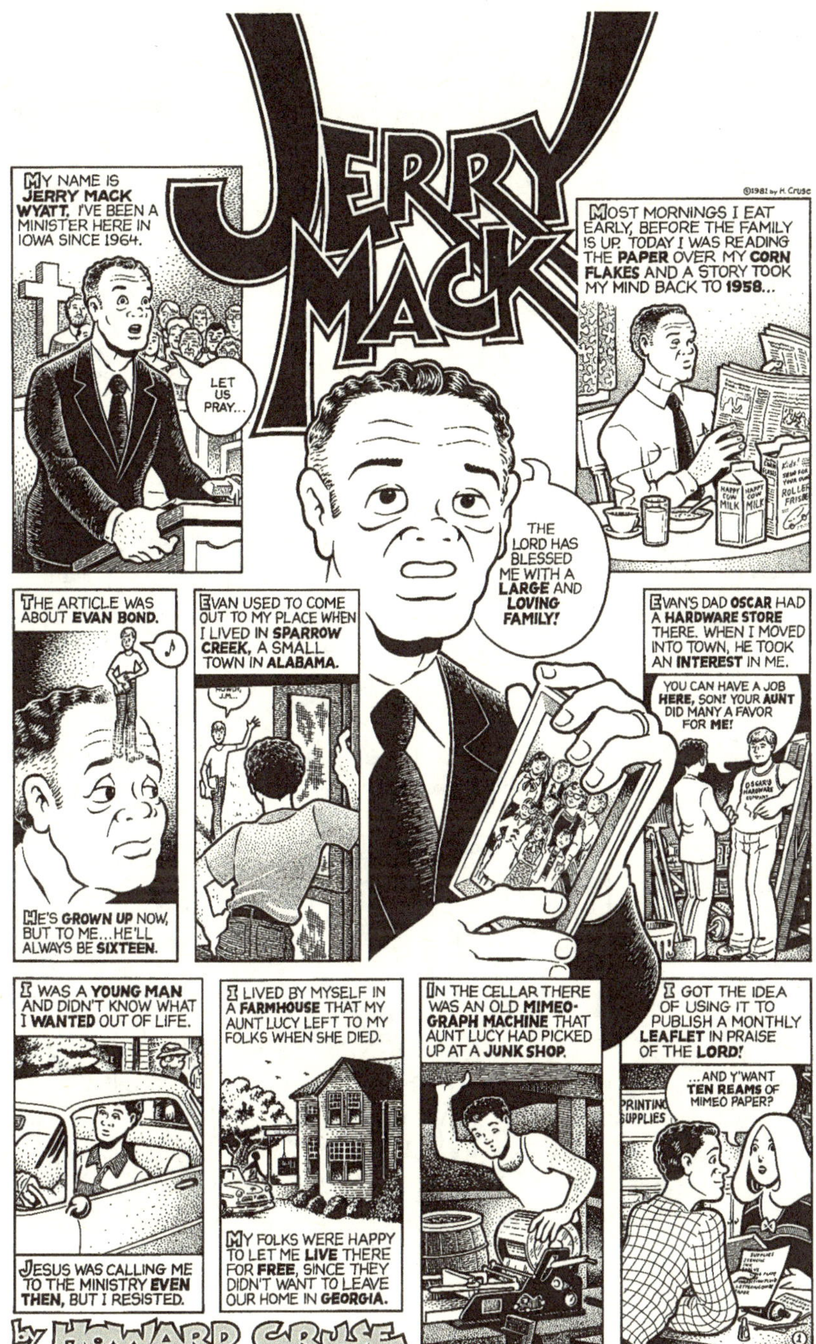
JERRY MACK
©1981 by H. Cruse
MY NAME IS JERRY MACK WYATT. I'VE BEEN A MINISTER HERE IN IOWA SINCE 1964.
LET US PRAY...
MOST MORNINGS I EAT EARLY, BEFORE THE FAMILY IS UP. TODAY I WAS READING THE PAPER OVER MY CORN FLAKES AND A STORY TOOK MY MIND BACK TO 1958...
HAPPY COW MILK
HAPPY COW MILK
THE LORD HAS BLESSED ME WITH A LARGE AND LOVING FAMILY!
THE ARTICLE WAS ABOUT EVAN BOND.
♪
HE'S GROWN UP NOW, BUT TO ME... HE'LL ALWAYS BE SIXTEEN.
EVAN USED TO COME OUT TO MY PLACE WHEN I LIVED IN SPARROW CREEK, A SMALL TOWN IN ALABAMA.
EVAN'S DAD OSCAR HAD A HARDWARE STORE THERE. WHEN I MOVED INTO TOWN, HE TOOK AN INTEREST IN ME.
YOU CAN HAVE A JOB HERE, SON! YOUR AUNT DID MANY A FAVOR FOR ME!
I WAS A YOUNG MAN AND DIDN'T KNOW WHAT I WANTED OUT OF LIFE.
JESUS WAS CALLING ME TO THE MINISTRY EVEN THEN, BUT I RESISTED.
I LIVED BY MYSELF IN A FARMHOUSE THAT MY AUNT LUCY LEFT TO MY FOLKS WHEN SHE DIED.
MY FOLKS WERE HAPPY TO LET ME LIVE THERE FOR FREE, SINCE THEY DIDN'T WANT TO LEAVE OUR HOME IN GEORGIA.
IN THE CELLAR THERE WAS AN OLD MIMEOGRAPH MACHINE THAT AUNT LUCY HAD PICKED UP AT A JUNK SHOP.
I GOT THE IDEA OF USING IT TO PUBLISH A MONTHLY LEAFLET IN PRAISE OF THE LORD!
PRINTING SUPPLIES
...AND Y'WANT TEN REAMS OF MIMEO PAPER?
1
by HOWARD CRUSE

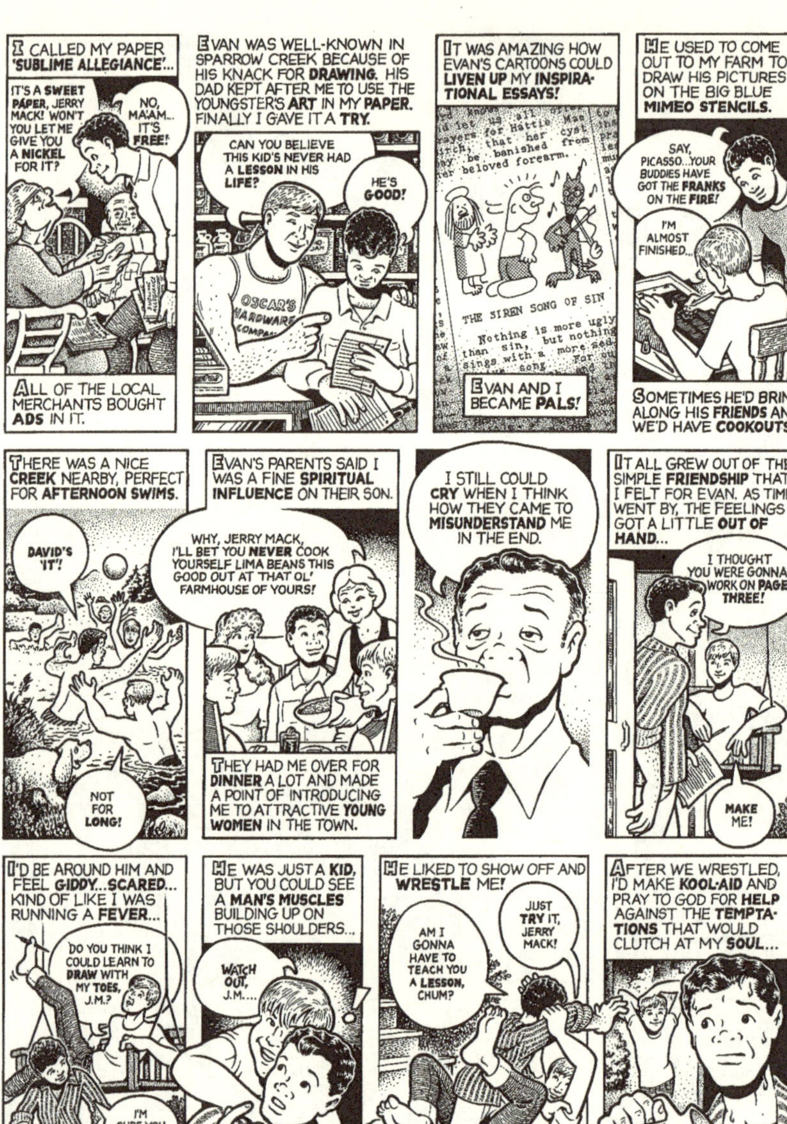

I CALLED MY PAPER 'SUBLIME ALLEGIANCE'...
IT'S A SWEET PAPER, JERRY MACK! WON'T YOU LET ME GIVE YOU A NICKEL FOR IT?
NO, MA'AM... IT'S FREE!
ALL OF THE LOCAL MERCHANTS BOUGHT ADS IN IT.
EVAN WAS WELL-KNOWN IN SPARROW CREEK BECAUSE OF HIS KNACK FOR DRAWING. HIS DAD KEPT AFTER ME TO USE THE YOUNGSTER'S ART IN MY PAPER. FINALLY I GAVE IT A TRY.
CAN YOU BELIEVE THIS KID'S NEVER HAD A LESSON IN HIS LIFE?
HE'S GOOD!
OSCAR'S HARDWARE
IT WAS AMAZING HOW EVAN'S CARTOONS COULD LIVEN UP MY INSPIRATIONAL ESSAYS!
THE SIREN SONG OF SIN
Nothing is more ugly than sin, but nothing sings with a more
EVAN AND I BECAME PALS!
HE USED TO COME OUT TO MY FARM TO DRAW HIS PICTURES ON THE BIG BLUE MIMEO STENCILS.
SAY, PICASSO...YOUR BUDDIES HAVE GOT THE FRANKS ON THE FIRE!
I'M ALMOST FINISHED...
SOMETIMES HE'D BRING ALONG HIS FRIENDS AND WE'D HAVE COOKOUTS.
THERE WAS A NICE CREEK NEARBY, PERFECT FOR AFTERNOON SWIMS.
DAVID'S 'IT'!
NOT FOR LONG!
EVAN'S PARENTS SAID I WAS A FINE SPIRITUAL INFLUENCE ON THEIR SON.
WHY, JERRY MACK, I'LL BET YOU NEVER COOK YOURSELF LIMA BEANS THIS GOOD OUT AT THAT OL' FARMHOUSE OF YOURS!
THEY HAD ME OVER FOR DINNER A LOT AND MADE A POINT OF INTRODUCING ME TO ATTRACTIVE YOUNG WOMEN IN THE TOWN.
I STILL COULD CRY WHEN I THINK HOW THEY CAME TO MISUNDERSTAND ME IN THE END.
IT ALL GREW OUT OF THE SIMPLE FRIENDSHIP THAT I FELT FOR EVAN. AS TIME WENT BY, THE FEELINGS GOT A LITTLE OUT OF HAND...
I THOUGHT YOU WERE GONNA WORK ON PAGE THREE!
MAKE ME!
I'D BE AROUND HIM AND FEEL GIDDY...SCARED... KIND OF LIKE I WAS RUNNING A FEVER...
DO YOU THINK I COULD LEARN TO DRAW WITH MY TOES, J.M.?
I'M SURE YOU COULD!
HE WAS JUST A KID, BUT YOU COULD SEE A MAN'S MUSCLES BUILDING UP ON THOSE SHOULDERS...
WATCH OUT, J.M....
HE LIKED TO SHOW OFF AND WRESTLE ME!
AM I GONNA HAVE TO TEACH YOU A LESSON, CHUM?
JUST TRY IT, JERRY MACK!
OH, I'D PIN HIM DOWN—I WAS SEVEN YEARS OLDER, AFTER ALL! BUT THAT KID COULD PUT UP A WOOLY FIGHT!
AFTER WE WRESTLED, I'D MAKE KOOL-AID AND PRAY TO GOD FOR HELP AGAINST THE TEMPTATIONS THAT WOULD CLUTCH AT MY SOUL...
2

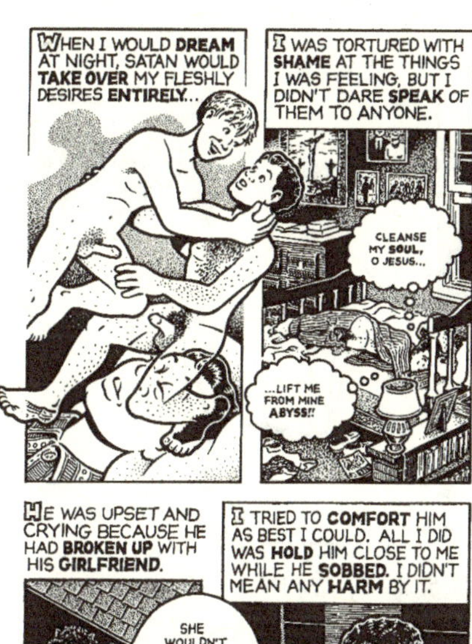

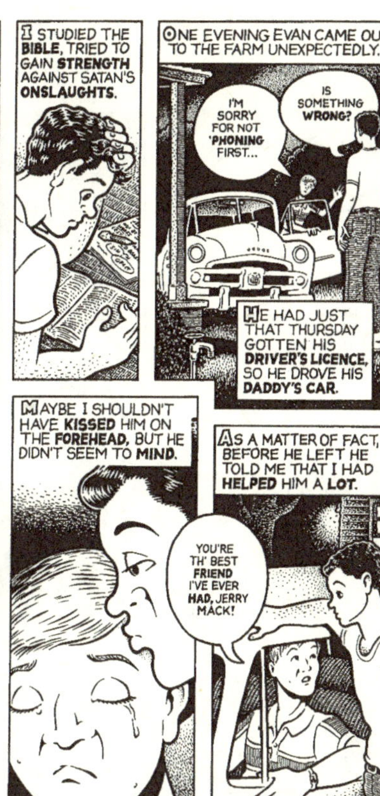

HE WAS UPSET AND CRYING BECAUSE HE HAD **BROKEN UP** WITH HIS **GIRLFRIEND**.

SHE WOULDN'T **LISTEN** TO ME! I WAS JUST TRYIN' TO **EXPLAIN** TO HER...

I TRIED TO **COMFORT** HIM AS BEST I COULD. ALL I DID WAS **HOLD** HIM CLOSE TO ME WHILE HE **SOBBED**. I DIDN'T MEAN ANY **HARM** BY IT.

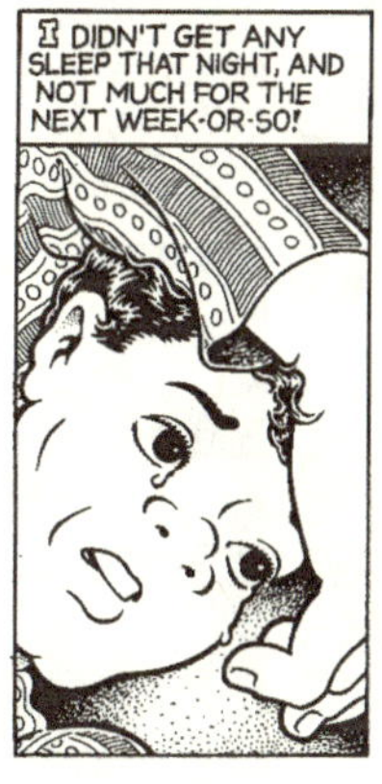

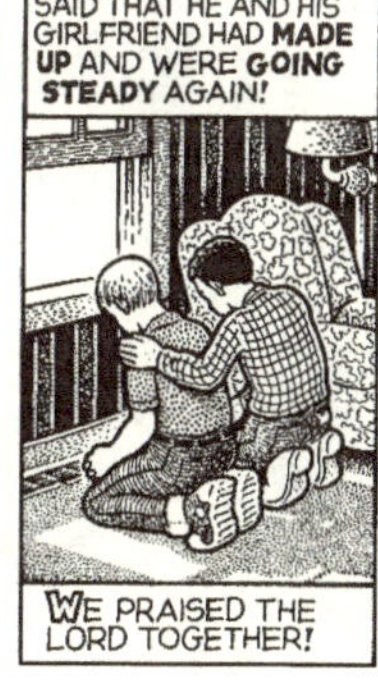

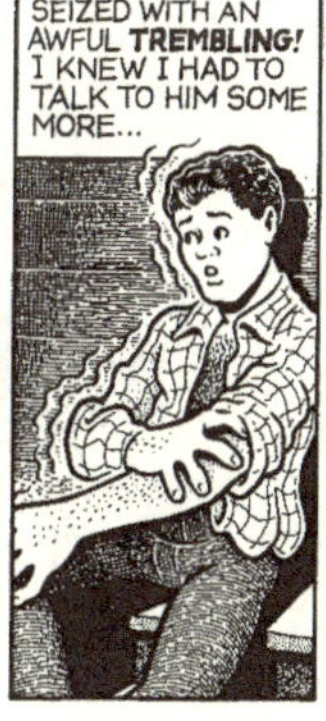

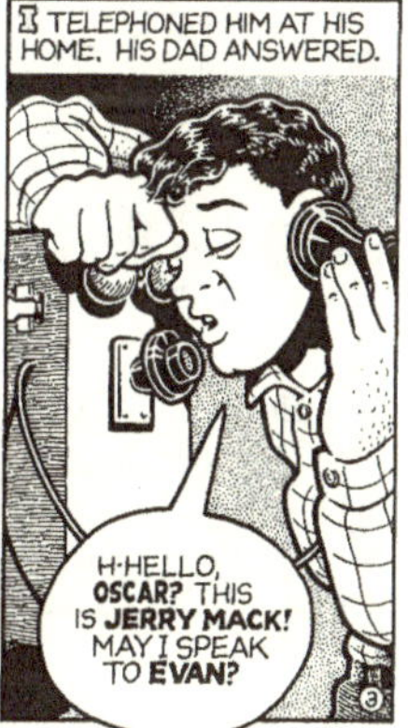

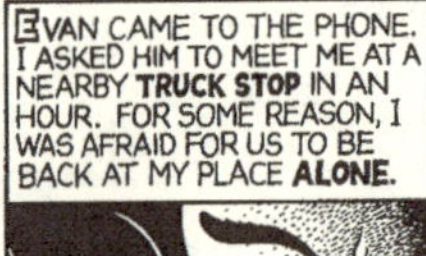

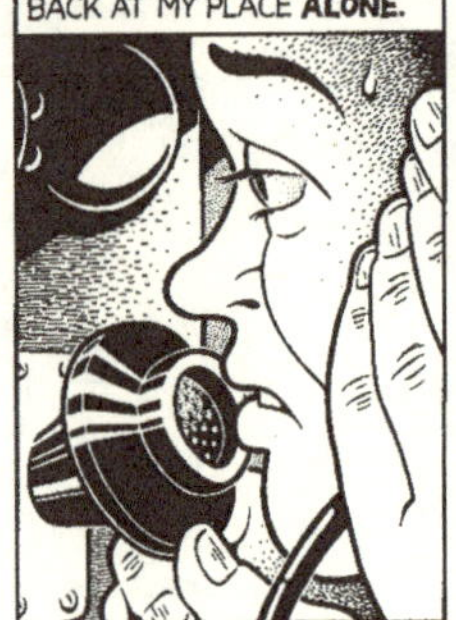

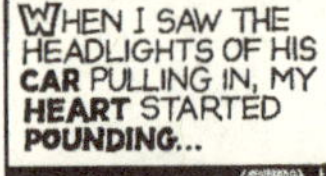

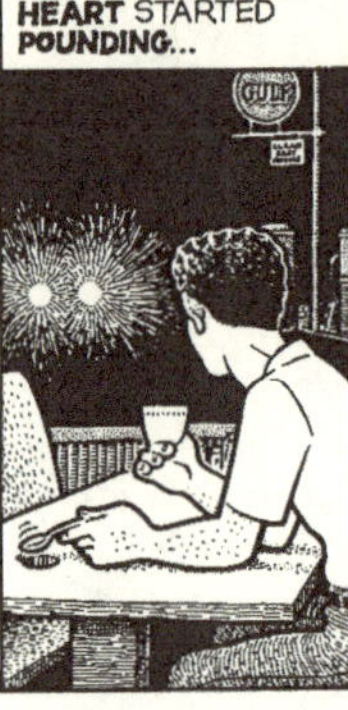

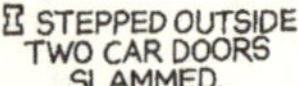

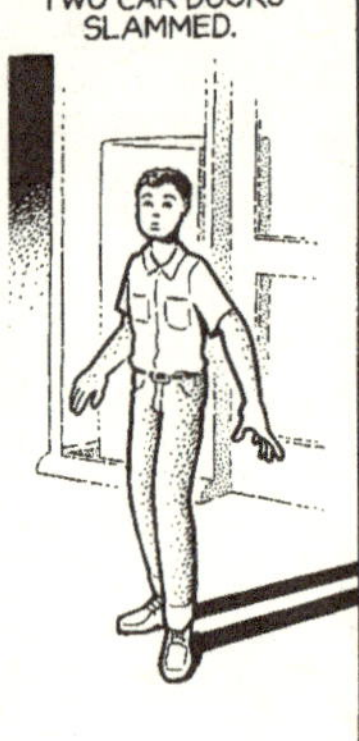

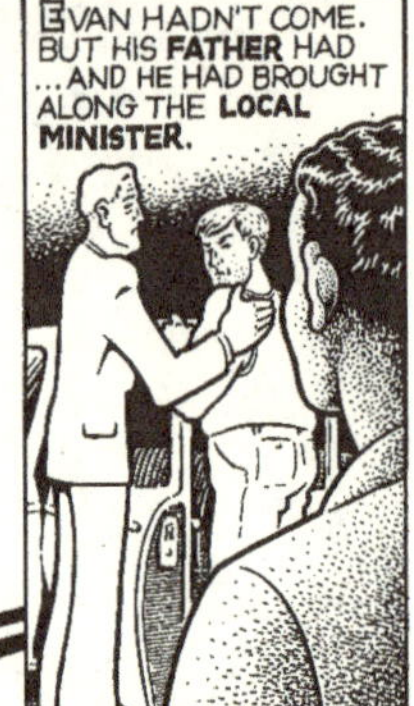

OSCAR WALKED UP TO ME AND STARTED **YELLING** AND **HITTING** ME IN THE **FACE**...

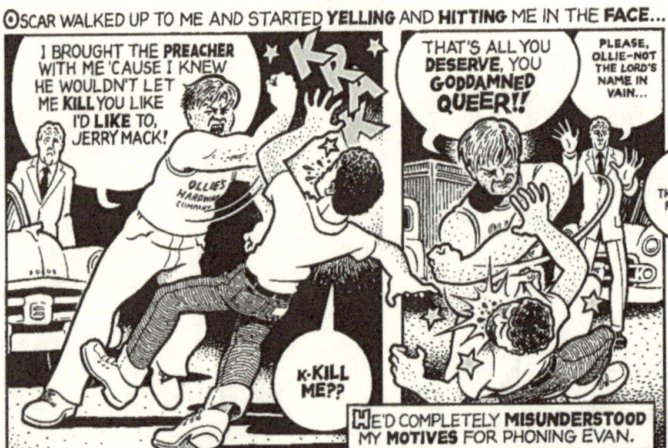

I WANT YOU **OUT** OF THIS TOWN BY **TOMORROW** OR, BY GOD, YOUR **ASS'LL** BE SWINGIN' FROM THE **TOWN HALL LAMP POST!**

...PARDON TH' LANGUAGE, PREACHER!...

THAT'S ALL RIGHT, SON...

...AND DON'T YOU EVER **SPEAK** OR **WRITE A WORD** TO MY BOY **AGAIN!**

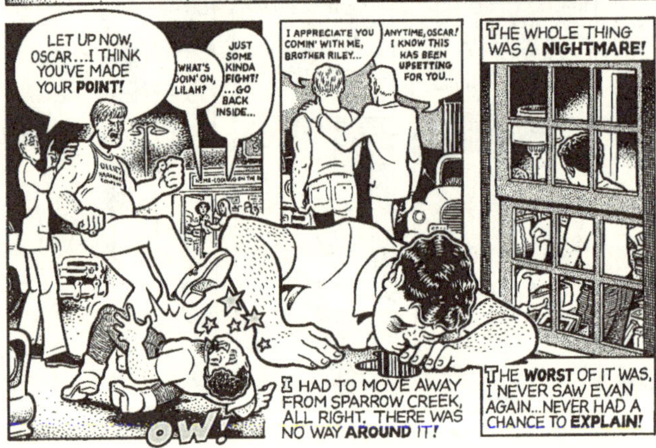

CONSIDERING HOW **LOW** I FELT AT THE TIME, IT'S A MIRACLE THAT I **EVER** GOT MY LIFE TOGETHER AGAIN...

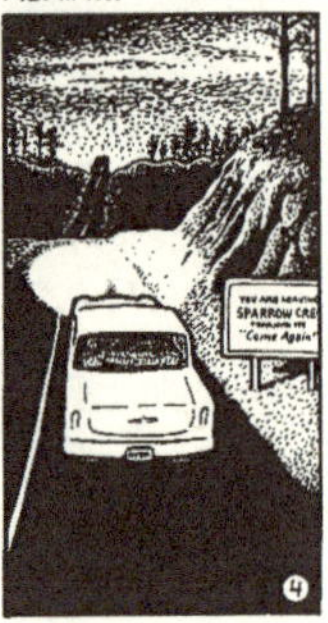

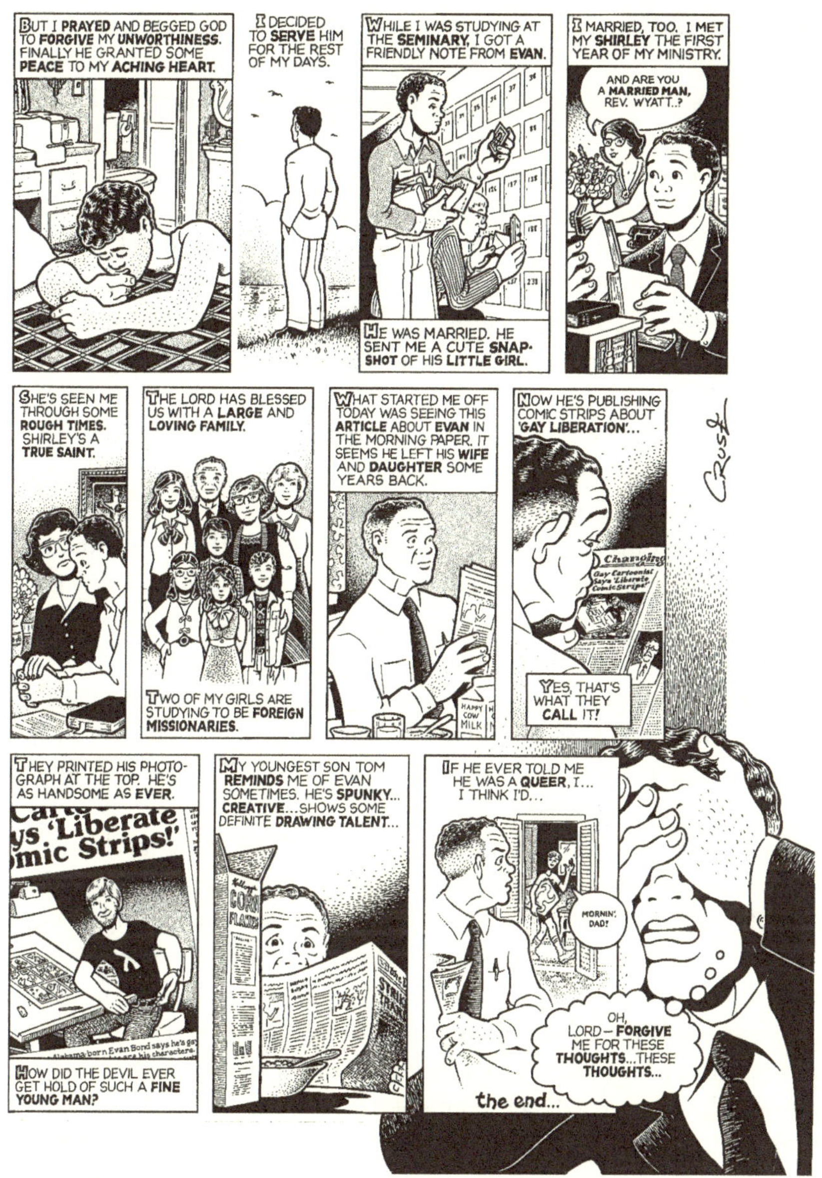
BUT I PRAYED AND BEGGED GOD TO FORGIVE MY UNWORTHINESS. FINALLY HE GRANTED SOME PEACE TO MY ACHING HEART.
I DECIDED TO SERVE HIM FOR THE REST OF MY DAYS.
WHILE I WAS STUDYING AT THE SEMINARY, I GOT A FRIENDLY NOTE FROM EVAN.
HE WAS MARRIED. HE SENT ME A CUTE SNAPSHOT OF HIS LITTLE GIRL.
I MARRIED, TOO. I MET MY SHIRLEY THE FIRST YEAR OF MY MINISTRY.
AND ARE YOU A MARRIED MAN, REV. WYATT..?
SHE'S SEEN ME THROUGH SOME ROUGH TIMES. SHIRLEY'S A TRUE SAINT.
THE LORD HAS BLESSED US WITH A LARGE AND LOVING FAMILY.
TWO OF MY GIRLS ARE STUDYING TO BE FOREIGN MISSIONARIES.
WHAT STARTED ME OFF TODAY WAS SEEING THIS ARTICLE ABOUT EVAN IN THE MORNING PAPER. IT SEEMS HE LEFT HIS WIFE AND DAUGHTER SOME YEARS BACK.
HAPPY COW MILK
NOW HE'S PUBLISHING COMIC STRIPS ABOUT 'GAY LIBERATION'...
Changing
Gay Cartoonist Says 'Liberate Comic Strips!'
YES, THAT'S WHAT THEY CALL IT!
CRUSE
THEY PRINTED HIS PHOTOGRAPH AT THE TOP. HE'S AS HANDSOME AS EVER.
ys 'Liberate mic Strips!'
Alabama-born Evan Bond says he's gay
HOW DID THE DEVIL EVER GET HOLD OF SUCH A FINE YOUNG MAN?
MY YOUNGEST SON TOM REMINDS ME OF EVAN SOMETIMES. HE'S SPUNKY... CREATIVE...SHOWS SOME DEFINITE DRAWING TALENT...
Kellogg's CORN FLAKES
IF HE EVER TOLD ME HE WAS A QUEER, I... I THINK I'D...
MORNIN', DAD!
OH, LORD – FORGIVE ME FOR THESE THOUGHTS...THESE THOUGHTS...
the end...

"Unfinished Pictures"

When it appeared in *Bizarre Sex* 4 (October 1975), "Unfinished Pictures" was one of Cruse's first attempts to move away from *Barefootz* and into more personal, autobiographical comics. His style here seems like a transitional phase between *Barefootz* and later comics for *Gay Comix*. Remnants of the bigfoot style are still present in the disproportionate heads and large eyes, and his avatar differs from the one he would use later. The absurdist tone carries over from *Barefootz*, and there is a sex-positive element that also runs through Cruse's work. Despite the anxiety and shame about premature orgasms that young Howard faces when he draws, the story is ultimately nostalgic about adolescent sexuality: in the end, the older Howard regrets that he trained himself (through behaviorism, electric shock, and aversion therapy) to stop finding his artwork arousing.

Though one can't determine to any precise degree just how "true" this story is in autobiographical terms, it has, at its core, a "truth" about how easy it is to arouse most adolescent boys. The humor lies in Cruse's frank acknowledgment of that, accompanied by the fact that all of the orgasms are conspicuous. Underlining this point, each of young Howard's ejaculations is accompanied by a unique sound effect: "Ka-Sploit!" "Ptui!!" "Splort!" "Spurt!" "Gush!" and "Splurt."

However, the story is not completely open when it comes to sexuality. At the time he created the story, Cruse had not yet come out as a gay cartoonist, and "Unfinished Pictures" may reveal some of his anxieties along those lines. Cruse is somewhat ambiguous about the content of his erotic drawings. There are only a couple of indicators that he is composing scenes of straight sex: his thoughts about "asses . . . cocks . . . boobs . . . cervixes . . ." at the bottom of the first page, and young Howard inviting classmate Mary Juniper to his bedroom for a bout of mutual drawing (Mary's Katy Keene sketch setting Howard off even before he can start drawing). Otherwise, the only drawing we see is Howard's perfect mimicry of Ernie Bushmiller's Nancy and Sluggo, which he considers "totally sexless."[3] (This panel also anticipates Cruse's sexualizing of Little Lulu in "The Nightmares of Little L*l*" as well as the satirical "Raising Nancies.") Following that moment, the mere act of drawing, regardless of the subject, arouses him, to the point where he dreams of having sex with a genderless rubber eraser.

Cruse included "Unfinished Pictures" in his collection *The Other Sides of Howard Cruse*, which contained what he considered to be his nongay comics. Nevertheless, a certain queerness remains in this story, perhaps only evident through hindsight, and Cruse would go on to draw many more ejaculating penises in future work.

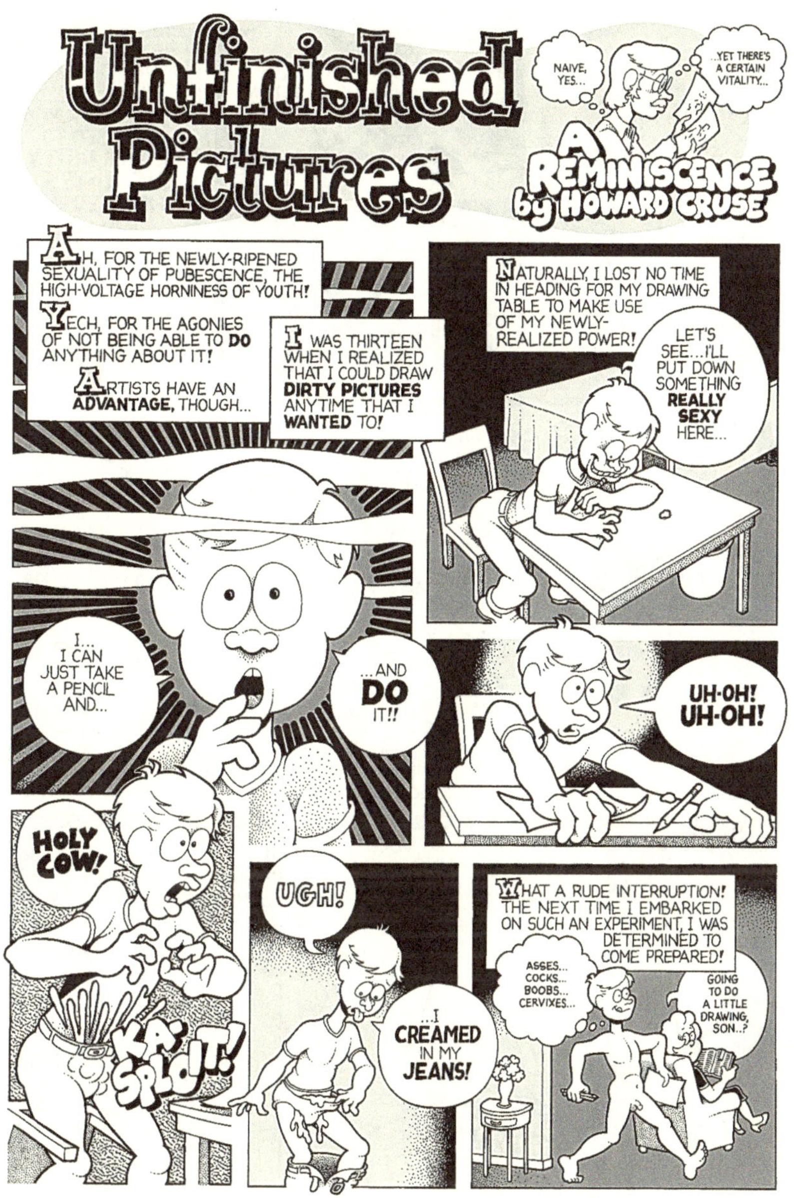

Unfinished Pictures
NAIVE, YES...
...YET THERE'S A CERTAIN VITALITY...
A REMINISCENCE by HOWARD CRUSE
AH, FOR THE NEWLY-RIPENED SEXUALITY OF PUBESCENCE, THE HIGH-VOLTAGE HORNINESS OF YOUTH!
YECH, FOR THE AGONIES OF NOT BEING ABLE TO DO ANYTHING ABOUT IT!
ARTISTS HAVE AN ADVANTAGE, THOUGH...
I WAS THIRTEEN WHEN I REALIZED THAT I COULD DRAW DIRTY PICTURES ANYTIME THAT I WANTED TO!
I... I CAN JUST TAKE A PENCIL AND...
...AND DO IT!!
NATURALLY, I LOST NO TIME IN HEADING FOR MY DRAWING TABLE TO MAKE USE OF MY NEWLY-REALIZED POWER!
LET'S SEE...I'LL PUT DOWN SOMETHING REALLY SEXY HERE...
UH-OH! UH-OH!
HOLY COW!
KA-SPLOOT!
UGH!
...I CREAMED IN MY JEANS!
WHAT A RUDE INTERRUPTION! THE NEXT TIME I EMBARKED ON SUCH AN EXPERIMENT, I WAS DETERMINED TO COME PREPARED!
ASSES... COCKS... BOOBS... CERVIXES...
GOING TO DO A LITTLE DRAWING, SON..?

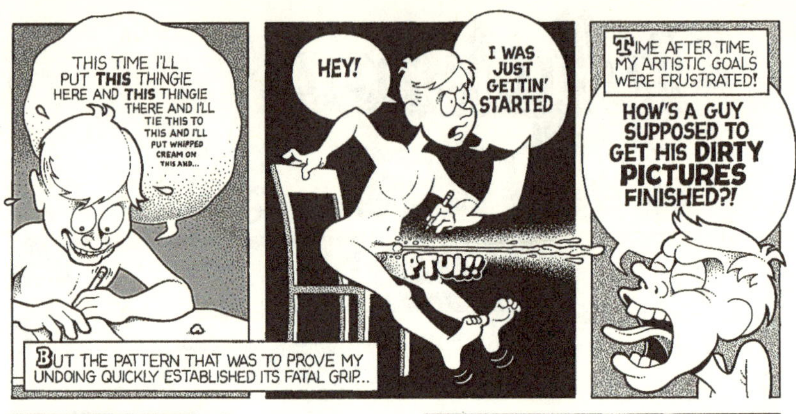
THIS TIME I'LL PUT THIS THINGIE HERE AND THIS THINGIE THERE AND I'LL TIE THIS TO THIS AND I'LL PUT WHIPPED CREAM ON THIS AND...
BUT THE PATTERN THAT WAS TO PROVE MY UNDOING QUICKLY ESTABLISHED ITS FATAL GRIP...
HEY!
I WAS JUST GETTIN' STARTED
PTUI!!
TIME AFTER TIME, MY ARTISTIC GOALS WERE FRUSTRATED!
HOW'S A GUY SUPPOSED TO GET HIS DIRTY PICTURES FINISHED?!

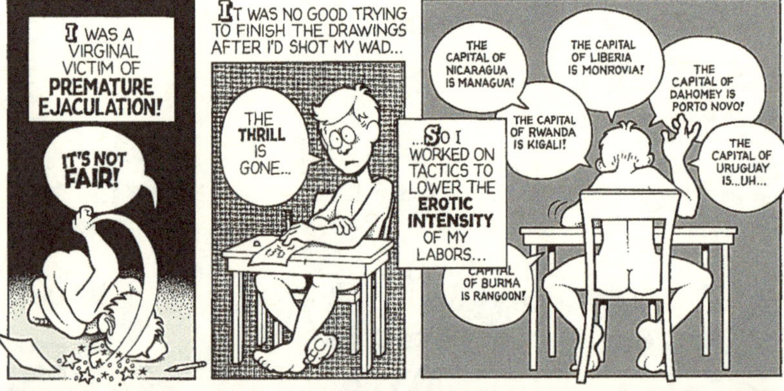
I WAS A VIRGINAL VICTIM OF PREMATURE EJACULATION!
IT'S NOT FAIR!
IT WAS NO GOOD TRYING TO FINISH THE DRAWINGS AFTER I'D SHOT MY WAD...
THE THRILL IS GONE...
...SO I WORKED ON TACTICS TO LOWER THE EROTIC INTENSITY OF MY LABORS...
THE CAPITAL OF NICARAGUA IS MANAGUA!
THE CAPITAL OF LIBERIA IS MONROVIA!
THE CAPITAL OF DAHOMEY IS PORTO NOVO!
THE CAPITAL OF RWANDA IS KIGALI!
THE CAPITAL OF URUGUAY IS...UH...
CAPITAL OF BURMA IS RANGOON!

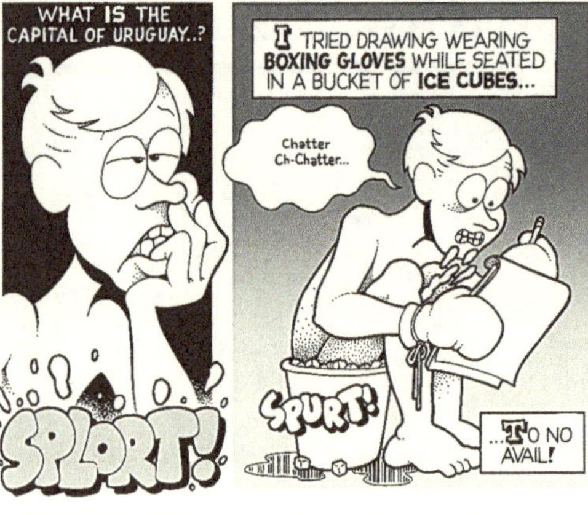
WHAT IS THE CAPITAL OF URUGUAY..?
SPLORT!
I TRIED DRAWING WEARING BOXING GLOVES WHILE SEATED IN A BUCKET OF ICE CUBES...
Chatter Ch-Chatter...
SPURT!
...TO NO AVAIL!

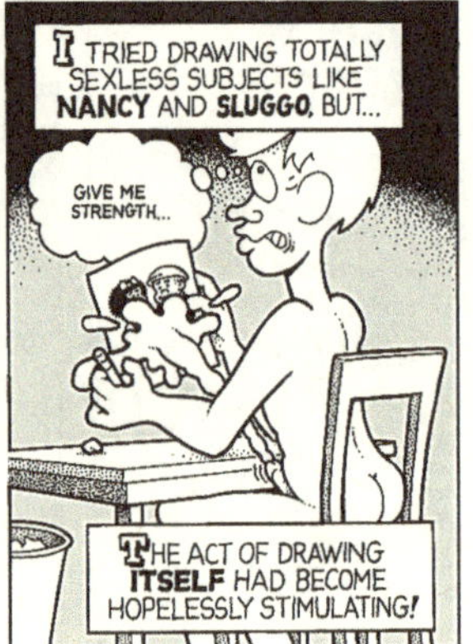
I TRIED DRAWING TOTALLY SEXLESS SUBJECTS LIKE NANCY AND SLUGGO, BUT...
GIVE ME STRENGTH...
THE ACT OF DRAWING ITSELF HAD BECOME HOPELESSLY STIMULATING!

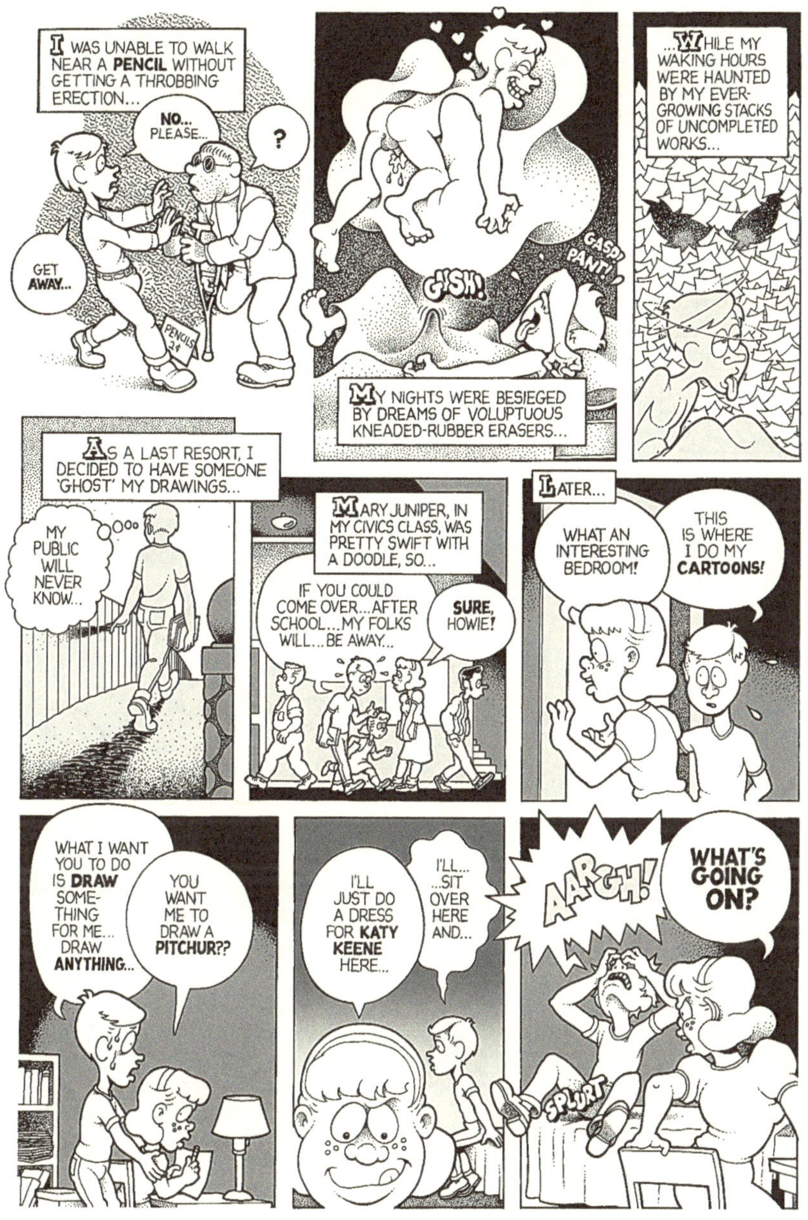
I WAS UNABLE TO WALK NEAR A PENCIL WITHOUT GETTING A THROBBING ERECTION...
NO... PLEASE...
?
GET AWAY...
PENCILS 2¢
MY NIGHTS WERE BESIEGED BY DREAMS OF VOLUPTUOUS KNEADED-RUBBER ERASERS...
GUSH!
GASP! PANT!
...WHILE MY WAKING HOURS WERE HAUNTED BY MY EVER-GROWING STACKS OF UNCOMPLETED WORKS...
AS A LAST RESORT, I DECIDED TO HAVE SOMEONE 'GHOST' MY DRAWINGS...
MY PUBLIC WILL NEVER KNOW...
MARY JUNIPER, IN MY CIVICS CLASS, WAS PRETTY SWIFT WITH A DOODLE, SO...
IF YOU COULD COME OVER...AFTER SCHOOL...MY FOLKS WILL...BE AWAY...
SURE, HOWIE!
LATER...
WHAT AN INTERESTING BEDROOM!
THIS IS WHERE I DO MY CARTOONS!
WHAT I WANT YOU TO DO IS DRAW SOMETHING FOR ME... DRAW ANYTHING...
YOU WANT ME TO DRAW A PITCHUR??
I'LL JUST DO A DRESS FOR KATY KEENE HERE...
I'LL... ...SIT OVER HERE AND...
AARGH!
WHAT'S GOING ON?
SPLURT

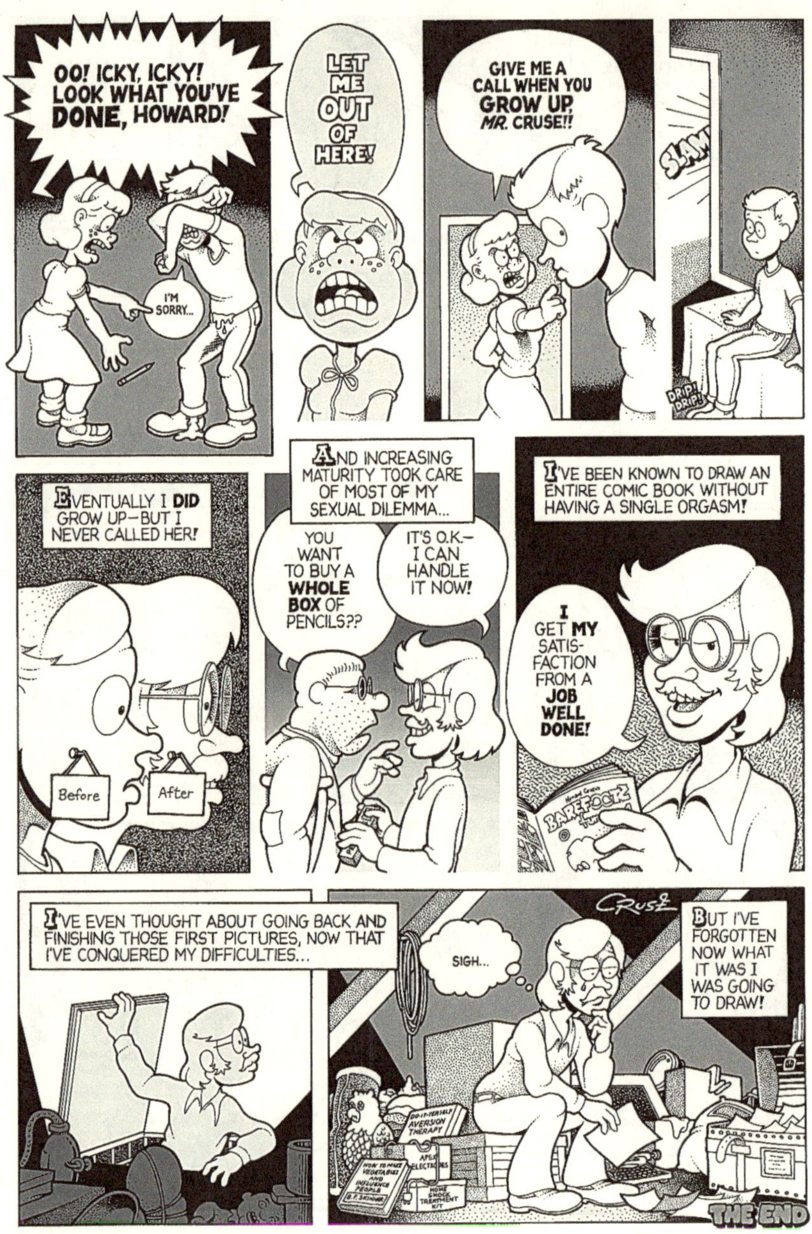

"Unfinished Pictures" copyright the estate of Howard Cruse. Used by permission.

"The Guide"

This story originally appeared in Kitchen Sink's *Dope Comix* 3 (June 1981) and is often identified as "My First Acid Trip" due to the way Cruse designed the opening splash panel. It had been accepted for publication by Kitchen in March 1979. In April 1977, Kitchen pitched the idea of Cruse creating a story for the *Dope Comix* series, but Cruse was hesitant to do it: "Dope isn't playing enough of a part in my current lifestyle to provide me with fresh ideas for drug-related comedy; consequently, when I go hunting specifically for story ideas in that area, I find myself re-hashing old, stale Sixties stuff" (23 May 1977 letter). However, Cruse ended up publishing stories in the first three issues of the series: "Big Marvy," "Li'l Nirvana Sees God," and "The Guide."

Cruse refers to "The Guide" as a "mock-reminiscence" (*Other Sides* 145), in that it feels like a true autobiographical story until the horribly violent twist ending. This is perhaps the most extreme example of Cruse playing with the "autobiographical pact"—he includes a version of himself in the story, he admits to taking LSD, and so on—which collectively lure in readers to buy the autobiographical claims. This approach to autobiography anticipates later cartoonists like Julie Doucet and Gabrielle Bell, who often make uncued shifts from autobiography to fantasy in their works, or Seth's *It's a Good Life, if You Don't Weaken*, where Seth creates a graphic novel about his search for an obscure *New Yorker* cartoonist who, in reality, does not exist.

"The Guide" is also a part of an autobiographical tradition in underground comix, where the artists document their first acid trip or other drug experience. As Jared Gardner shows, drug trip stories formed some of the earliest examples of autobiography in the underground, like Robert Crumb's early stories "The Trip" (1965) and "Big Freakout on Detroit Ave." (1967) and Art Spiegelman's "Little Harold Sunshine" (1967). Gardner explains why LSD and the comics medium go together so well: "Comics, with its emphasis on the nonverbal and its openness to nonlinear storytelling, was also latched on to as the ideal medium to tell the unique and uniquely untranslatable experience of taking LSD" (*Projections* 120).[4]

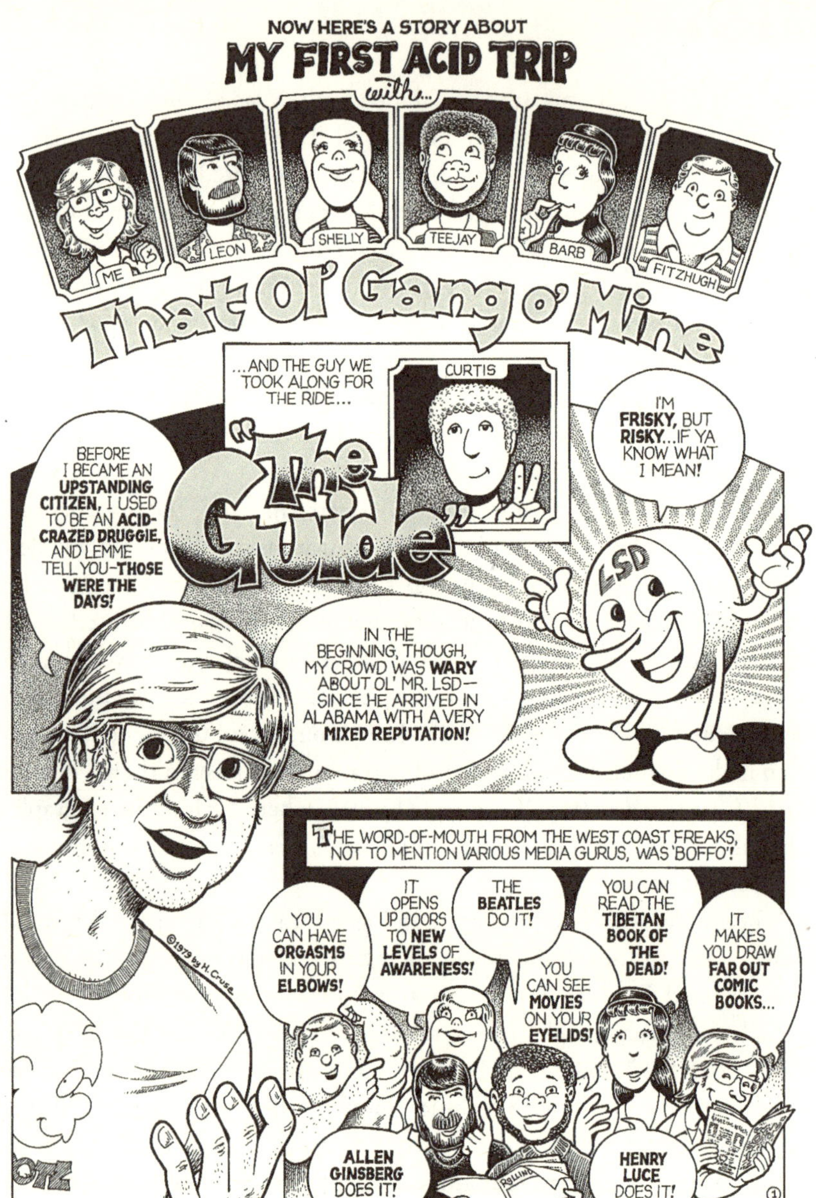
NOW HERE'S A STORY ABOUT
MY FIRST ACID TRIP
with...
ME
LEON
SHELLY
TEEJAY
BARB
FITZHUGH
That Ol' Gang o' Mine
...AND THE GUY WE TOOK ALONG FOR THE RIDE...
CURTIS
"The Guide"
BEFORE I BECAME AN UPSTANDING CITIZEN, I USED TO BE AN ACID-CRAZED DRUGGIE, AND LEMME TELL YOU–THOSE WERE THE DAYS!
I'M FRISKY, BUT RISKY...IF YA KNOW WHAT I MEAN!
LSD
IN THE BEGINNING, THOUGH, MY CROWD WAS WARY ABOUT OL' MR. LSD–SINCE HE ARRIVED IN ALABAMA WITH A VERY MIXED REPUTATION!
THE WORD-OF-MOUTH FROM THE WEST COAST FREAKS, NOT TO MENTION VARIOUS MEDIA GURUS, WAS 'BOFFO'!
YOU CAN HAVE ORGASMS IN YOUR ELBOWS!
IT OPENS UP DOORS TO NEW LEVELS OF AWARENESS!
THE BEATLES DO IT!
YOU CAN SEE MOVIES ON YOUR EYELIDS!
YOU CAN READ THE TIBETAN BOOK OF THE DEAD!
IT MAKES YOU DRAW FAR OUT COMIC BOOKS...
ALLEN GINSBERG DOES IT!
HENRY LUCE DOES IT!
©1979 by H. Cruse
1

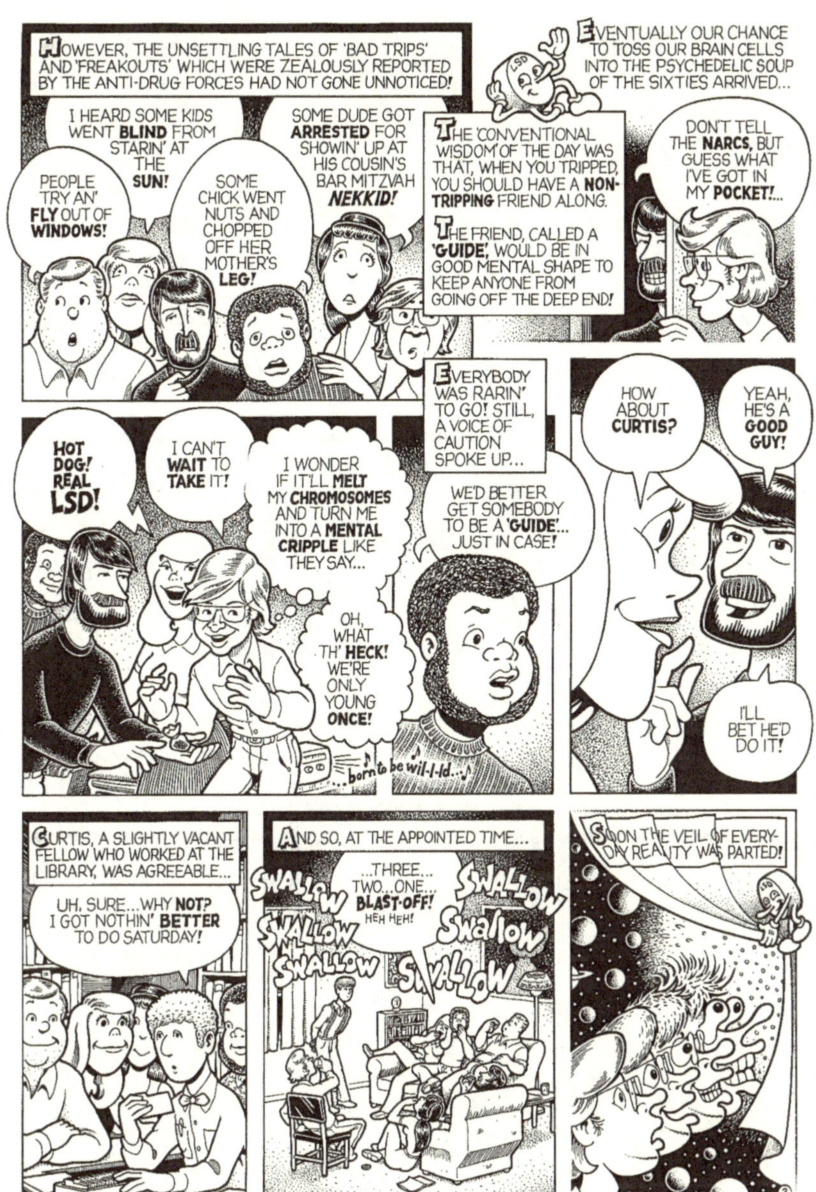
HOWEVER, THE UNSETTLING TALES OF 'BAD TRIPS' AND 'FREAKOUTS' WHICH WERE ZEALOUSLY REPORTED BY THE ANTI-DRUG FORCES HAD NOT GONE UNNOTICED!
I HEARD SOME KIDS WENT BLIND FROM STARIN' AT THE SUN!
SOME DUDE GOT ARRESTED FOR SHOWIN' UP AT HIS COUSIN'S BAR MITZVAH NEKKID!
PEOPLE TRY AN' FLY OUT OF WINDOWS!
SOME CHICK WENT NUTS AND CHOPPED OFF HER MOTHER'S LEG!
EVENTUALLY OUR CHANCE TO TOSS OUR BRAIN CELLS INTO THE PSYCHEDELIC SOUP OF THE SIXTIES ARRIVED...
LSD
THE 'CONVENTIONAL WISDOM' OF THE DAY WAS THAT, WHEN YOU TRIPPED, YOU SHOULD HAVE A NON-TRIPPING FRIEND ALONG.
THE FRIEND, CALLED A 'GUIDE', WOULD BE IN GOOD MENTAL SHAPE TO KEEP ANYONE FROM GOING OFF THE DEEP END!
DON'T TELL THE NARCS, BUT GUESS WHAT I'VE GOT IN MY POCKET!...
HOT DOG! REAL LSD!
I CAN'T WAIT TO TAKE IT!
I WONDER IF IT'LL MELT MY CHROMOSOMES AND TURN ME INTO A MENTAL CRIPPLE LIKE THEY SAY...
OH, WHAT TH' HECK! WE'RE ONLY YOUNG ONCE!
...born to be wil-l-ld...
EVERYBODY WAS RARIN' TO GO! STILL, A VOICE OF CAUTION SPOKE UP...
WE'D BETTER GET SOMEBODY TO BE A 'GUIDE'... JUST IN CASE!
HOW ABOUT CURTIS?
YEAH, HE'S A GOOD GUY!
I'LL BET HE'D DO IT!
CURTIS, A SLIGHTLY VACANT FELLOW WHO WORKED AT THE LIBRARY, WAS AGREEABLE...
UH, SURE... WHY NOT? I GOT NOTHIN' BETTER TO DO SATURDAY!
AND SO, AT THE APPOINTED TIME...
...THREE... TWO...ONE... BLAST-OFF! HEH HEH!
SWALLOW
SWALLOW
SWALLOW
SWALLOW
SWALLOW
SWALLOW
SOON THE VEIL OF EVERY-DAY REALITY WAS PARTED!
LSD
2

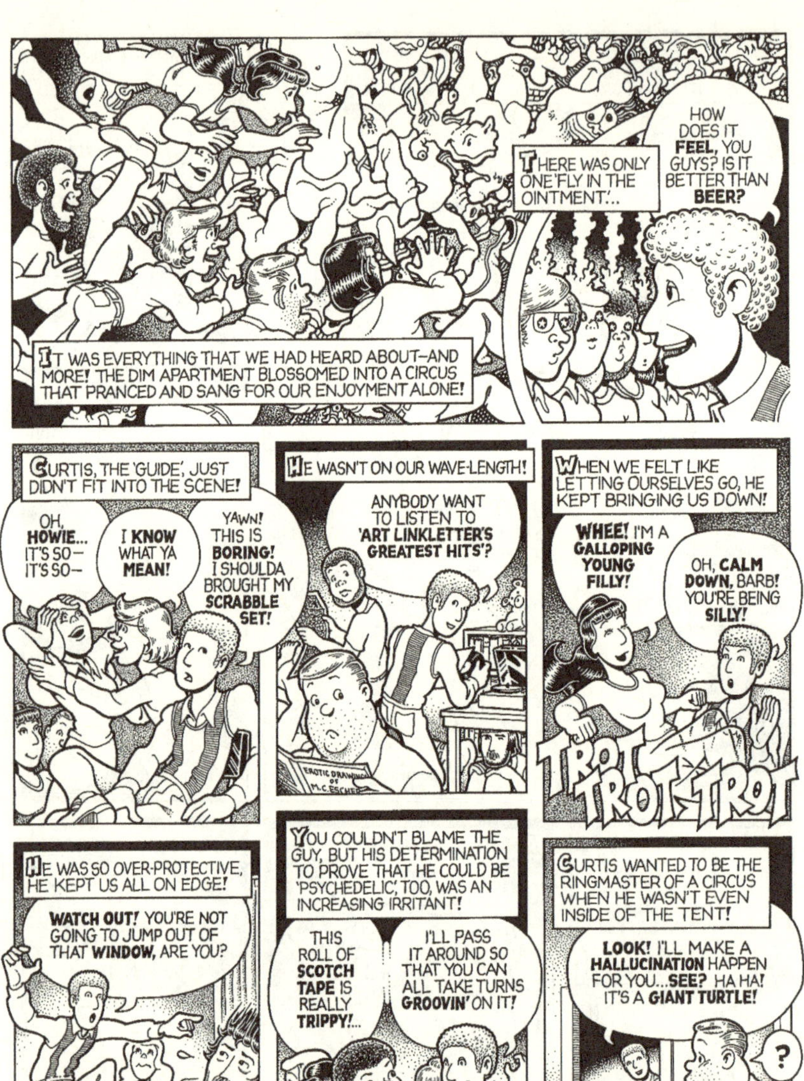
IT WAS EVERYTHING THAT WE HAD HEARD ABOUT—AND MORE! THE DIM APARTMENT BLOSSOMED INTO A CIRCUS THAT PRANCED AND SANG FOR OUR ENJOYMENT ALONE!
THERE WAS ONLY ONE 'FLY IN THE OINTMENT'...
HOW DOES IT FEEL, YOU GUYS? IS IT BETTER THAN BEER?
CURTIS, THE 'GUIDE', JUST DIDN'T FIT INTO THE SCENE!
OH, HOWIE... IT'S SO— IT'S SO—
I KNOW WHAT YA MEAN!
YAWN! THIS IS BORING! I SHOULDA BROUGHT MY SCRABBLE SET!
HE WASN'T ON OUR WAVE-LENGTH!
ANYBODY WANT TO LISTEN TO 'ART LINKLETTER'S GREATEST HITS'?
EROTIC DRAWINGS OF M.C. ESCHER
WHEN WE FELT LIKE LETTING OURSELVES GO, HE KEPT BRINGING US DOWN!
WHEE! I'M A GALLOPING YOUNG FILLY!
OH, CALM DOWN, BARB! YOU'RE BEING SILLY!
TROT TROT TROT
HE WAS SO OVER-PROTECTIVE, HE KEPT US ALL ON EDGE!
WATCH OUT! YOU'RE NOT GOING TO JUMP OUT OF THAT WINDOW, ARE YOU?
YOU COULDN'T BLAME THE GUY, BUT HIS DETERMINATION TO PROVE THAT HE COULD BE 'PSYCHEDELIC', TOO, WAS AN INCREASING IRRITANT!
THIS ROLL OF SCOTCH TAPE IS REALLY TRIPPY!...
I'LL PASS IT AROUND SO THAT YOU CAN ALL TAKE TURNS GROOVIN' ON IT!
CURTIS WANTED TO BE THE RINGMASTER OF A CIRCUS WHEN HE WASN'T EVEN INSIDE OF THE TENT!
LOOK! I'LL MAKE A HALLUCINATION HAPPEN FOR YOU...SEE? HA HA! IT'S A GIANT TURTLE!
?
3

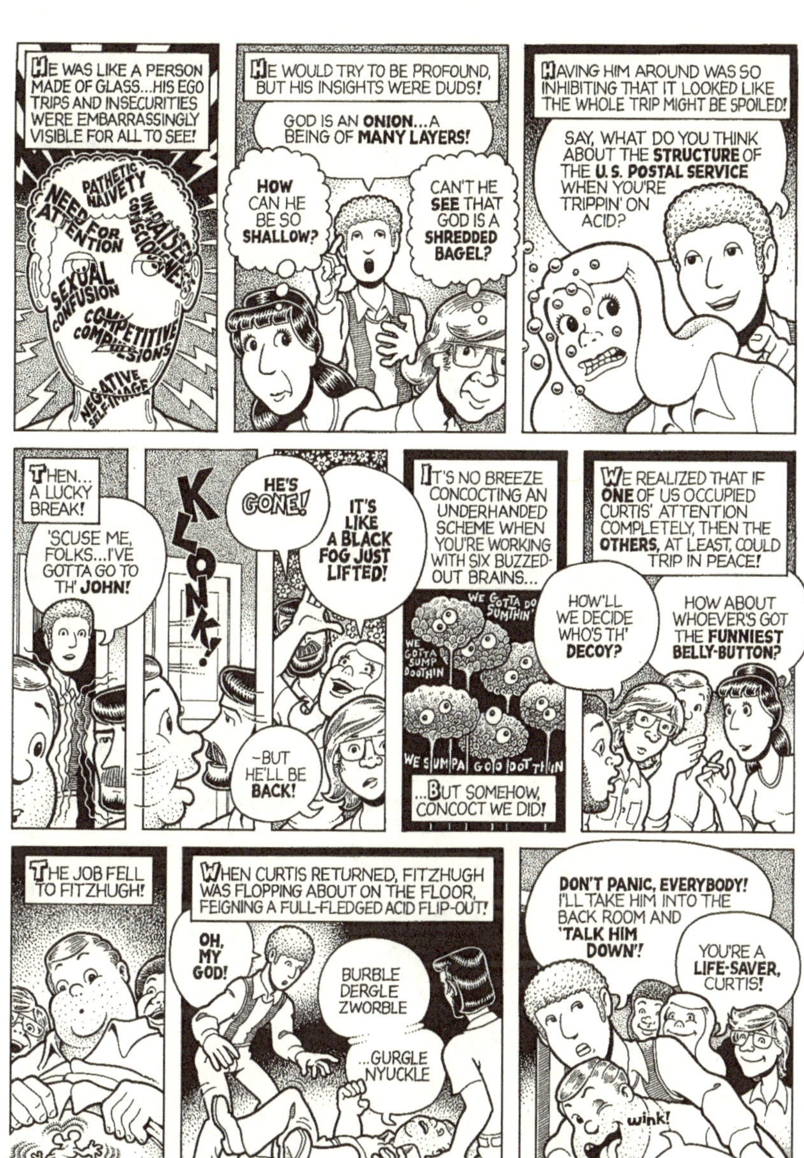
HE WAS LIKE A PERSON MADE OF GLASS...HIS EGO TRIPS AND INSECURITIES WERE EMBARRASSINGLY VISIBLE FOR ALL TO SEE!
PATHETIC NAIVETY
NEED FOR ATTENTION
UN-RAISED CONSCIOUSNESS
SEXUAL CONFUSION
COMPETITIVE COMPULSIONS
NEGATIVE SELF-IMAGE
HE WOULD TRY TO BE PROFOUND, BUT HIS INSIGHTS WERE DUDS!
GOD IS AN ONION...A BEING OF MANY LAYERS!
HOW CAN HE BE SO SHALLOW?
CAN'T HE SEE THAT GOD IS A SHREDDED BAGEL?
HAVING HIM AROUND WAS SO INHIBITING THAT IT LOOKED LIKE THE WHOLE TRIP MIGHT BE SPOILED!
SAY, WHAT DO YOU THINK ABOUT THE STRUCTURE OF THE U.S. POSTAL SERVICE WHEN YOU'RE TRIPPIN' ON ACID?
THEN... A LUCKY BREAK!
'SCUSE ME, FOLKS...I'VE GOTTA GO TO TH' JOHN!
KLONK!
HE'S GONE!
IT'S LIKE A BLACK FOG JUST LIFTED!
-BUT HE'LL BE BACK!
IT'S NO BREEZE CONCOCTING AN UNDERHANDED SCHEME WHEN YOU'RE WORKING WITH SIX BUZZED-OUT BRAINS...
WE GOTTA DO SUMTHIN
WE GOTTA SUMP DOOTHIN
WE SUMPA GOO DOTTHIN
...BUT SOMEHOW, CONCOCT WE DID!
WE REALIZED THAT IF ONE OF US OCCUPIED CURTIS' ATTENTION COMPLETELY, THEN THE OTHERS, AT LEAST, COULD TRIP IN PEACE!
HOW'LL WE DECIDE WHO'S TH' DECOY?
HOW ABOUT WHOEVER'S GOT THE FUNNIEST BELLY-BUTTON?
THE JOB FELL TO FITZHUGH!
WHEN CURTIS RETURNED, FITZHUGH WAS FLOPPING ABOUT ON THE FLOOR, FEIGNING A FULL-FLEDGED ACID FLIP-OUT!
OH, MY GOD!
BURBLE DERGLE ZWORBLE
...GURGLE NYUCKLE
TSK TSK!
DON'T PANIC, EVERYBODY! I'LL TAKE HIM INTO THE BACK ROOM AND 'TALK HIM DOWN'!
YOU'RE A LIFE-SAVER, CURTIS!
wink!
GORBLE JERKLE MRUMFUMP...
4

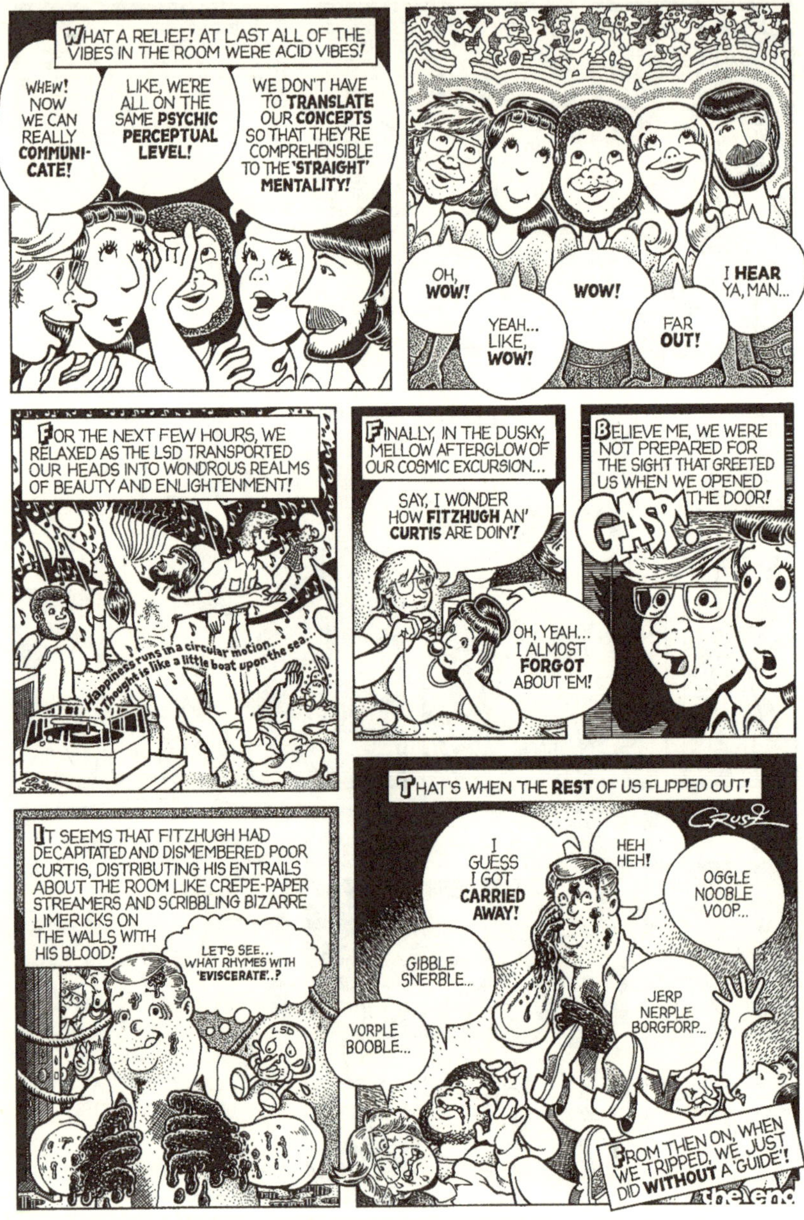
WHAT A RELIEF! AT LAST ALL OF THE VIBES IN THE ROOM WERE ACID VIBES!
WHEW! NOW WE CAN REALLY COMMUNI-CATE!
LIKE, WE'RE ALL ON THE SAME PSYCHIC PERCEPTUAL LEVEL!
WE DON'T HAVE TO TRANSLATE OUR CONCEPTS SO THAT THEY'RE COMPREHENSIBLE TO THE 'STRAIGHT' MENTALITY!
OH, WOW!
YEAH... LIKE, WOW!
WOW!
FAR OUT!
I HEAR YA, MAN...
FOR THE NEXT FEW HOURS, WE RELAXED AS THE LSD TRANSPORTED OUR HEADS INTO WONDROUS REALMS OF BEAUTY AND ENLIGHTENMENT!
Happiness runs in a circular motion...
Thought is like a little boat upon the sea...
FINALLY, IN THE DUSKY, MELLOW AFTERGLOW OF OUR COSMIC EXCURSION...
SAY, I WONDER HOW FITZHUGH AN' CURTIS ARE DOIN'?
OH, YEAH... I ALMOST FORGOT ABOUT 'EM!
BELIEVE ME, WE WERE NOT PREPARED FOR THE SIGHT THAT GREETED US WHEN WE OPENED THE DOOR!
GASP!
IT SEEMS THAT FITZHUGH HAD DECAPITATED AND DISMEMBERED POOR CURTIS, DISTRIBUTING HIS ENTRAILS ABOUT THE ROOM LIKE CREPE-PAPER STREAMERS AND SCRIBBLING BIZARRE LIMERICKS ON THE WALLS WITH HIS BLOOD!
LET'S SEE... WHAT RHYMES WITH 'EVISCERATE'..?
LSD
THAT'S WHEN THE REST OF US FLIPPED OUT!
I GUESS I GOT CARRIED AWAY!
HEH HEH!
OGGLE NOOBLE VOOP...
GIBBLE SNERBLE...
JERP NERPLE BORGFORP...
VORPLE BOOBLE...
FROM THEN ON, WHEN WE TRIPPED, WE JUST DID WITHOUT A 'GUIDE'!

"I Always Cry at Movies . . ."

This emotionally resonant memoir, from *Gay Comix* 3, focuses on the end of Cruse's relationship with Don Higdon, some eight or nine years after their breakup. The dialogue that Howard hears from the movie screen comes from the final moment of that relationship, as Don left Birmingham, Alabama, to pursue an acting career in California. The words clearly still hurt.

In the first panel, Cruse makes his avatar stand out from the rest of the movie audience by drawing himself in a sharply different style. Howard is haloed and drawn with a solid ink line and no shading, while the surrounding figures sit in the dark and feature extensive cross-hatching and almost pointillistic shading. This is not only an effective technique for this story, but it is also notable because it anticipates the style that Cruse would later use to greater effect in *Stuck Rubber Baby*.

The two-page story is deceptively simple and highlights Cruse's mastery of the comics medium. In most panels, Howard is framed in a close-up, where we can see his emotional reactions to the dialogue. These close-ups erase the background, so we never see at what point Howard transitions from the movie theater of the first page to the living room sofa of the final panel. At one point, a small, naked male figure reaches across panel borders to smash a chair into Howard's face. This inventive technique provides a visual metaphor for the traumatic memory that Howard re-experiences. The traumatic nature of the memory is reinforced by a subtle change in the shape of the word balloons. For most of the story, the balloons are shaped with jagged edges that denote an electronic source for the dialogue, like a movie theater speaker, and they also exceed the boundaries of the panel borders. However, in the final tier, the more conventional, rounded balloon appears, implying that the speaker is present in the room and no longer electronically broadcast. In a final, subtle touch, Howard sets his glasses down on the sofa, but they continue to shed tears and sniffle.

In the last panel, behind Howard's head, a framed picture hangs containing a photo of a naked man with his arms outstretched. This image is a fragment of a larger picture, which serves as a motif that appears in Cruse's early work, notably *Barefootz*. In his introduction to *Early Barefootz*, Cruse describes the origin of the image: "Sometime in 1971 as I recall, I got the idea for a psychedelic poster that would mix the imagery of religion as I had known it when I was growing up, with the ecstatic feelings of spirituality that I had experienced under the influence of psilocybin. The poster would be dominated by the image of a naked male figure with arms outstretched in a position that called to mind Christ on the cross but that could as easily be seen as a sublimely liberated human in flight" (15). In order to achieve a more realistic image than Cruse could draw, he used a photograph of Don in this pose and then turned it into a high-contrast drawing. Though Cruse never made the planned psychedelic poster, the image served its duty in the background of a particularly trippy *Barefootz* story, "The Eclipse," and later appeared throughout most of the series. The realistic, photo-based drawing stands in sharp contrast to Cruse's cartooning style in *Barefootz*. In "I Always Cry at Movies . . . ," Cruse has moved into a more realistic style, but the contrast is still there. By referring back to his *Barefootz* days, Cruse also contrasts the innocence of those strips with the emotional weight of this story. But if the picture is also, as Cruse described, an image of liberation, then its inclusion leaves a lingering question: What does that freedom mean in the context of this story? In other words, who is liberated in the end?

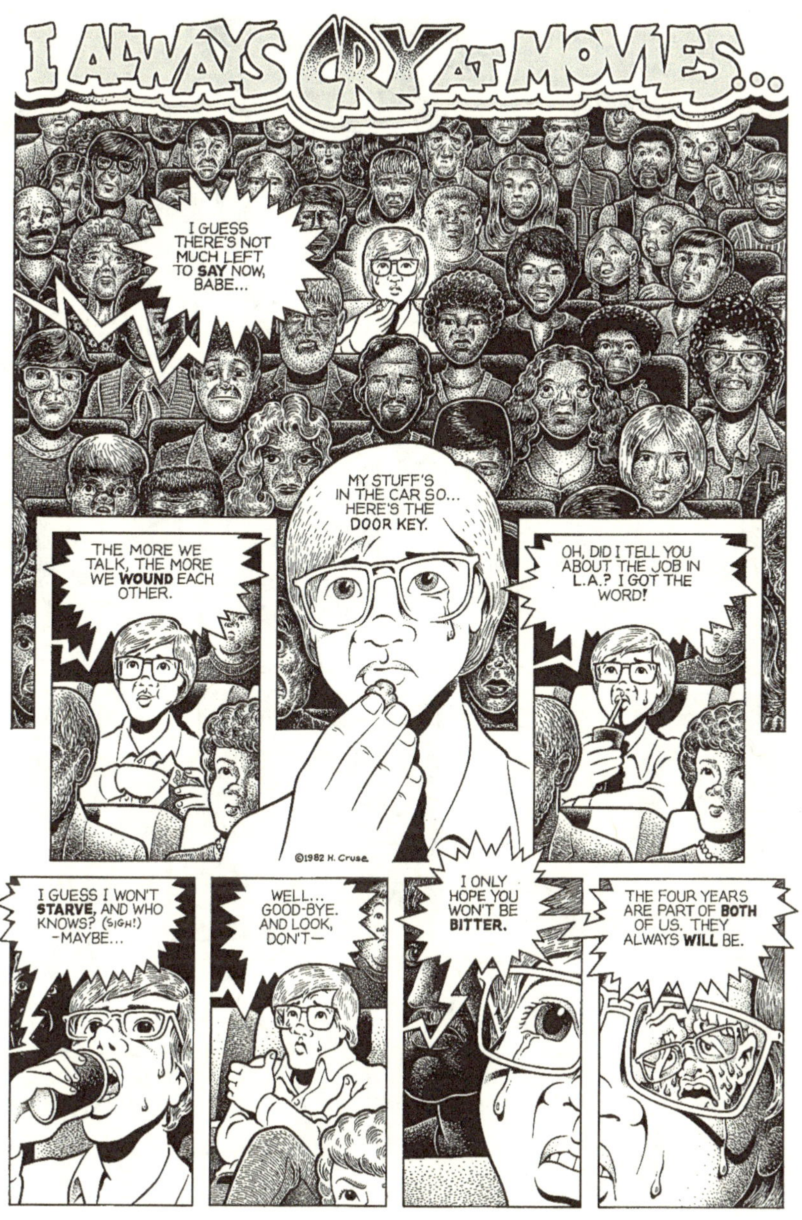
I ALWAYS CRY AT MOVIES...
I GUESS THERE'S NOT MUCH LEFT TO SAY NOW, BABE...
MY STUFF'S IN THE CAR SO... HERE'S THE DOOR KEY.
THE MORE WE TALK, THE MORE WE WOUND EACH OTHER.
OH, DID I TELL YOU ABOUT THE JOB IN L.A.? I GOT THE WORD!
©1982 H. Cruse
I GUESS I WON'T STARVE, AND WHO KNOWS? (SIGH!) -MAYBE...
WELL... GOOD-BYE. AND LOOK, DON'T—
I ONLY HOPE YOU WON'T BE BITTER.
THE FOUR YEARS ARE PART OF BOTH OF US. THEY ALWAYS WILL BE.

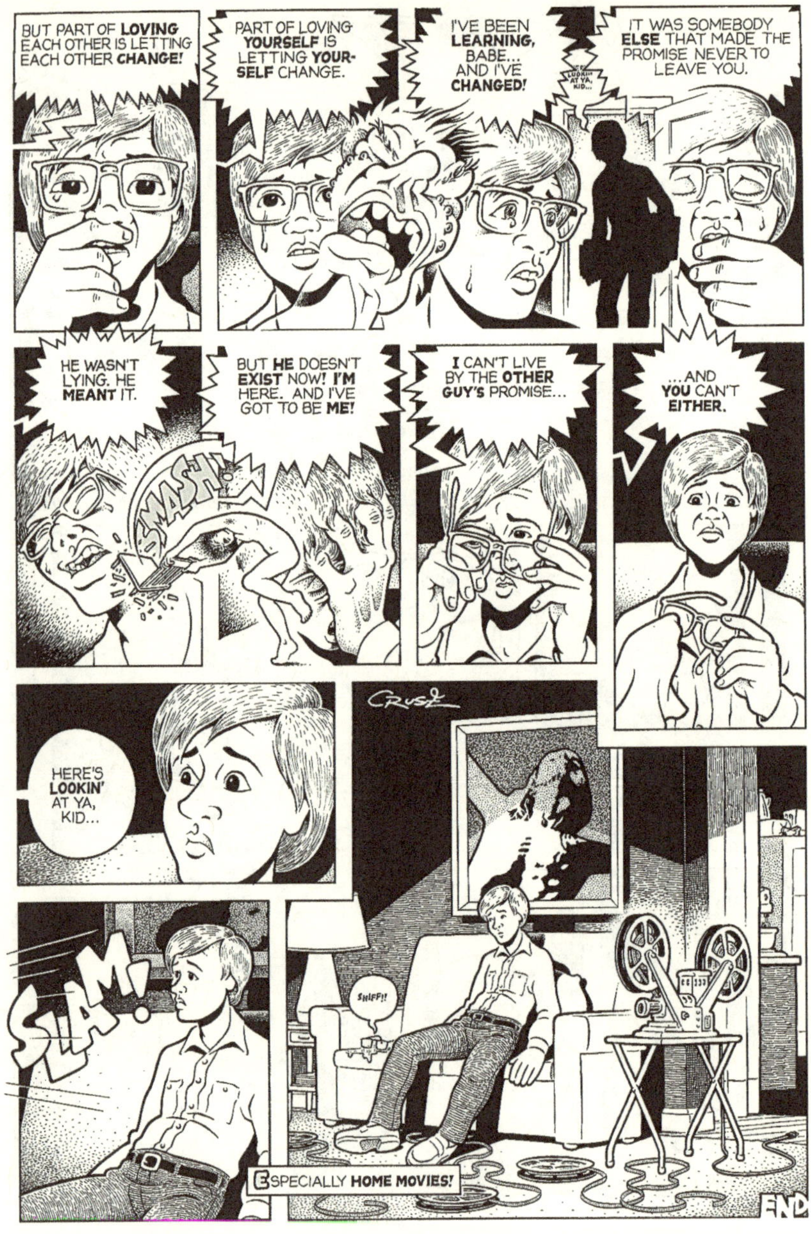

"I Always Cry at Movies . . ." copyright the estate of Howard Cruse. Used by permission.

"That Night at the Stonewall"

One of Howard Cruse's claims to fame is that he was present for the Stonewall Riots in New York City on June 28, 1969. However, as this story shows, his involvement was accidental and awkwardly timed to an LSD trip he was experiencing following a Tiny Tim concert. It's done in six concise panels, which don't overplay Cruse's involvement in this monumental event.

This story appears in multiple forms. In the online version on his website and the version reprinted in *From Headrack to Claude*, Cruse added color to panel five in order to capture the acid-influenced perspective on the experience. The online version uses a psychedelic color palate with a pastiche of American Revolution imagery, mainly from John Trumbull paintings. The *Headrack* one also has a pastiche of American Revolution paintings—primarily John Trumbull's *The Death of General Mercer at the Battle of Princeton*—but with the original color. These two images also reflect the revolutionary potential of the event. The version here reproduces the original black and white as it first appeared in the *Village Voice* in 1982.

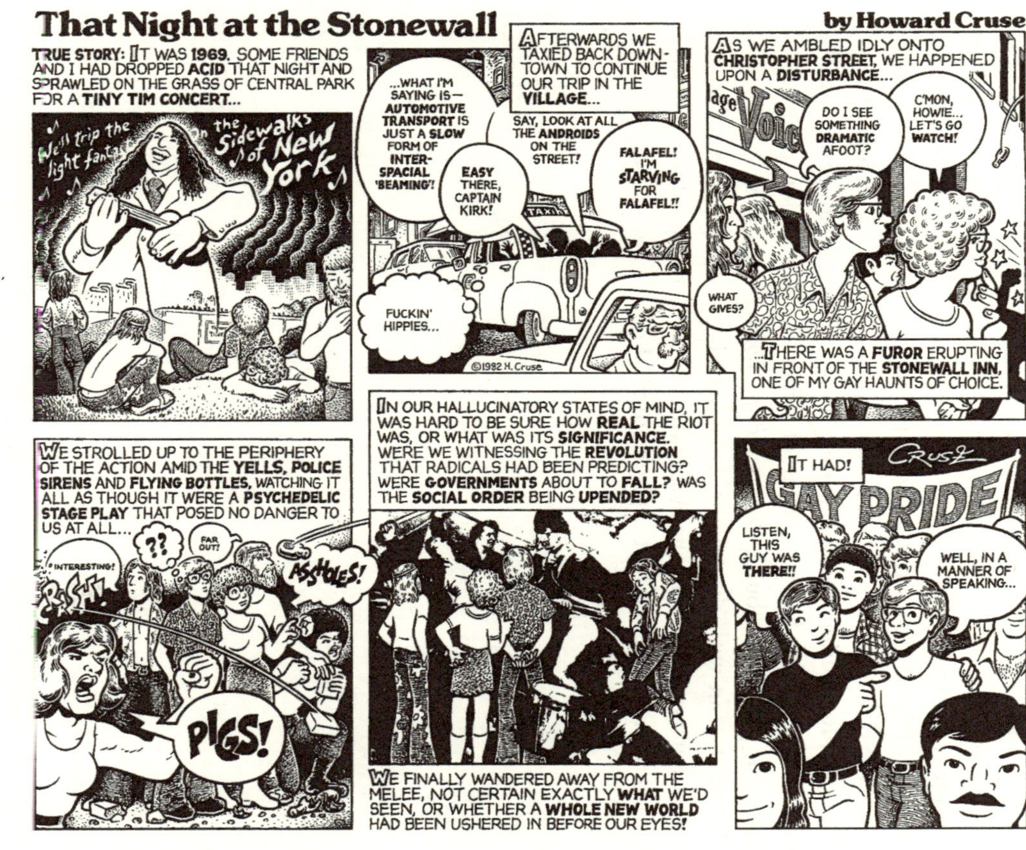

"That Night at the Stonewall" copyright the estate of Howard Cruse. Used by permission.

"Then There Was Claude"

"Then There Was Claude" appeared in the comics anthology *Book of Boy Trouble, Vol. 2: Born to Trouble*, edited by Robert Kirby and David Kelly for Green Candy Press in 2008, where it was originally published in color. It's an example of the style of short-form autobiographical comics Cruse created later in his career, after publishing *Stuck Rubber Baby*. In the early 2000s, Cruse was invited to contribute to numerous queer comics anthologies, to which he would lend his name and status as the "Godfather of Gay Comics" for support.

This personal story is presented in a straightforward manner—Cruse isn't playing with the genre as he did in early examples. It also covers a theme that Cruse has addressed in past comics, including "Jerry Mack" and *Stuck Rubber Baby*: the incompatible mixture of organized Christianity and homosexuality. Claude's solution to his dilemma of being a gay minister—that he would be queer every day but Sunday—is unsustainable, but rather than being the tragic denial of identity that we see in "Jerry Mack," it's played for laughs. Howard in the comic quickly realizes that Claude's plan won't work, neither for Claude nor for Howard in a long-term relationship, but he goes ahead and continues with the sex anyway. The visual style contains the cross-hatching used in *Stuck Rubber Baby*, but the figure drawing is definitely the later style that Cruse adopted, still with a humorous look but not quite the same as the *Wendel* days.

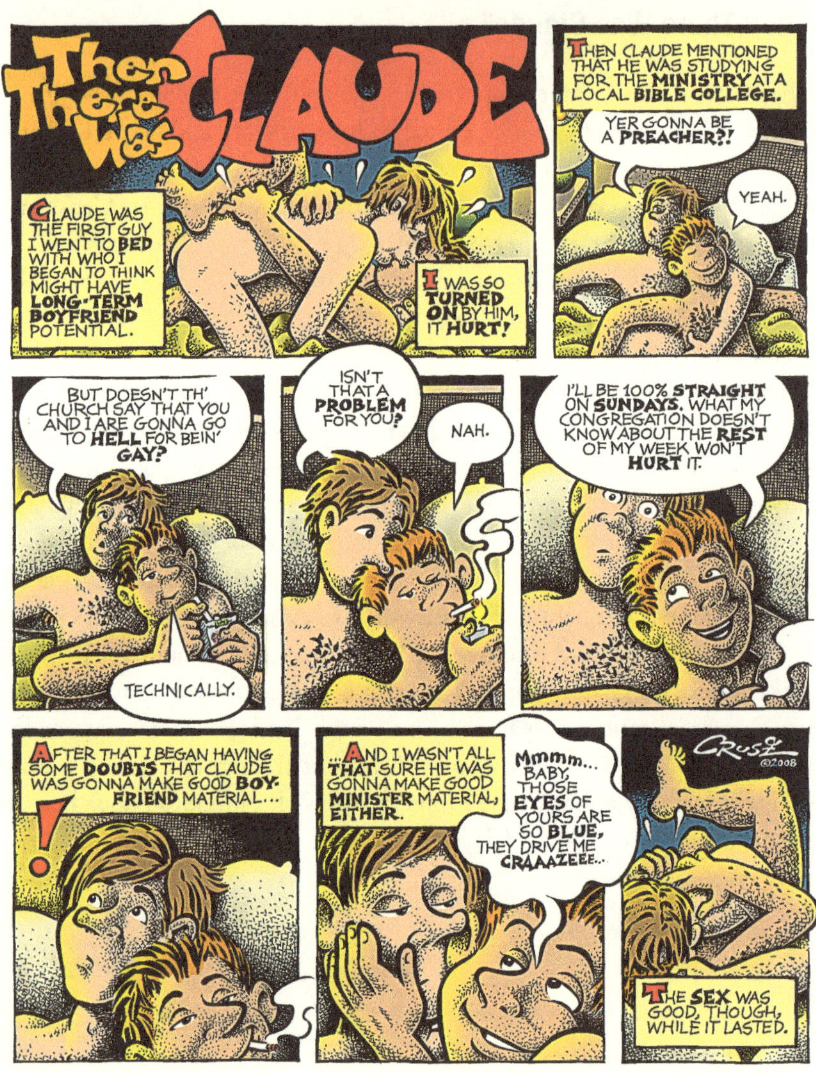

"Then There Was Claude" copyright the estate of Howard Cruse. Used by permission.

3

Commentary and Satire

●●●●●●●●●●●●●●

Throughout his career, Howard Cruse engaged with political, social, and cultural issues, but especially in the 1980s, when Reagan-era conservatism dominated U.S. politics. During this period, Cruse covers topics like AIDS, homophobia, censorship, the news media, and gay activism. However, because such work was so overtly topical, the impact of the strips can be lost for contemporary audiences who lack the memory or experience of the specific contexts.

For such commentary, Cruse developed a type of comics essay that was not common to the medium at the time that he created these strips. The genre has its origins in political cartooning and in educational comics. However, the comics essay doesn't really emerge as a popular genre until the underground comix era, especially in the more politically charged anthologies like *Wimmen's Comix* and Leonard Rifas's *All-Atomic Comics* (1976), which parodies the educational comics of the 1950s and 1960s by having a frog with an extra leg explain the dangers of nuclear power. Lee Marrs's contributions to the early issues of *Wimmen's Comix* serve as good examples of the comics essay genre as well, especially "So, Ya Wanna Be an Artist" (issue 2) and "Cyberfenetics" (issue 4), which explores women's connections to technology.

The comics essay frees up a creator from the requirements of a linear narrative structure; instead, the comic can be organized with an introduction, body, and conclusion in the same sense as a prose essay. This argumentative structure is evident in "Safe Sex," "Sometimes I Get So Mad . . . ," "The Gay in the Street," and "My Life as a TV Pundit." These stories feature the Howard avatar as a narrator and organizing principle, a figure who also appears in many of Cruse's autobiographical comics. In these instances, the Howard avatar is an exaggeration of the real Howard Cruse, often used for comic and satirical effect.

In these comics essays, Cruse also exhibits some of his most creative artistic choices, especially in the unconventional panel borders of "Safe Sex" and the dense page layout of "Sometimes I Get So Mad . . ." Cruse's expressive and inventive lettering skills are also on display here—a talent for which Cruse does not receive a lot of credit or attention (see especially the third panel of "The Gay in the Street," where Cruse is able to depict changes in volume, confusion, and uncertainty in one balloon).

"Safe Sex," "The Gay in the Street," and "Death" exemplify Cruse's tendency toward improvisation in his creative process, in which he would begin a strip without a set plan for what he would say, where it would go, or how long it would be. That can explain how many of his comics essays read like stream of consciousness, where ideas in one panel seem to inspire the next, and so on.

"Billy Goes Out" is a primary exception to the nonnarrative comics essays in this chapter. Here, Cruse provides an empathic view of one gay man's experience, including memories of homophobic relatives, his struggles with competing desires, and so on, all of which offers a snapshot of gay urban life in the early 1980s, at the advent of the AIDS crisis. As such, it makes a commentary on a particular time, place, and social milieu.

"Billy Goes Out"

"Billy Goes Out" is Cruse's contribution to the first issue of *Gay Comix* and, as such, is one of his earliest works to fall outside of the *Barefootz* series. Cruse envisioned a dual audience for *Gay Comix*: an insider gay readership looking for authentic narratives by gay creators that reflected and validated their experiences, and an outsider straight audience who needed to be educated about and made familiar with queerness. Cruse even put a statement to this effect in his solicitation letter to potential creators. In a letter to Jackie Urbanovic regarding *Gay Comix* 4 (to which she was one of the contributors), Cruse wrote about his goals for the series: "hopefully letting the nongay readers see that gay men and lesbians are not weird species from Mars but rather human beings whose range of feelings are very similar to theirs" (24 Jan. 1983). To this end, as his first contribution to the series, "Billy Goes Out" serves as a kind of mission statement for Cruse's editorial vision as he attempts to navigate these two audiences. On the one hand, it reflects a specific but common gay male experience in the late 1970s, fulfilling the mandate that gay readers could see their experiences reflected in the stories; on the other hand, it reveals to straight readers the conflicts and complexity of that otherwise little known experience.

The story starts with Billy watching what looks like a television interview with a husband and a wife that reinforces the dominance of heteronormativity in popular culture, while Billy looks nonplussed at the screen. As Billy starts to get ready for his night out, the inane question of the TV interview ("Who's the boss in your home—you or your wife?") is transformed into an imagined interview between Billy and his penis, who both declare a shared, mutual understanding in which neither is the boss. After a phone call from his mother about the death of an uncle, Billy remembers homophobic comments that his uncle made about Billy staying in the closet. His memory then moves to how Billy has followed that advice in his current workplace. Later, Billy will return to even more homophobic comments from his uncle. By placing these memories early in the story, Cruse builds sympathy for Billy, especially with straight readers who can be horrified by the way that Billy has been treated. The memories also reveal fragments of a long-term relationship that Billy had with Brad, but one that ended in an unspecified tragedy probably involving a gay-bashing incident where Brad is killed at a gay pride parade.

On the surface, then, Billy's reckless promiscuity later in the story may seem to feed gay male stereotypes, but his internal life presented through the innovative use of thought balloons reveals his struggles, his traumatic experiences, and the social forces that affect his daily existence. Billy's daily life requires a disconnect between his public and private selves, and the tragic loss of his lover Brad has sent him back to the anonymous sex of cruising gay bars. Therefore, Cruse does not shy away from the more graphic elements of Billy's sex life.

Along with "Jerry Mack," "Billy Goes Out" represents the high point of Cruse's work during the *Gay Comix* period. It is highly innovative in both form and content. The story builds across seven pages, with every page consistently divided into six tall and narrow panels. Cruse takes advantage of unique elements of the medium, where each panel juxtaposes Billy's evening out with his internal life of memory and fantasy. That juxtaposition creates sympathy for Billy and reveals a depth of experience. Therefore, in addition to its groundbreaking content, "Billy Goes Out" is also a master class in comics form.

In the end, "Billy Goes Out" was a critical and personal success for Cruse, and it proved that he was on the right track with his career. In a January 31, 1981, letter to friends Nancy and Jon, he explained: "'Billy Goes Out' has been the best-received thing I've ever done. . . . It was one of those things where I was drawing the mask from my own face, and somehow I hit a nerve in the process for a lot of people." Letters to *Gay Comix* from readers also bear out the story's positive reception by singling it out as a high point for the first issue.

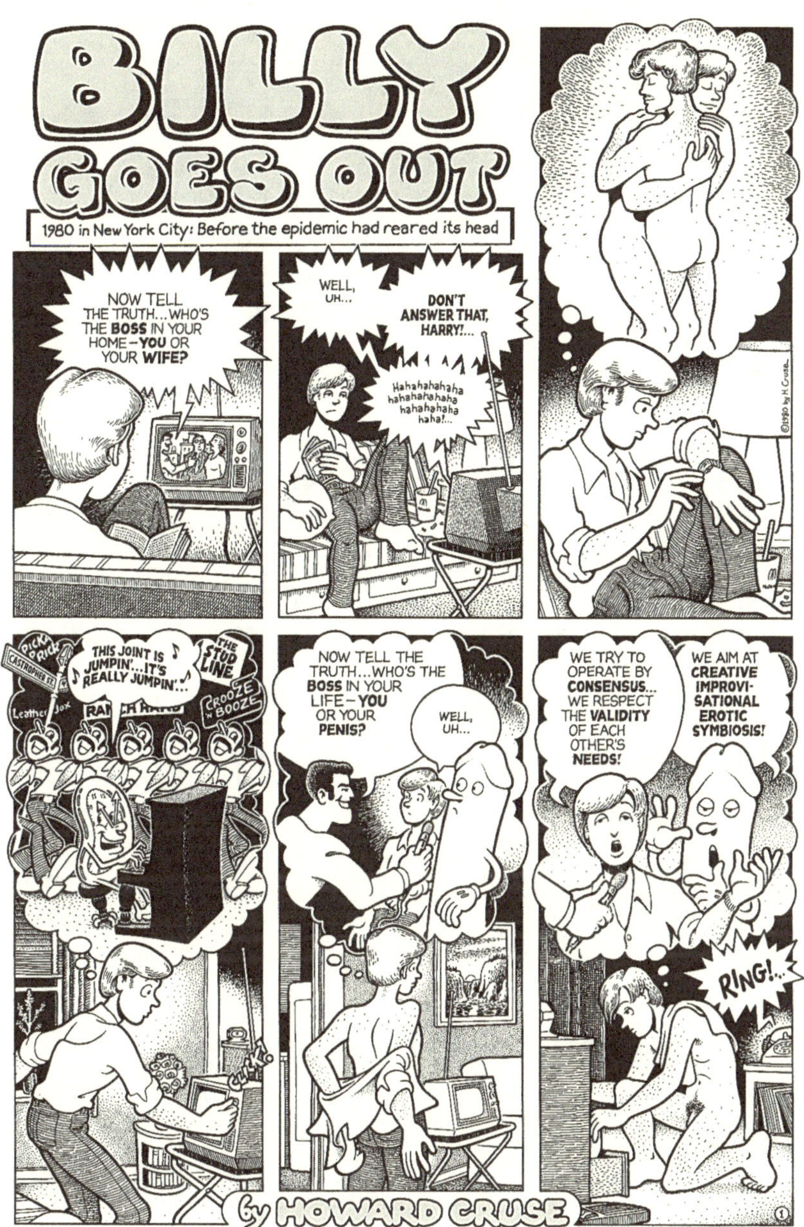
BILLY GOES OUT
1980 in New York City: Before the epidemic had reared its head
NOW TELL THE TRUTH... WHO'S THE BOSS IN YOUR HOME—YOU OR YOUR WIFE?
WELL, UH...
DON'T ANSWER THAT, HARRY!...
Hahahahahaha hahahahahaha hahahahaha haha!...
CASTROPHER ST.
THIS JOINT IS JUMPIN'... IT'S REALLY JUMPIN'...
THE STUD LINE
CROOZE 'N BOOZE
NOW TELL THE TRUTH... WHO'S THE BOSS IN YOUR LIFE—YOU OR YOUR PENIS?
WELL, UH...
WE TRY TO OPERATE BY CONSENSUS... WE RESPECT THE VALIDITY OF EACH OTHER'S NEEDS!
WE AIM AT CREATIVE IMPROVISATIONAL EROTIC SYMBIOSIS!
RING!...
by HOWARD CRUSE
1

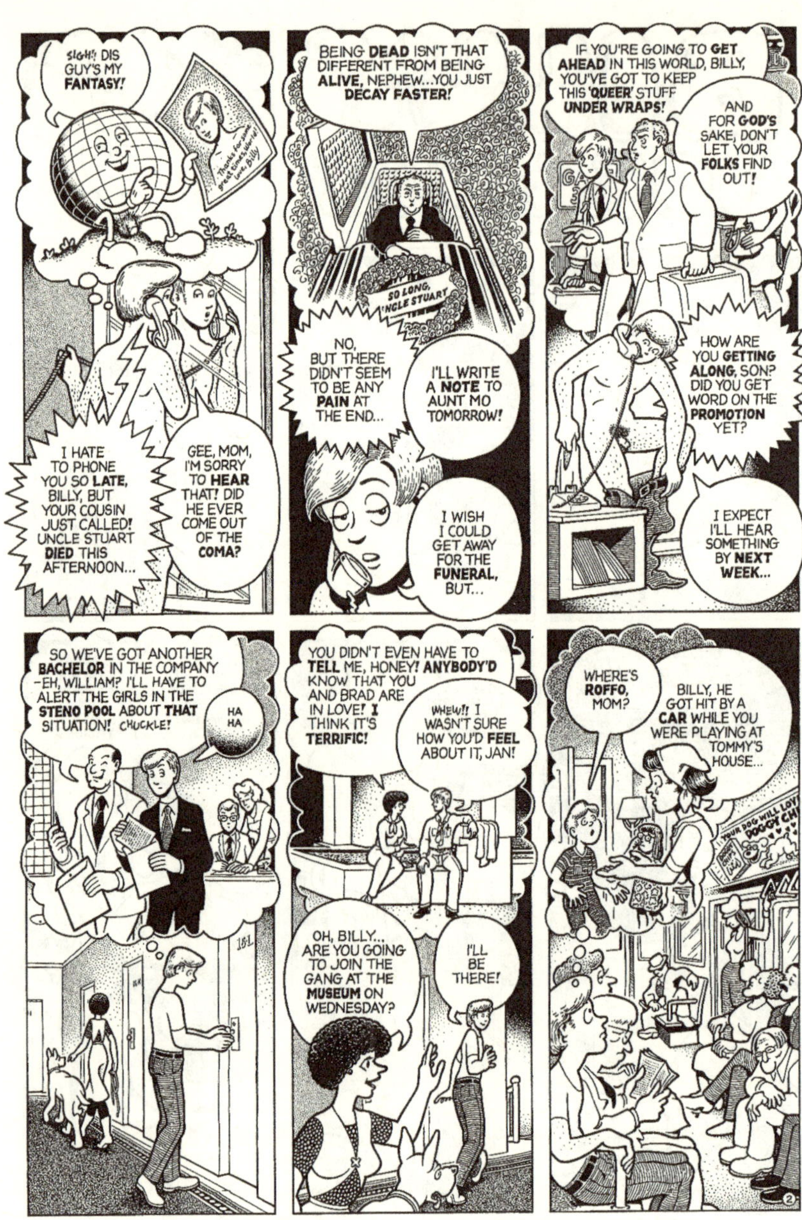
SIGH! DIS GUY'S MY FANTASY!
Thanks for some great times. Warm love, Billy
I HATE TO PHONE YOU SO LATE, BILLY, BUT YOUR COUSIN JUST CALLED! UNCLE STUART DIED THIS AFTERNOON...
GEE, MOM, I'M SORRY TO HEAR THAT! DID HE EVER COME OUT OF THE COMA?
BEING DEAD ISN'T THAT DIFFERENT FROM BEING ALIVE, NEPHEW...YOU JUST DECAY FASTER!
SO LONG, UNCLE STUART
NO, BUT THERE DIDN'T SEEM TO BE ANY PAIN AT THE END...
I'LL WRITE A NOTE TO AUNT MO TOMORROW!
I WISH I COULD GET AWAY FOR THE FUNERAL, BUT...
IF YOU'RE GOING TO GET AHEAD IN THIS WORLD, BILLY, YOU'VE GOT TO KEEP THIS 'QUEER' STUFF UNDER WRAPS!
AND FOR GOD'S SAKE, DON'T LET YOUR FOLKS FIND OUT!
HOW ARE YOU GETTING ALONG, SON? DID YOU GET WORD ON THE PROMOTION YET?
I EXPECT I'LL HEAR SOMETHING BY NEXT WEEK...
SO WE'VE GOT ANOTHER BACHELOR IN THE COMPANY –EH, WILLIAM? I'LL HAVE TO ALERT THE GIRLS IN THE STENO POOL ABOUT THAT SITUATION! CHUCKLE!
HA HA
YOU DIDN'T EVEN HAVE TO TELL ME, HONEY! ANYBODY'D KNOW THAT YOU AND BRAD ARE IN LOVE! I THINK IT'S TERRIFIC!
WHEW!! I WASN'T SURE HOW YOU'D FEEL ABOUT IT, JAN!
OH, BILLY... ARE YOU GOING TO JOIN THE GANG AT THE MUSEUM ON WEDNESDAY?
I'LL BE THERE!
WHERE'S ROFFO, MOM?
BILLY, HE GOT HIT BY A CAR WHILE YOU WERE PLAYING AT TOMMY'S HOUSE...
YOUR DOG WILL LOVE DOGGY CH

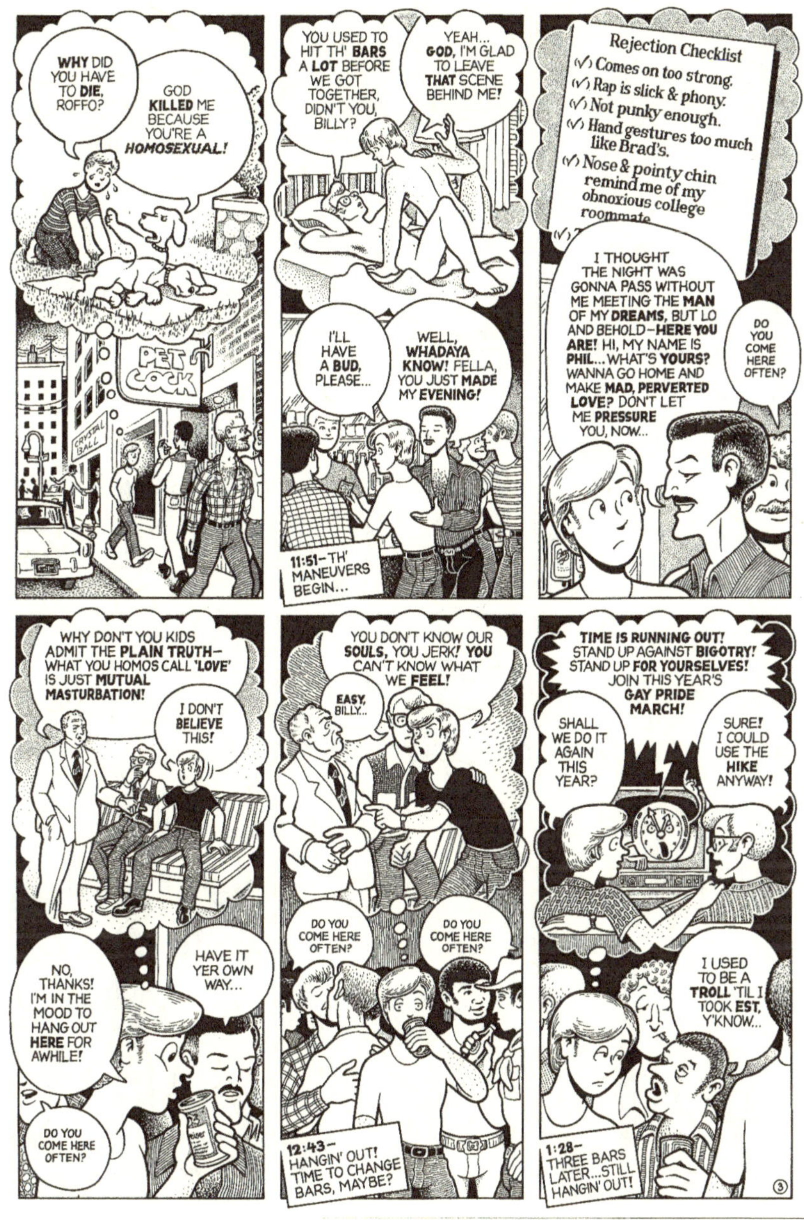
WHY DID YOU HAVE TO DIE, ROFFO?
GOD KILLED ME BECAUSE YOU'RE A HOMOSEXUAL!
PET COCK
CRYSTAL BALL
YOU USED TO HIT TH' BARS A LOT BEFORE WE GOT TOGETHER, DIDN'T YOU, BILLY?
YEAH... GOD, I'M GLAD TO LEAVE THAT SCENE BEHIND ME!
I'LL HAVE A BUD, PLEASE...
WELL, WHADAYA KNOW! FELLA, YOU JUST MADE MY EVENING!
11:51—TH' MANEUVERS BEGIN...
Rejection Checklist
(✓) Comes on too strong.
(✓) Rap is slick & phony.
(✓) Not punky enough.
(✓) Hand gestures too much like Brad's.
(✓) Nose & pointy chin remind me of my obnoxious college roommate
I THOUGHT THE NIGHT WAS GONNA PASS WITHOUT ME MEETING THE MAN OF MY DREAMS, BUT LO AND BEHOLD—HERE YOU ARE! HI, MY NAME IS PHIL... WHAT'S YOURS? WANNA GO HOME AND MAKE MAD, PERVERTED LOVE? DON'T LET ME PRESSURE YOU, NOW...
DO YOU COME HERE OFTEN?
WHY DON'T YOU KIDS ADMIT THE PLAIN TRUTH—WHAT YOU HOMOS CALL 'LOVE' IS JUST MUTUAL MASTURBATION!
I DON'T BELIEVE THIS!
NO, THANKS! I'M IN THE MOOD TO HANG OUT HERE FOR AWHILE!
HAVE IT YER OWN WAY...
DO YOU COME HERE OFTEN?
YOU DON'T KNOW OUR SOULS, YOU JERK! YOU CAN'T KNOW WHAT WE FEEL!
EASY, BILLY...
DO YOU COME HERE OFTEN?
DO YOU COME HERE OFTEN?
12:43—HANGIN' OUT! TIME TO CHANGE BARS, MAYBE?
TIME IS RUNNING OUT! STAND UP AGAINST BIGOTRY! STAND UP FOR YOURSELVES! JOIN THIS YEAR'S GAY PRIDE MARCH!
SHALL WE DO IT AGAIN THIS YEAR?
SURE! I COULD USE THE HIKE ANYWAY!
I USED TO BE A TROLL 'TIL I TOOK EST, Y'KNOW...
1:28—THREE BARS LATER...STILL HANGIN' OUT!
3

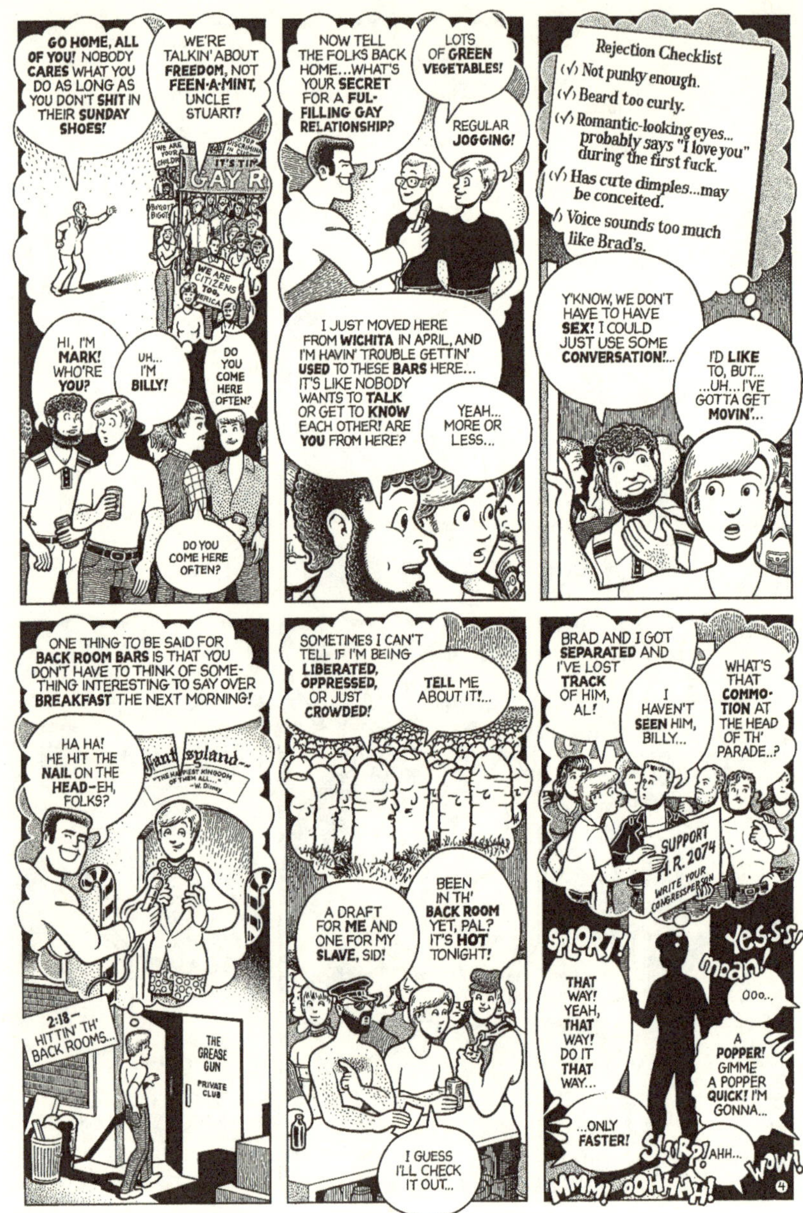
GO HOME, ALL OF YOU! NOBODY CARES WHAT YOU DO AS LONG AS YOU DON'T SHIT IN THEIR SUNDAY SHOES!
WE'RE TALKIN' ABOUT FREEDOM, NOT FEEN-A-MINT, UNCLE STUART!
WE ARE CITIZENS TOO,
NOW TELL THE FOLKS BACK HOME... WHAT'S YOUR SECRET FOR A FUL-FILLING GAY RELATIONSHIP?
LOTS OF GREEN VEGETABLES!
REGULAR JOGGING!
Rejection Checklist
(√) Not punky enough.
(√) Beard too curly.
(√) Romantic-looking eyes... probably says "I love you" during the first fuck.
(√) Has cute dimples...may be conceited.
(√) Voice sounds too much like Brad's.
HI, I'M MARK! WHO'RE YOU?
UH... I'M BILLY!
DO YOU COME HERE OFTEN?
DO YOU COME HERE OFTEN?
I JUST MOVED HERE FROM WICHITA IN APRIL, AND I'M HAVIN' TROUBLE GETTIN' USED TO THESE BARS HERE... IT'S LIKE NOBODY WANTS TO TALK OR GET TO KNOW EACH OTHER! ARE YOU FROM HERE?
YEAH... MORE OR LESS...
Y'KNOW, WE DON'T HAVE TO HAVE SEX! I COULD JUST USE SOME CONVERSATION!...
I'D LIKE TO, BUT... ...UH... I'VE GOTTA GET MOVIN'...
ONE THING TO BE SAID FOR BACK ROOM BARS IS THAT YOU DON'T HAVE TO THINK OF SOME-THING INTERESTING TO SAY OVER BREAKFAST THE NEXT MORNING!
HA HA! HE HIT THE NAIL ON THE HEAD—EH, FOLKS?
Fantasyland
2:18— HITTIN' TH' BACK ROOMS...
THE GREASE GUN PRIVATE CLUB
SOMETIMES I CAN'T TELL IF I'M BEING LIBERATED, OPPRESSED, OR JUST CROWDED!
TELL ME ABOUT IT!...
A DRAFT FOR ME AND ONE FOR MY SLAVE, SID!
BEEN IN TH' BACK ROOM YET, PAL? IT'S HOT TONIGHT!
I GUESS I'LL CHECK IT OUT...
BRAD AND I GOT SEPARATED AND I'VE LOST TRACK OF HIM, AL!
I HAVEN'T SEEN HIM, BILLY...
WHAT'S THAT COMMO-TION AT THE HEAD OF TH' PARADE..?
SUPPORT H.R. 2074 WRITE YOUR CONGRESSPERSON
SPLORT!
YES-S-S!
MOAN!
OOO...
THAT WAY! YEAH, THAT WAY! DO IT THAT WAY...
A POPPER! GIMME A POPPER QUICK! I'M GONNA...
...ONLY FASTER!
SLURP!
AHH...
WOW!
MMM!
OOHHHAH!
4

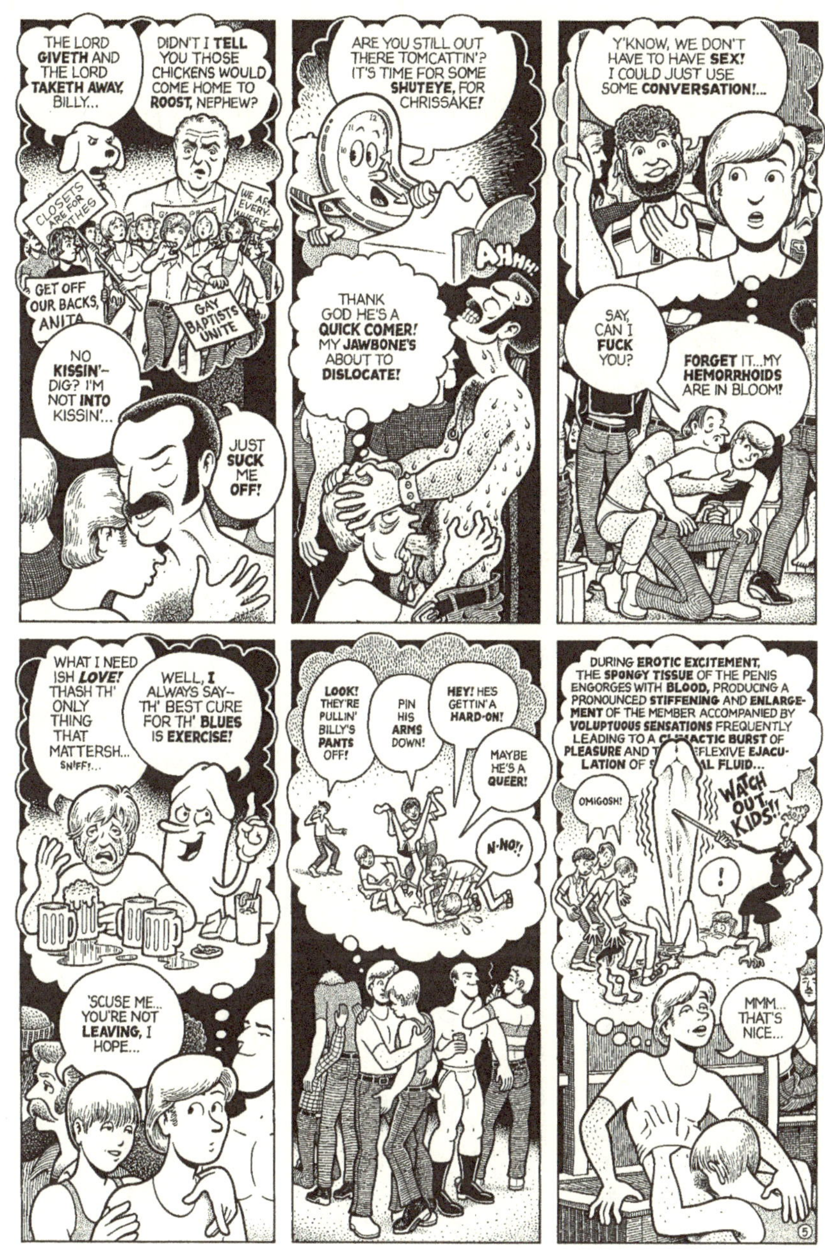
THE LORD GIVETH AND THE LORD TAKETH AWAY, BILLY...
DIDN'T I TELL YOU THOSE CHICKENS WOULD COME HOME TO ROOST, NEPHEW?
CLOSETS ARE FOR CLOTHES
WE ARE EVERYWHERE
GET OFF OUR BACKS, ANITA
GAY BAPTISTS UNITE
NO KISSIN'– DIG? I'M NOT INTO KISSIN'...
JUST SUCK ME OFF!
ARE YOU STILL OUT THERE TOMCATTIN'? IT'S TIME FOR SOME SHUTEYE, FOR CHRISSAKE!
AHHH!
THANK GOD HE'S A QUICK COMER! MY JAWBONE'S ABOUT TO DISLOCATE!
Y'KNOW, WE DON'T HAVE TO HAVE SEX! I COULD JUST USE SOME CONVERSATION!...
SAY, CAN I FUCK YOU?
FORGET IT...MY HEMORRHOIDS ARE IN BLOOM!
WHAT I NEED ISH LOVE! THASH TH' ONLY THING THAT MATTERSH... SNIFF!...
WELL, I ALWAYS SAY-- TH' BEST CURE FOR TH' BLUES IS EXERCISE!
'SCUSE ME... YOU'RE NOT LEAVING, I HOPE...
LOOK! THEY'RE PULLIN' BILLY'S PANTS OFF!
PIN HIS ARMS DOWN!
HEY! HE'S GETTIN' A HARD-ON!
MAYBE HE'S A QUEER!
N-NO!!
DURING EROTIC EXCITEMENT, THE SPONGY TISSUE OF THE PENIS ENGORGES WITH BLOOD, PRODUCING A PRONOUNCED STIFFENING AND ENLARGEMENT OF THE MEMBER ACCOMPANIED BY VOLUPTUOUS SENSATIONS FREQUENTLY LEADING TO A CLIMACTIC BURST OF PLEASURE AND THE REFLEXIVE EJACULATION OF SEMINAL FLUID...
OMIGOSH!
WATCH OUT, KIDS!!
!
MMM... THAT'S NICE...
5

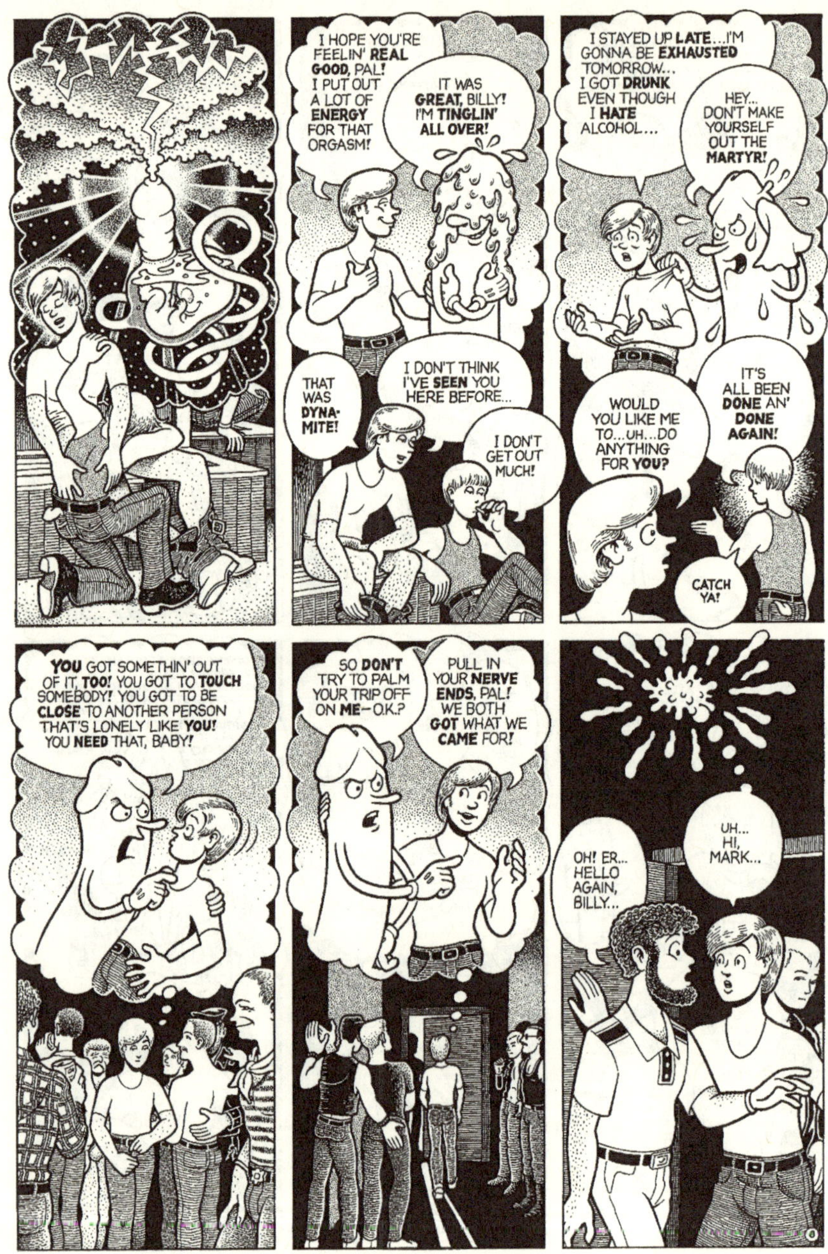
I HOPE YOU'RE FEELIN' REAL GOOD, PAL! I PUT OUT A LOT OF ENERGY FOR THAT ORGASM!
IT WAS GREAT, BILLY! I'M TINGLIN' ALL OVER!
THAT WAS DYNA-MITE!
I DON'T THINK I'VE SEEN YOU HERE BEFORE...
I DON'T GET OUT MUCH!
I STAYED UP LATE...I'M GONNA BE EXHAUSTED TOMORROW... I GOT DRUNK EVEN THOUGH I HATE ALCOHOL...
HEY... DON'T MAKE YOURSELF OUT THE MARTYR!
WOULD YOU LIKE ME TO...UH...DO ANYTHING FOR YOU?
IT'S ALL BEEN DONE AN' DONE AGAIN!
CATCH YA!
YOU GOT SOMETHIN' OUT OF IT, TOO! YOU GOT TO TOUCH SOMEBODY! YOU GOT TO BE CLOSE TO ANOTHER PERSON THAT'S LONELY LIKE YOU! YOU NEED THAT, BABY!
SO DON'T TRY TO PALM YOUR TRIP OFF ON ME—O.K.?
PULL IN YOUR NERVE ENDS, PAL! WE BOTH GOT WHAT WE CAME FOR!
UH... HI, MARK...
OH! ER... HELLO AGAIN, BILLY...

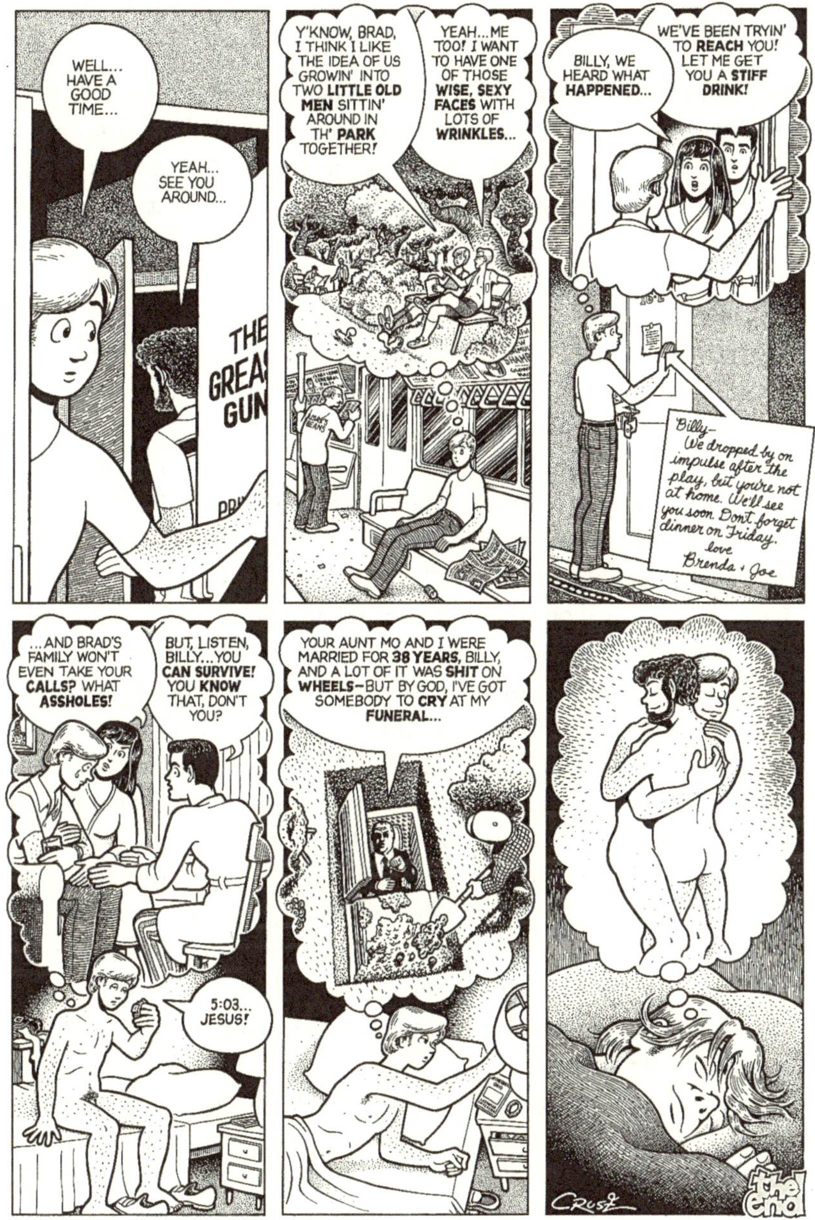

"Billy Goes Out" copyright the estate of Howard Cruse. Used by permission.

"Dirty Old Lovers"

"Dirty Old Lovers" first appeared in issue 3 of *Gay Comix* (Dec. 1982). Like many of the comics Cruse produced for *Gay Comix*, including "Safe Sex," he satirizes aspects of queer culture from the inside. While "Safe Sex" targets some of the irrational gay panic involving the AIDS epidemic, its intent is ultimately serious. "Dirty Old Lovers," however, is farcical, aimed at the generational divide in which the younger generation takes itself too seriously.

Luke Tewba and Clark Stobber seem loosely based on Cruse and his lover Eddie Sedarbaum, respectively, or at least an imagined version of their future. By day, the couple is celebrated for their activism and community service, but at night, they are shunned for their lewd behavior and constant sexual innuendos (even the narrator is embarrassed by their behavior). In the end, they become the targets of the younger generation's "Gays for Righteous Image Management" (GRIM), who find their behavior "an unacceptable liability to the Movement."

Cruse had planned on continuing the misadventures of Clark and Luke in their own series before he settled on *Wendel*. A continuation of "Dirty Old Lovers" was even part of the package that Cruse pitched to the editors at the *Advocate*. He had enough affection for the characters to bring them back in *Wendel*, with Luke as Wendel's uncle. In his introduction to the *Wendel* collection, Cruse lamented not using these characters more in the series because they were so fun to write (*Complete Wendel* 13). But he had made the decision to locate Luke and Clark far away from Wendel's home, and so they couldn't easily drop into Wendel's life on a regular basis. Still, Cruse's enjoyment in writing these characters is evident from this first story, and it's easy to see why Cruse wanted to return to them: they are fully realized characters from the outset, and they allow Cruse to exercise his talents with dialogue and verbal humor.

The "president's son" mentioned on the splash page is a reference to Ron Reagan, youngest son of President Ronald Reagan. During his father's presidency, rumors spread that Ron Jr., as he was known, was gay, mainly due to his stint as a ballet dancer and the stereotype associated with that profession.

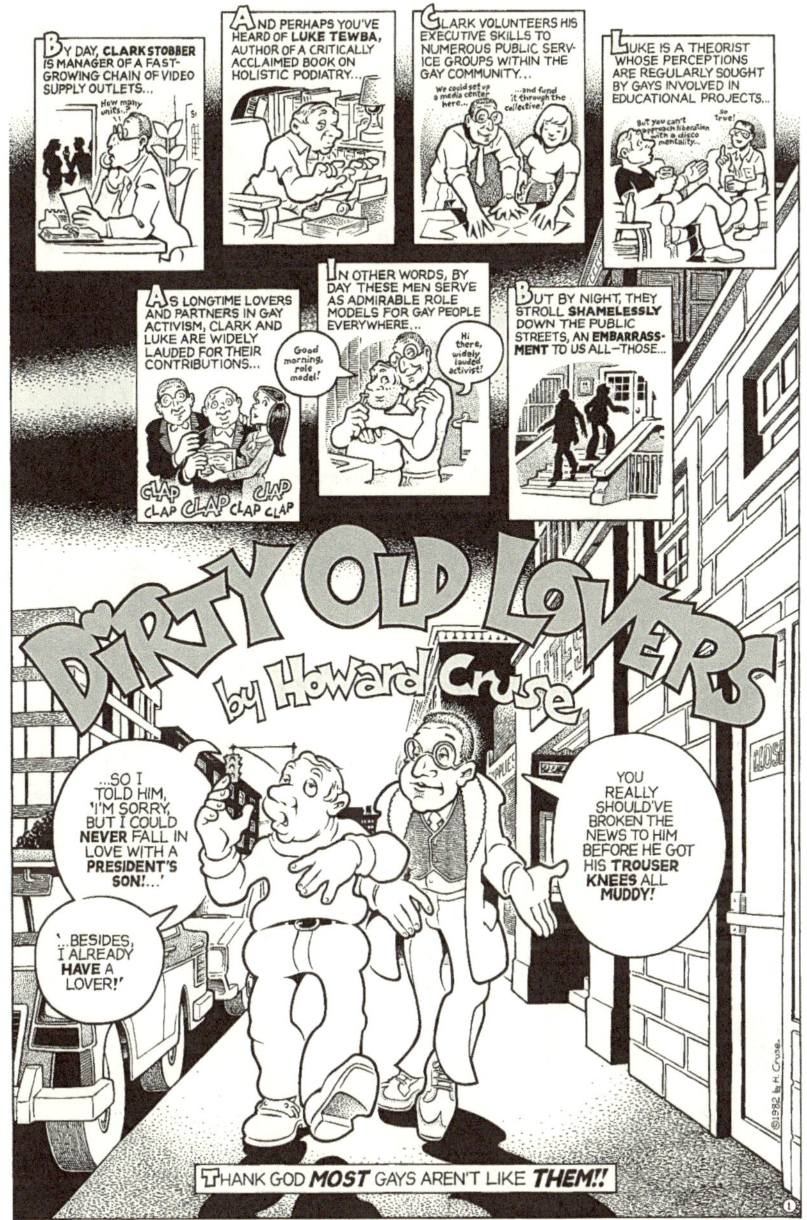

BY DAY, CLARK STOBBER IS MANAGER OF A FAST-GROWING CHAIN OF VIDEO SUPPLY OUTLETS...
How many units..?
AND PERHAPS YOU'VE HEARD OF LUKE TEWBA, AUTHOR OF A CRITICALLY ACCLAIMED BOOK ON HOLISTIC PODIATRY...
CLARK VOLUNTEERS HIS EXECUTIVE SKILLS TO NUMEROUS PUBLIC SERVICE GROUPS WITHIN THE GAY COMMUNITY...
We could set up a media center here...
...and fund it through the collective!
LUKE IS A THEORIST WHOSE PERCEPTIONS ARE REGULARLY SOUGHT BY GAYS INVOLVED IN EDUCATIONAL PROJECTS...
But you can't approach liberation with a disco mentality...
So true!
AS LONGTIME LOVERS AND PARTNERS IN GAY ACTIVISM, CLARK AND LUKE ARE WIDELY LAUDED FOR THEIR CONTRIBUTIONS...
CLAP CLAP CLAP CLAP CLAP CLAP
IN OTHER WORDS, BY DAY THESE MEN SERVE AS ADMIRABLE ROLE MODELS FOR GAY PEOPLE EVERYWHERE...
Good morning, role model!
Hi there, widely lauded activist!
BUT BY NIGHT, THEY STROLL SHAMELESSLY DOWN THE PUBLIC STREETS, AN EMBARRASSMENT TO US ALL—THOSE...
DIRTY OLD LOVERS
by Howard Cruse
...SO I TOLD HIM, 'I'M SORRY, BUT I COULD NEVER FALL IN LOVE WITH A PRESIDENT'S SON!...'
'...BESIDES, I ALREADY HAVE A LOVER!'
YOU REALLY SHOULD'VE BROKEN THE NEWS TO HIM BEFORE HE GOT HIS TROUSER KNEES ALL MUDDY!
©1982 by H. Cruse
THANK GOD MOST GAYS AREN'T LIKE THEM!!
1

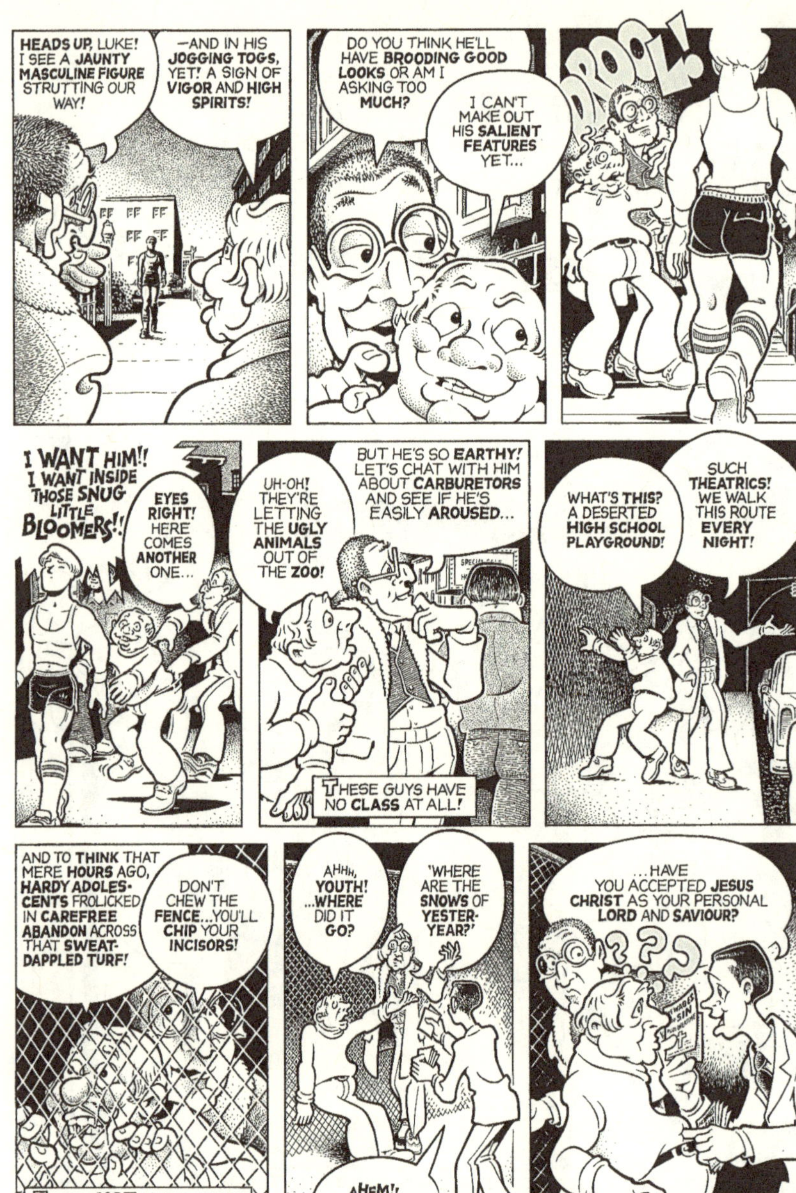
HEADS UP, LUKE! I SEE A JAUNTY MASCULINE FIGURE STRUTTING OUR WAY!
—AND IN HIS JOGGING TOGS, YET! A SIGN OF VIGOR AND HIGH SPIRITS!
DO YOU THINK HE'LL HAVE BROODING GOOD LOOKS OR AM I ASKING TOO MUCH?
I CAN'T MAKE OUT HIS SALIENT FEATURES YET...
DROOL!
I WANT HIM!! I WANT INSIDE THOSE SNUG LITTLE BLOOMERS!!
EYES RIGHT! HERE COMES ANOTHER ONE...
UH-OH! THEY'RE LETTING THE UGLY ANIMALS OUT OF THE ZOO!
BUT HE'S SO EARTHY! LET'S CHAT WITH HIM ABOUT CARBURETORS AND SEE IF HE'S EASILY AROUSED...
THESE GUYS HAVE NO CLASS AT ALL!
WHAT'S THIS? A DESERTED HIGH SCHOOL PLAYGROUND!
SUCH THEATRICS! WE WALK THIS ROUTE EVERY NIGHT!
AND TO THINK THAT MERE HOURS AGO, HARDY ADOLESCENTS FROLICKED IN CAREFREE ABANDON ACROSS THAT SWEAT-DAPPLED TURF!
DON'T CHEW THE FENCE...YOU'LL CHIP YOUR INCISORS!
THIS IS NOT A 'POLITICALLY CORRECT' CONVERSATION!!
AHHH, YOUTH! ...WHERE DID IT GO?
'WHERE ARE THE SNOWS OF YESTER-YEAR?'
AHEM!! I BEG YOUR PARDON...
...HAVE YOU ACCEPTED JESUS CHRIST AS YOUR PERSONAL LORD AND SAVIOUR?
2

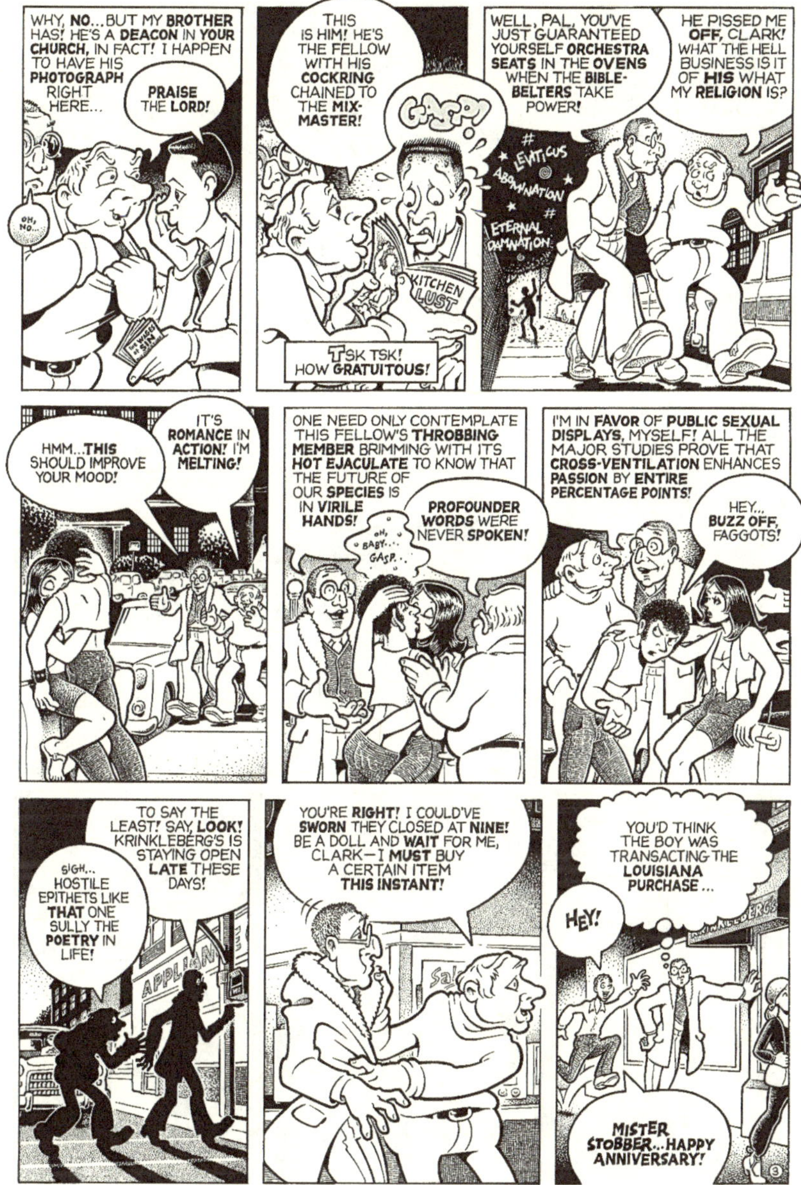

WHY, NO... BUT MY BROTHER HAS! HE'S A DEACON IN YOUR CHURCH, IN FACT! I HAPPEN TO HAVE HIS PHOTOGRAPH RIGHT HERE...
PRAISE THE LORD!
OH, NO...
THE WAGES OF SIN
THIS IS HIM! HE'S THE FELLOW WITH HIS COCKRING CHAINED TO THE MIX-MASTER!
GASP!
KITCHEN LUST
TSK TSK! HOW GRATUITOUS!
WELL, PAL, YOU'VE JUST GUARANTEED YOURSELF ORCHESTRA SEATS IN THE OVENS WHEN THE BIBLE-BELTERS TAKE POWER!
HE PISSED ME OFF, CLARK! WHAT THE HELL BUSINESS IS IT OF HIS WHAT MY RELIGION IS?
LEVITICUS
ABOMINATION
ETERNAL DAMNATION
HMM... THIS SHOULD IMPROVE YOUR MOOD!
IT'S ROMANCE IN ACTION! I'M MELTING!
ONE NEED ONLY CONTEMPLATE THIS FELLOW'S THROBBING MEMBER BRIMMING WITH ITS HOT EJACULATE TO KNOW THAT THE FUTURE OF OUR SPECIES IS IN VIRILE HANDS!
OH, BABY... GASP...
PROFOUNDER WORDS WERE NEVER SPOKEN!
I'M IN FAVOR OF PUBLIC SEXUAL DISPLAYS, MYSELF! ALL THE MAJOR STUDIES PROVE THAT CROSS-VENTILATION ENHANCES PASSION BY ENTIRE PERCENTAGE POINTS!
HEY... BUZZ OFF, FAGGOTS!
SIGH... HOSTILE EPITHETS LIKE THAT ONE SULLY THE POETRY IN LIFE!
TO SAY THE LEAST! SAY, LOOK! KRINKLEBERG'S IS STAYING OPEN LATE THESE DAYS!
YOU'RE RIGHT! I COULD'VE SWORN THEY CLOSED AT NINE! BE A DOLL AND WAIT FOR ME, CLARK—I MUST BUY A CERTAIN ITEM THIS INSTANT!
YOU'D THINK THE BOY WAS TRANSACTING THE LOUISIANA PURCHASE...
HEY!
MISTER STOBBER... HAPPY ANNIVERSARY!
3

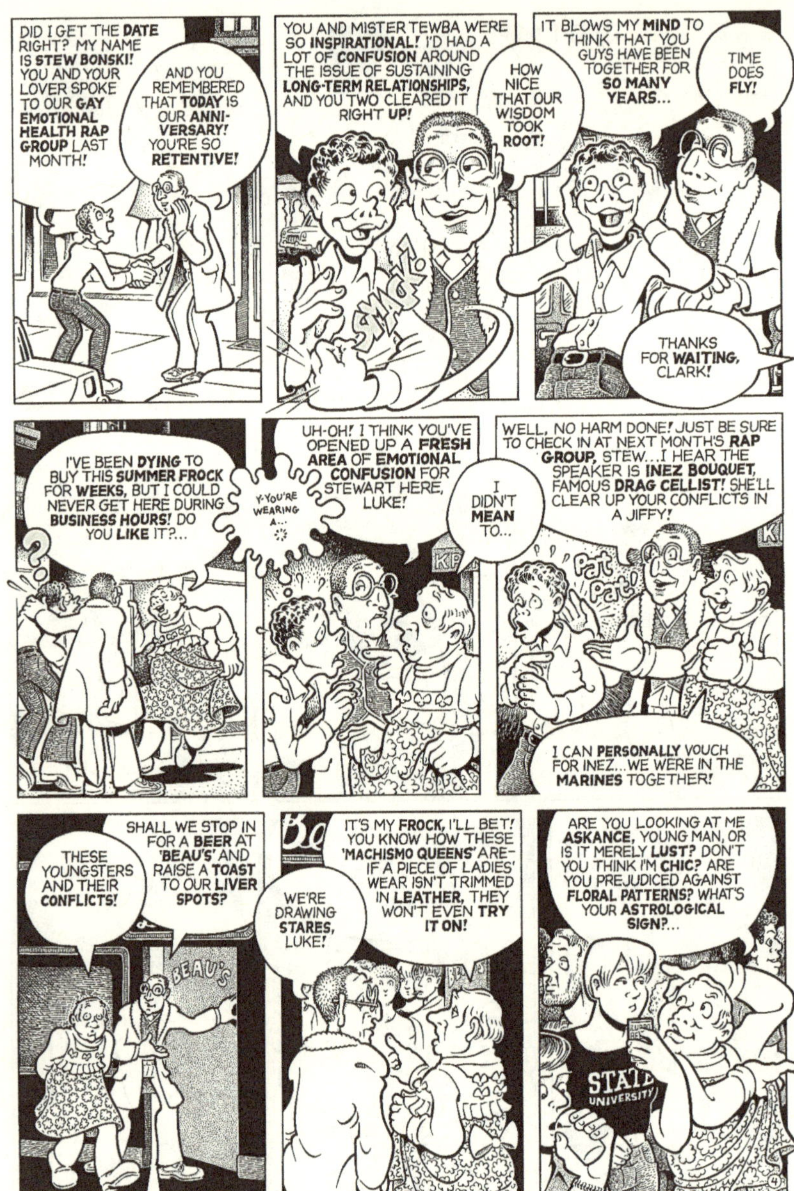
DID I GET THE DATE RIGHT? MY NAME IS STEW BONSKI! YOU AND YOUR LOVER SPOKE TO OUR GAY EMOTIONAL HEALTH RAP GROUP LAST MONTH!
AND YOU REMEMBERED THAT TODAY IS OUR ANNI-VERSARY! YOU'RE SO RETENTIVE!
YOU AND MISTER TEWBA WERE SO INSPIRATIONAL! I'D HAD A LOT OF CONFUSION AROUND THE ISSUE OF SUSTAINING LONG-TERM RELATIONSHIPS, AND YOU TWO CLEARED IT RIGHT UP!
HOW NICE THAT OUR WISDOM TOOK ROOT!
SMACK!
IT BLOWS MY MIND TO THINK THAT YOU GUYS HAVE BEEN TOGETHER FOR SO MANY YEARS...
TIME DOES FLY!
THANKS FOR WAITING, CLARK!
I'VE BEEN DYING TO BUY THIS SUMMER FROCK FOR WEEKS, BUT I COULD NEVER GET HERE DURING BUSINESS HOURS! DO YOU LIKE IT?...
Y-YOU'RE WEARING A...
UH-OH! I THINK YOU'VE OPENED UP A FRESH AREA OF EMOTIONAL CONFUSION FOR STEWART HERE, LUKE!
I DIDN'T MEAN TO...
WELL, NO HARM DONE! JUST BE SURE TO CHECK IN AT NEXT MONTH'S RAP GROUP, STEW...I HEAR THE SPEAKER IS INEZ BOUQUET, FAMOUS DRAG CELLIST! SHE'LL CLEAR UP YOUR CONFLICTS IN A JIFFY!
Pat Pat!
I CAN PERSONALLY VOUCH FOR INEZ...WE WERE IN THE MARINES TOGETHER!
THESE YOUNGSTERS AND THEIR CONFLICTS!
SHALL WE STOP IN FOR A BEER AT 'BEAU'S' AND RAISE A TOAST TO OUR LIVER SPOTS?
BEAU'S
WE'RE DRAWING STARES, LUKE!
IT'S MY FROCK, I'LL BET! YOU KNOW HOW THESE 'MACHISMO QUEENS' ARE— IF A PIECE OF LADIES' WEAR ISN'T TRIMMED IN LEATHER, THEY WON'T EVEN TRY IT ON!
ARE YOU LOOKING AT ME ASKANCE, YOUNG MAN, OR IS IT MERELY LUST? DON'T YOU THINK I'M CHIC? ARE YOU PREJUDICED AGAINST FLORAL PATTERNS? WHAT'S YOUR ASTROLOGICAL SIGN?...
STATE UNIVERSITY
4

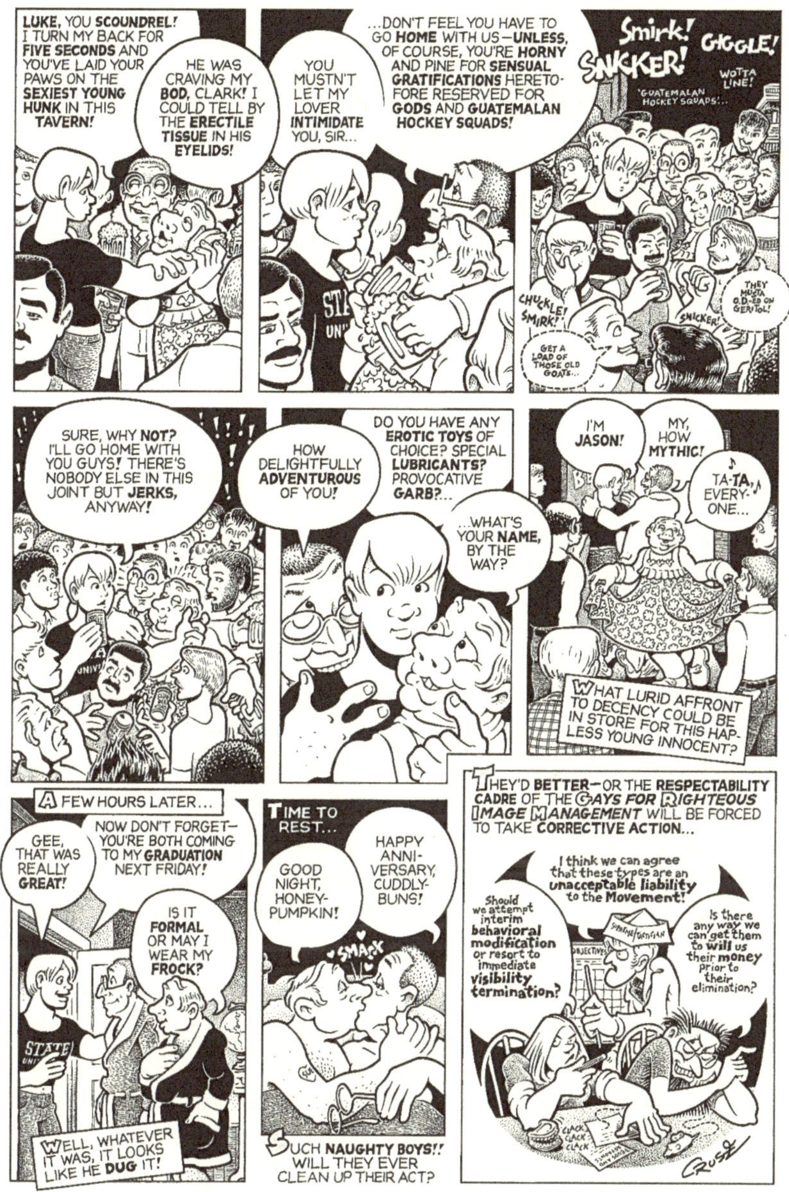

"Dirty Old Lovers" copyright the estate of Howard Cruse. Used by permission.

"Safe Sex"

"Safe Sex" originally appeared in *Gay Comix* 4 (1983). At the time, none of the contributors to *Gay Comix* had addressed the AIDS crisis, nor had Cruse even received a submission on the topic. Cruse felt strongly that a comic book devoted to the gay experience in the early 1980s should address the subject (Ringgenberg 77). In Cruse's initial attempts at the subject matter, he tried a narrative approach, similar to his earlier stories "Jerry Mack" and "Billy Goes Out," but they rang false because he lacked the personal experience of AIDS, even through his close circle of friends (77). The stories he was coming up with about AIDS patients were too maudlin—"disease-of-the-week," as he described them (Cruse, *From Headrack* 62). "Safe Sex," then, emerged from a desire to find a personal angle, which for Cruse at the time was the subject of AIDS panic and "the psychic chaos that we LGBT folks were going through" (65).

The result is a prime example of Cruse's social and satirical commentary in comics form, using a more essayistic approach to the subject that freed him from narrative restraints. It also establishes his voice as a social commentator: one that satirizes the foibles of the panic while also taking no prisoners with homophobic politicians, clergy, and others who neglected the crisis.

The freedom from the requirements of narrative storytelling also opens up Cruse's style and page layouts to greater experimentation. A satirical essay in comics form does not require the same progression from panel to panel that a narrative does. Each panel can serve as a snapshot of a specific point in the commentary, and so the panels don't need to be read in any particular order. In this story, panel borders don't conform to any conventional shape (and in some cases, Cruse leaves out the borders completely) but instead float seemingly haphazardly on the page, bumping into each other and overlapping. Also, these chaotic layouts visualize the cacophony of messages, myths, bad advice, and general panic that barraged gay men during the AIDS crisis. As Cruse describes these visual and layout choices, "It wasn't a narrative. It was an explosion of feelings. It was working through the jumble of feelings that hit me and many other gay people when we were first confronted with the AIDS epidemic" (Ringgenberg 77).

This is not to say that "Safe Sex" offers no progression through its six pages; instead, it builds to a dramatic and emotional climax. The final image pushes us to the future, to consider the place of the AIDS epidemic in "gay history." In this panel, Howard's penis requests, "Read to me again about the Stonewall Rebellion, Daddy!" like an innocent child asking for a comforting bedtime story. But Howard is busy making marginal notes in the book of "Gay History." That is, the activism and positive change resulting from the Stonewall Riots and other events seemed to indicate a progressive view of gay history toward greater freedom, acceptance, equality, and civil rights, but now that progressive history must be revised in the light of the AIDS epidemic.

While most of the images satirize the panic responses—like the young man worried because he's masturbating to a picture in "Steamy Studs" magazine and notices a blemish on the model's ankle—"Safe Sex" ends on a tragic note. A shadowed figure drawn in a more realistic register than the rest of the story states simply, "Billy's dead." In the 1986 interview with Steve Ringgenberg, Cruse confirmed that this line refers to the same character as in "Billy Goes Out": "The Billy that we all came to like in that story was doing exactly the kinds of things that we all later learned were dangerous" (77). A panel earlier in the story subtly foreshadows the news about Billy. The panel containing the caption "The trip downtown ain't what it used to be" comes directly from "Billy Goes Out," making a connection to the earlier story. This type of emotional shift from humor to pathos occurs regularly in Cruse's work—the humorous style lures us in and increases the emotional impact of the gut punch that is to come.

A few years later, the Australian magazine *Art & Text* commissioned a two-page addendum to "Safe Sex," titled "1986: An Interim Epilogue," to accompany the original strip. These two pages offer an ambivalent view on the "progress" made in the three years that followed the original story.

Note: On page 4, "Dear Ginny" refers to Virginia Apuzzo, executive director of the National Gay Task Force. The reference to "superstar Rock Jockman" on page 6 is not a direct reference to the death of actor Rock Hudson from complications related to AIDS, as it may first appear to be. Hudson died in 1985, two years after this story was published.

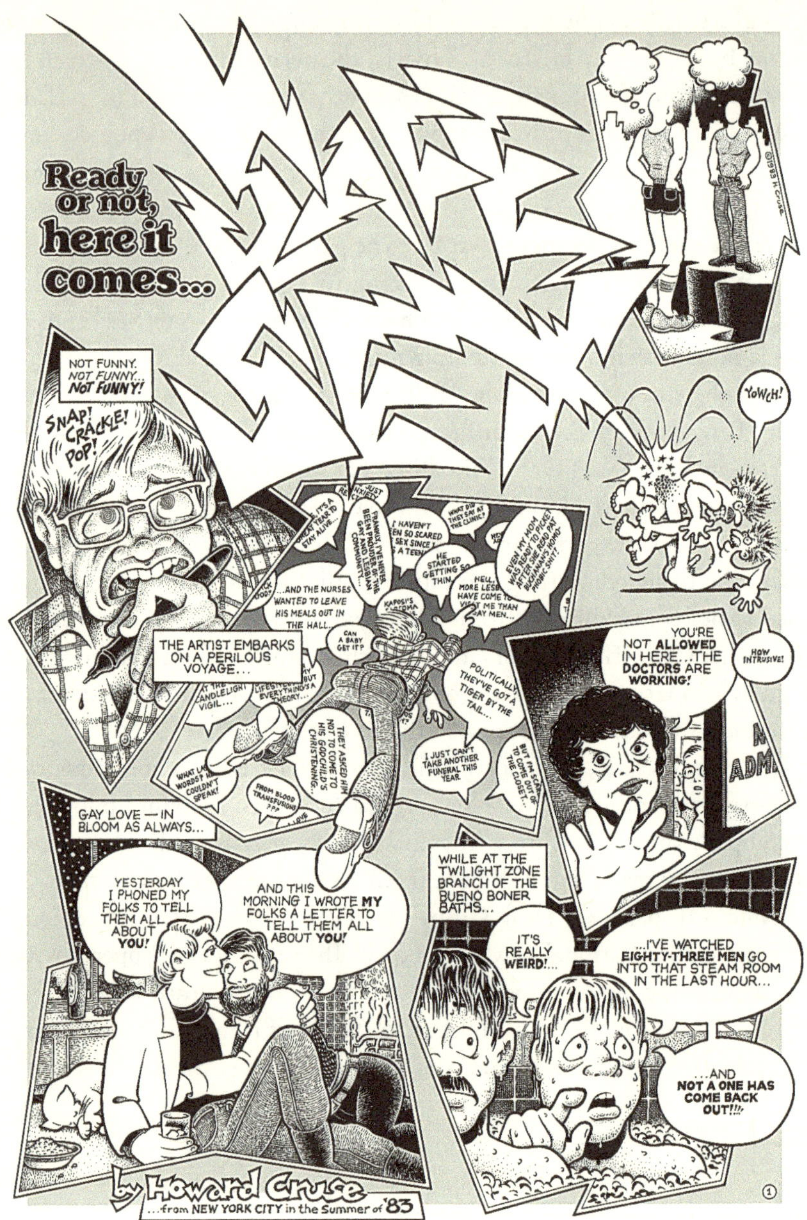

Ready or not, here it comes...
SAFE SEX
NOT FUNNY. NOT FUNNY... NOT FUNNY!
SNAP! CRACKLE! POP!
YOWCH!
FRANKLY, I'VE NEVER BEEN PROUDER OF THE GAY AND LESBIAN COMMUNITY...
WHAT DID THEY SAY AT THE CLINIC?
EVEN MY MOM WAS READY TO PICKET AFTER SHE READ PAT BUCHANAN'S HOMO-PHOBIC SHIT!
HE STARTED GETTING SO THIN.
...AND THE NURSES WANTED TO LEAVE HIS MEALS OUT IN THE HALL...
CAN A BABY GET IT?
THE ARTIST EMBARKS ON A PERILOUS VOYAGE...
POLITICALLY, THEY'VE GOT A TIGER BY THE TAIL...
THEY ASKED HIM NOT TO COME TO HIS GODCHILD'S CHRISTENING...
I JUST CAN'T TAKE ANOTHER FUNERAL THIS YEAR
FROM BLOOD TRANSFUSIONS ???
YOU'RE NOT ALLOWED IN HERE...THE DOCTORS ARE WORKING!
HOW INTRUSIVE!
GAY LOVE — IN BLOOM AS ALWAYS...
YESTERDAY I PHONED MY FOLKS TO TELL THEM ALL ABOUT YOU!
AND THIS MORNING I WROTE MY FOLKS A LETTER TO TELL THEM ALL ABOUT YOU!
WHILE AT THE TWILIGHT ZONE BRANCH OF THE BUENO BONER BATHS...
IT'S REALLY WEIRD!...
...I'VE WATCHED EIGHTY-THREE MEN GO INTO THAT STEAM ROOM IN THE LAST HOUR...
...AND NOT A ONE HAS COME BACK OUT!!!
by Howard Cruse
...from NEW YORK CITY in the Summer of '83
1

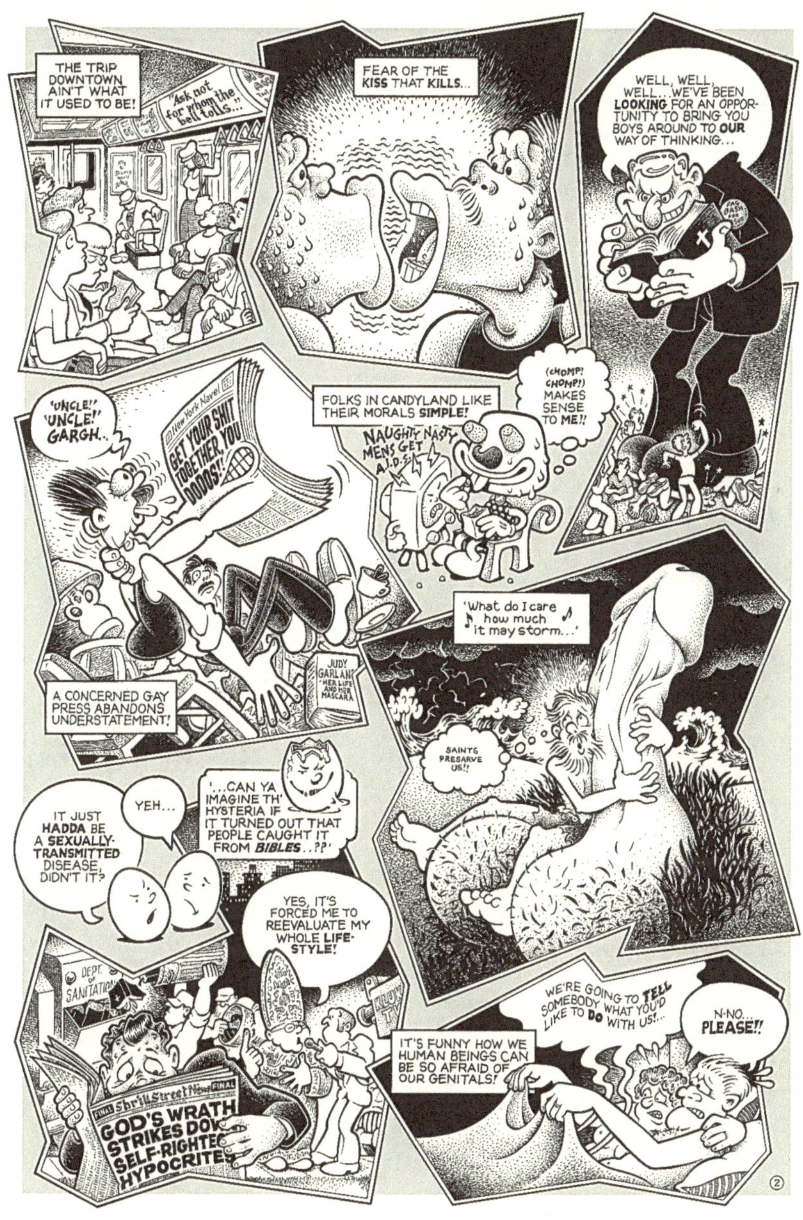
THE TRIP DOWNTOWN AIN'T WHAT IT USED TO BE!
"Ask not for whom the bell tolls..."
FEAR OF THE KISS THAT KILLS...
WELL, WELL, WELL... WE'VE BEEN LOOKING FOR AN OPPORTUNITY TO BRING YOU BOYS AROUND TO OUR WAY OF THINKING...
'UNCLE!' 'UNCLE!' GARGH..
New York Navel
GET YOUR SHIT TOGETHER, YOU DODOS!!
FOLKS IN CANDYLAND LIKE THEIR MORALS SIMPLE!
NAUGHTY NASTY MENS GET A.I.D.S.
(CHOMP! CHOMP!) MAKES SENSE TO ME!!
JUDY GARLAND "HER LIFE AND HER MASCARA"
A CONCERNED GAY PRESS ABANDONS UNDERSTATEMENT!
'What do I care how much it may storm...'
SAINTS PRESARVE US!!
IT JUST HADDA BE A SEXUALLY-TRANSMITTED DISEASE, DIDN'T IT?
YEH...
'...CAN YA IMAGINE TH' HYSTERIA IF IT TURNED OUT THAT PEOPLE CAUGHT IT FROM BIBLES..??'
YES, IT'S FORCED ME TO REEVALUATE MY WHOLE LIFE-STYLE!
DEPT. OF SANITATION
Shrill Street News FINAL
GOD'S WRATH STRIKES DOW SELF-RIGHTE HYPOCRITES
WE'RE GOING TO TELL SOMEBODY WHAT YOU'D LIKE TO DO WITH US!...
N-NO... PLEASE!!
IT'S FUNNY HOW WE HUMAN BEINGS CAN BE SO AFRAID OF OUR GENITALS!
2

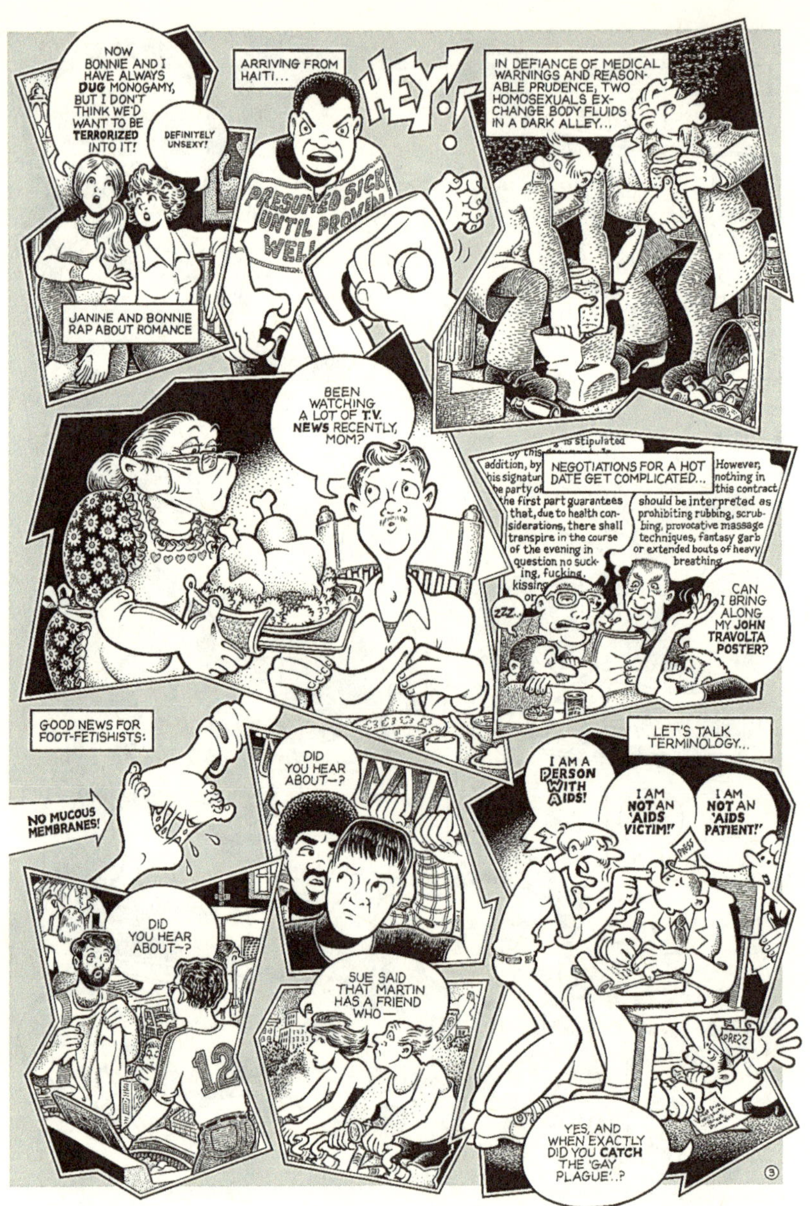

NOW BONNIE AND I HAVE ALWAYS **DUG** MONOGAMY, BUT I DON'T THINK WE'D WANT TO BE **TERRORIZED** INTO IT!
DEFINITELY UNSEXY!
JANINE AND BONNIE RAP ABOUT ROMANCE
ARRIVING FROM HAITI...
PRESUMED SICK UNTIL PROVEN WELL
HEY!
IN DEFIANCE OF MEDICAL WARNINGS AND REASONABLE PRUDENCE, TWO HOMOSEXUALS EXCHANGE BODY FLUIDS IN A DARK ALLEY...
BEEN WATCHING A LOT OF **T.V. NEWS** RECENTLY, MOM?
NEGOTIATIONS FOR A HOT DATE GET COMPLICATED...
is stipulated by this addition, by his signatur be party of the first part guarantees that, due to health considerations, there shall transpire in the course of the evening in question no sucking, fucking, kissing or
However, nothing in this contract should be interpreted as prohibiting rubbing, scrubbing, provocative massage techniques, fantasy garb or extended bouts of heavy breathing.
ZZZ...
CAN I BRING ALONG MY **JOHN TRAVOLTA POSTER?**
GOOD NEWS FOR FOOT-FETISHISTS:
NO MUCOUS MEMBRANES!
DID YOU HEAR ABOUT—?
DID YOU HEAR ABOUT—?
SUE SAID THAT MARTIN HAS A FRIEND WHO—
LET'S TALK TERMINOLOGY...
I AM A **PERSON WITH AIDS!**
I AM **NOT** AN **'AIDS VICTIM!'**
I AM **NOT** AN **'AIDS PATIENT!'**
PRESS
PRESS
YES, AND WHEN EXACTLY DID YOU **CATCH** THE 'GAY PLAGUE'..?
3

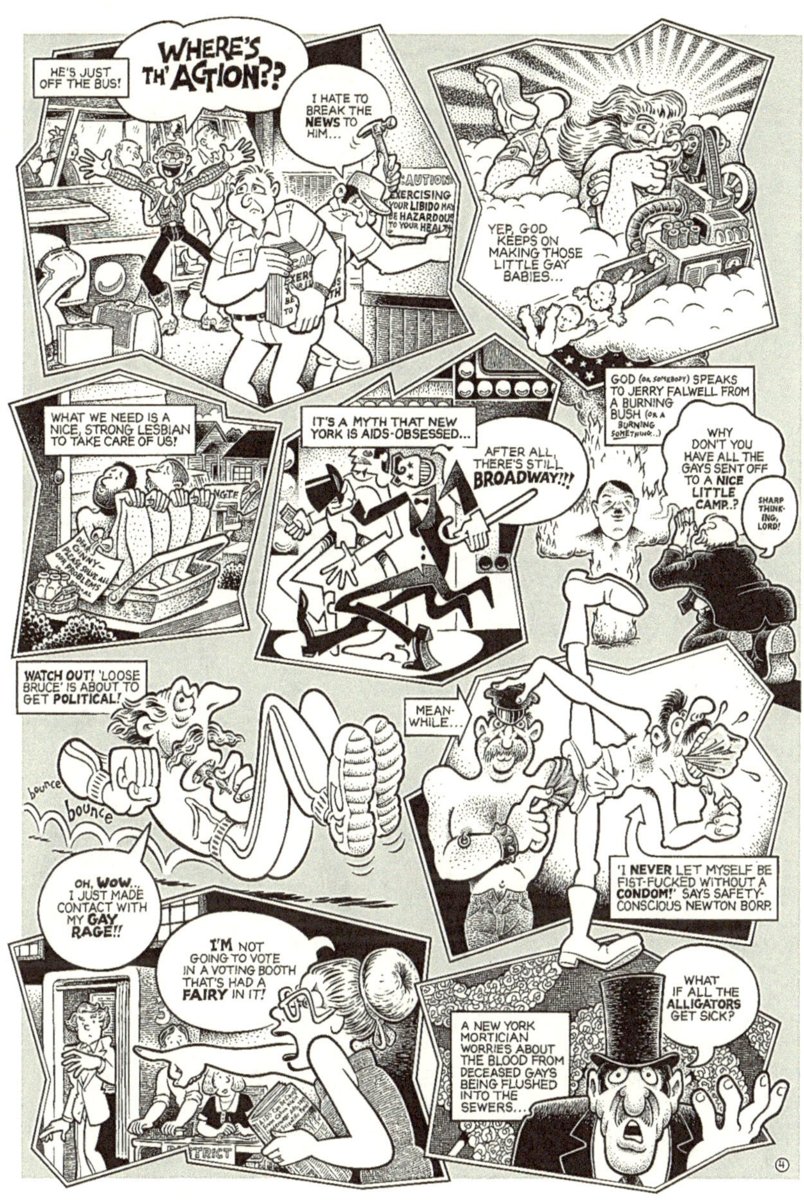

HE'S JUST OFF THE BUS!
WHERE'S TH' ACTION??
I HATE TO BREAK THE NEWS TO HIM...
YEP, GOD KEEPS ON MAKING THOSE LITTLE GAY BABIES...
WHAT WE NEED IS A NICE, STRONG LESBIAN TO TAKE CARE OF US!
IT'S A MYTH THAT NEW YORK IS AIDS-OBSESSED...
AFTER ALL, THERE'S STILL BROADWAY!!!
GOD (OR SOMEBODY) SPEAKS TO JERRY FALWELL FROM A BURNING BUSH (OR A BURNING SOMETHING...)
WHY DON'T YOU HAVE ALL THE GAYS SENT OFF TO A NICE LITTLE CAMP..?
SHARP THINK-ING, LORD!
WATCH OUT! 'LOOSE BRUCE' IS ABOUT TO GET POLITICAL!
bounce
bounce
OH, WOW... I JUST MADE CONTACT WITH MY GAY RAGE!!
MEAN-WHILE...
'I NEVER LET MYSELF BE FIST-FUCKED WITHOUT A CONDOM!' SAYS SAFETY-CONSCIOUS NEWTON BORP.
I'M NOT GOING TO VOTE IN A VOTING BOOTH THAT'S HAD A FAIRY IN IT!
A NEW YORK MORTICIAN WORRIES ABOUT THE BLOOD FROM DECEASED GAYS BEING FLUSHED INTO THE SEWERS...
WHAT IF ALL THE ALLIGATORS GET SICK?
4

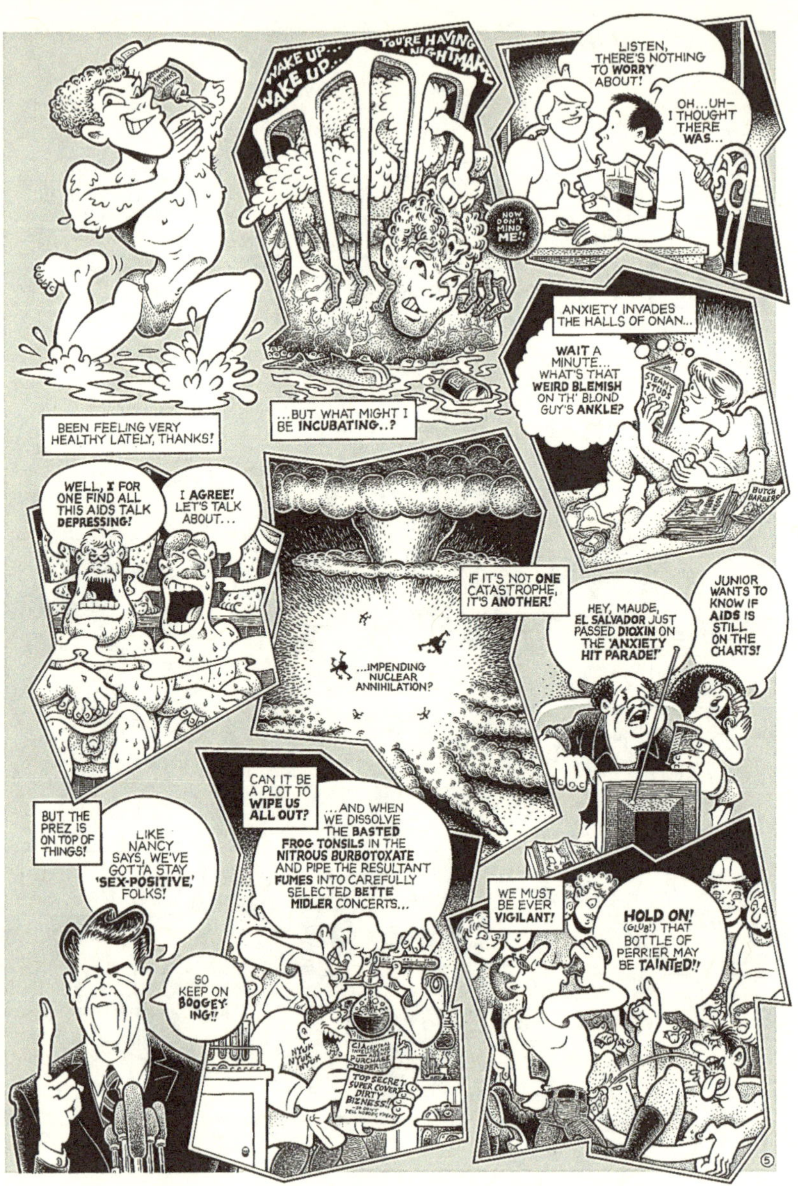
WAKE UP... WAKE UP... YOU'RE HAVING A NIGHTMARE
LISTEN, THERE'S NOTHING TO WORRY ABOUT!
OH...UH– I THOUGHT THERE WAS...
NOW DON'T MIND ME!!
BEEN FEELING VERY HEALTHY LATELY, THANKS!
...BUT WHAT MIGHT I BE INCUBATING..?
ANXIETY INVADES THE HALLS OF ONAN...
WAIT A MINUTE... WHAT'S THAT WEIRD BLEMISH ON 'TH' BLOND GUY'S ANKLE?
STEAMY STUDS
BUTCH BARBERS
WELL, I FOR ONE FIND ALL THIS AIDS TALK DEPRESSING!
I AGREE! LET'S TALK ABOUT...
...IMPENDING NUCLEAR ANNIHILATION?
IF IT'S NOT ONE CATASTROPHE, IT'S ANOTHER!
HEY, MAUDE, EL SALVADOR JUST PASSED DIOXIN ON THE 'ANXIETY HIT PARADE!'
JUNIOR WANTS TO KNOW IF AIDS IS STILL ON THE CHARTS!
BUT THE PREZ IS ON TOP OF THINGS!
LIKE NANCY SAYS, WE'VE GOTTA STAY 'SEX-POSITIVE,' FOLKS!
SO KEEP ON BOOGEY-ING!!
CAN IT BE A PLOT TO WIPE US ALL OUT?
...AND WHEN WE DISSOLVE THE BASTED FROG TONSILS IN THE NITROUS BURBOTOXATE AND PIPE THE RESULTANT FUMES INTO CAREFULLY SELECTED BETTE MIDLER CONCERTS...
NYUK NYUK NYUK
TOP SECRET SUPER COVERT DIRTY BIZNESS!!
WE MUST BE EVER VIGILANT!
HOLD ON! (GLUB!) THAT BOTTLE OF PERRIER MAY BE TAINTED!!
5

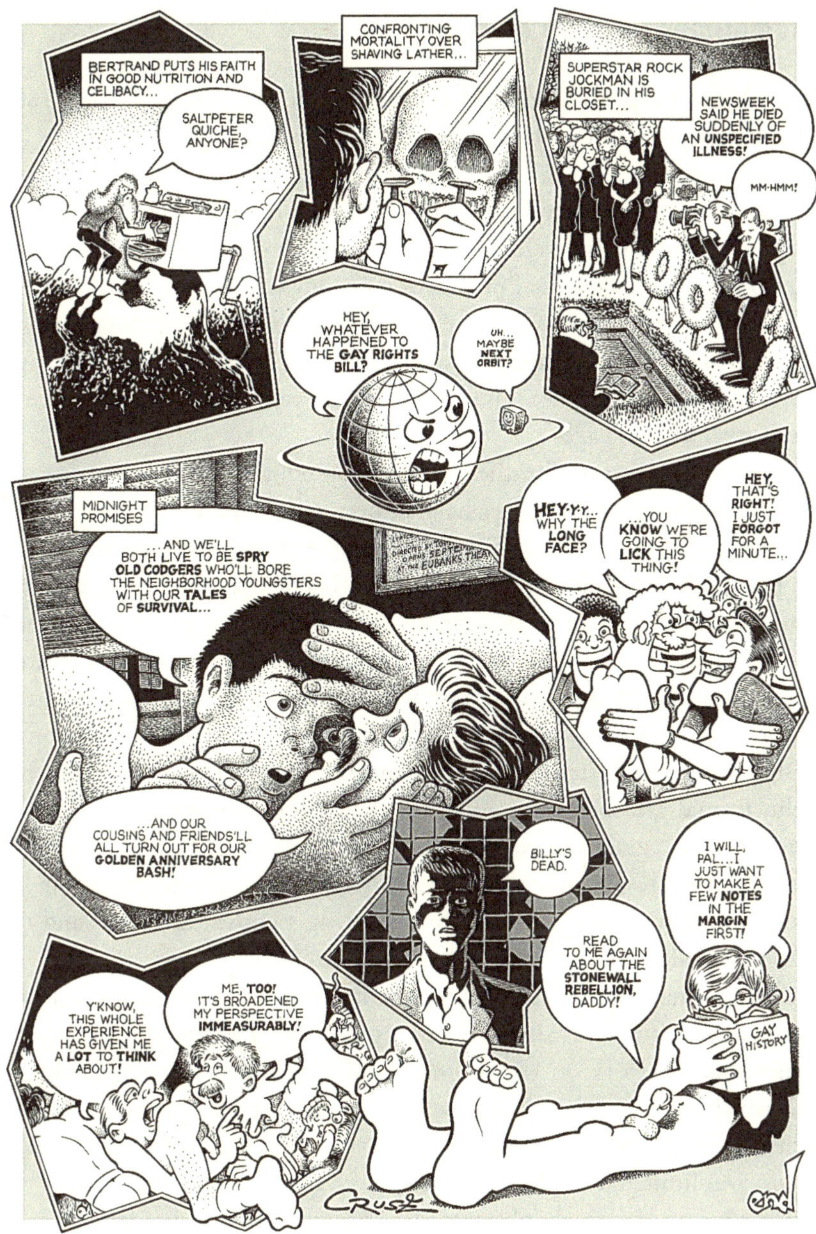
BERTRAND PUTS HIS FAITH IN GOOD NUTRITION AND CELIBACY...
SALTPETER QUICHE, ANYONE?
CONFRONTING MORTALITY OVER SHAVING LATHER...
SUPERSTAR ROCK JOCKMAN IS BURIED IN HIS CLOSET...
NEWSWEEK SAID HE DIED SUDDENLY OF AN UNSPECIFIED ILLNESS!
MM-HMM!
HEY, WHATEVER HAPPENED TO THE GAY RIGHTS BILL?
UH... MAYBE NEXT ORBIT?
MIDNIGHT PROMISES
...AND WE'LL BOTH LIVE TO BE SPRY OLD CODGERS WHO'LL BORE THE NEIGHBORHOOD YOUNGSTERS WITH OUR TALES OF SURVIVAL...
...AND OUR COUSINS AND FRIENDS'LL ALL TURN OUT FOR OUR GOLDEN ANNIVERSARY BASH!
HEY-Y-Y... WHY THE LONG FACE?
...YOU KNOW WE'RE GOING TO LICK THIS THING!
HEY, THAT'S RIGHT! I JUST FORGOT FOR A MINUTE...
BILLY'S DEAD.
Y'KNOW, THIS WHOLE EXPERIENCE HAS GIVEN ME A LOT TO THINK ABOUT!
ME, TOO! IT'S BROADENED MY PERSPECTIVE IMMEASURABLY!
READ TO ME AGAIN ABOUT THE STONEWALL REBELLION, DADDY!
I WILL, PAL...I JUST WANT TO MAKE A FEW NOTES IN THE MARGIN FIRST!
GAY HISTORY
CRUSE
end

"Sometimes I Get So Mad . . ."

"Sometimes I Get So Mad . . ." first appeared in the *Village Voice* in 1981. The newspaper's editors had solicited the strip from Cruse based on his editorship of *Gay Comix*. He was invited to comment on issues in gay culture at the time, and he was given free rein with his approach. Though the strip is printed on two pages here, as it is in the collection *Dancin' Nekkid with the Angels*, its original publication encompassed a single page in the tabloid-sized newspaper. Cruse's use of identically sized and shaped panels allows it to be broken up and rearranged this way, but the impact of twenty-one panels on a single page is much different than the reading experience of the story over two pages.

The story focuses on the dilemma between political outrage and creative productivity—that is, finding a balance between the potentially paralyzing anger at the rampant homophobia and bigotry that Cruse experiences and his need to be a productive cartoonist. To this extent, there is an unfortunately timeless element to this theme. As with so many of Cruse's stories, the formal elements of the strip visually represent his dilemma. The twenty-one identically sized panels show the cartoonist's attempt to control the material and his overwhelming anger. However, the word balloons often push out into the gutter beyond the panel borders. By the end, though, the tight, formal grid becomes a cage for the cartoonist: in the penultimate panel, Howard grabs the gutter like a prisoner shaking the bars of his cell, while his feet press against their constraints. In the final panel, however, his professionalism wins out as Howard, wearing a conservative suit and tie, enthusiastically turns the strip over to his editor.

"Sometimes I Get So Mad . . ." represents a watershed moment in Cruse's career for a variety of reasons. From a professional standpoint, it showed Cruse that his work on *Gay Comix* would expand his opportunities to publish elsewhere, rather than limit them. It also serves as the final point in Cruse's process of coming out as a gay artist: while the audience for *Gay Comix* was limited to readers of underground comix or those who found the series in gay and lesbian bookstores, the *Village Voice* was a mainstream publication with a broader audience, many of whom had not been exposed to Cruse's work in the past. The strip was also later reprinted in the *Advocate*, prompting Cruse to pitch a regular comic strip for that publication, which would result in *Wendel*.

SOMETIMES I GET SO MAD...

by HOWARD CRUSE

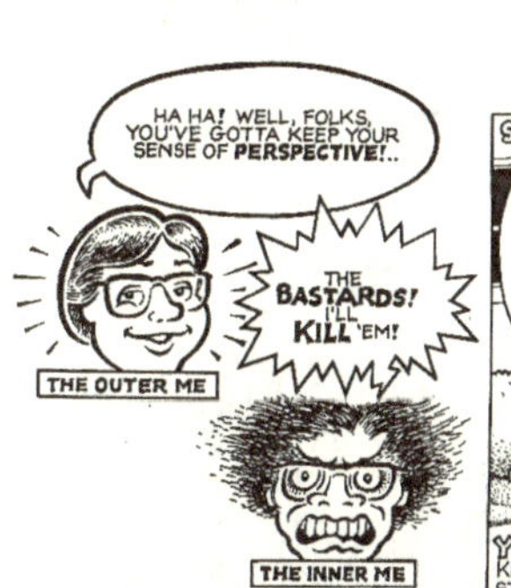

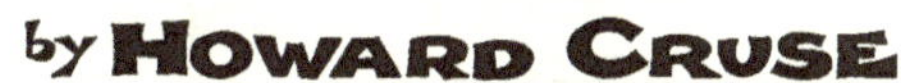

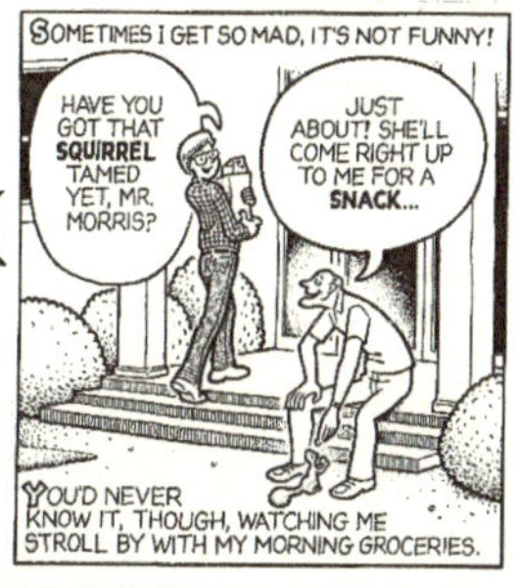

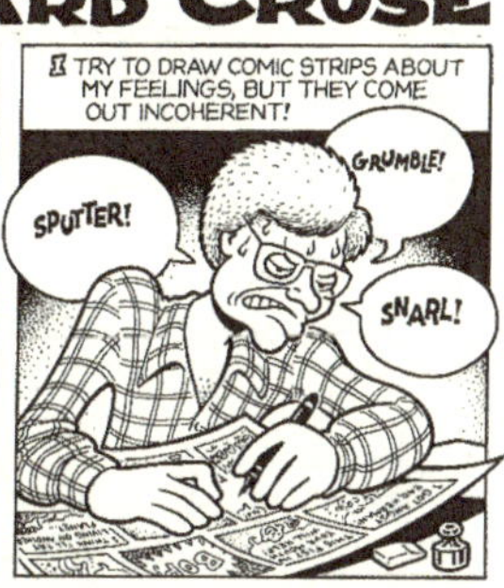

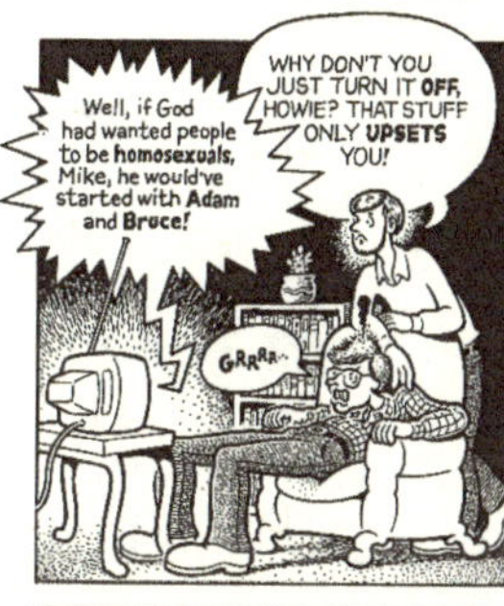

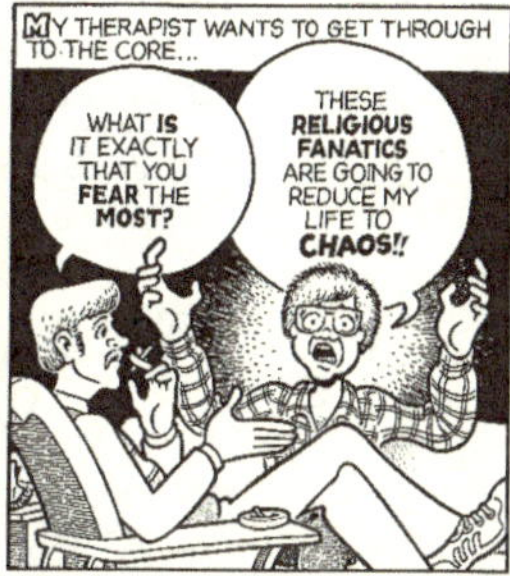

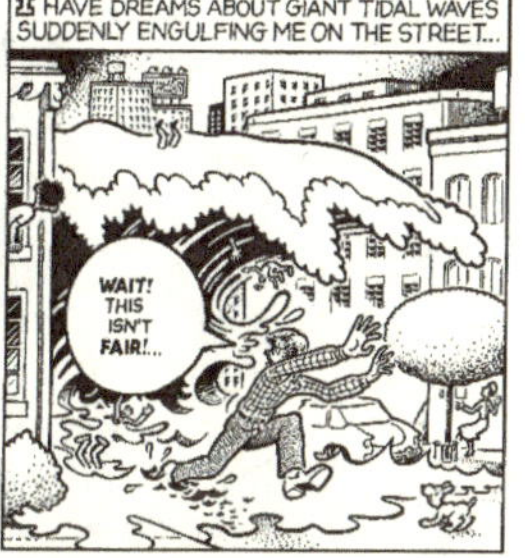

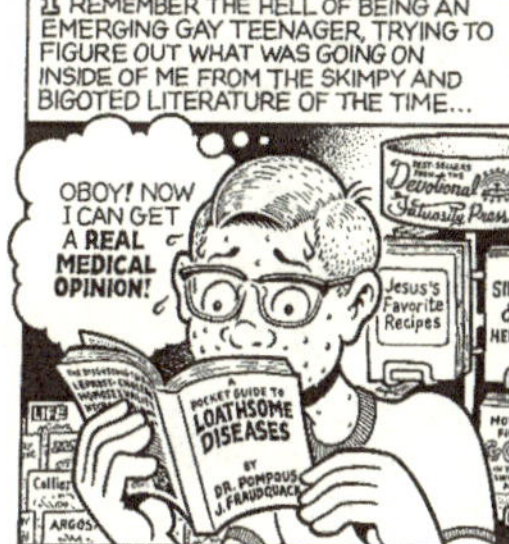

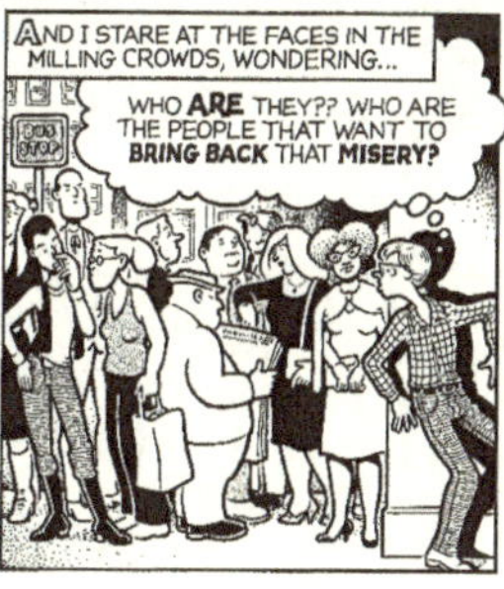

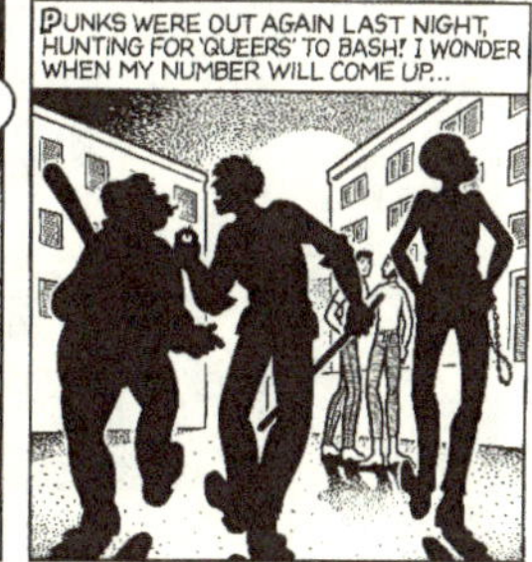

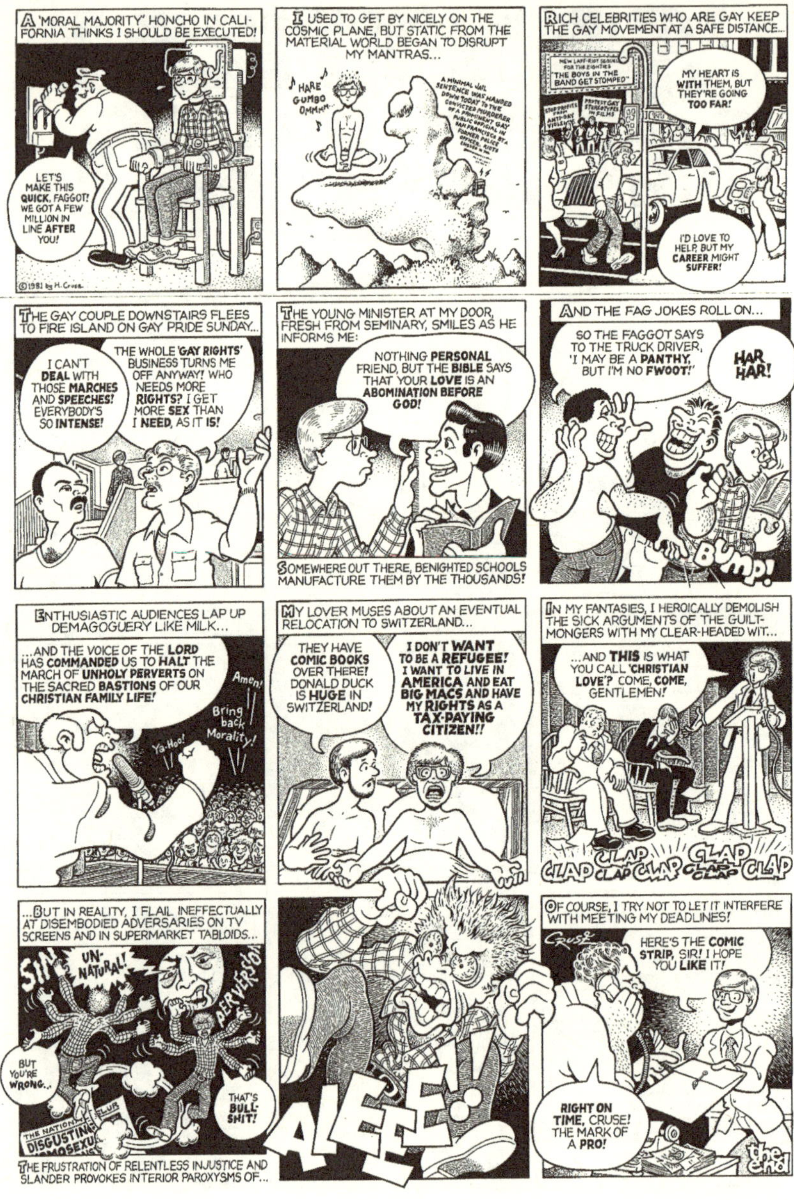

"Sometimes I Get So Mad . . ." copyright the estate of Howard Cruse. Used by permission.

"The Gay in the Street"

"The Gay in the Street," originally published in the *Village Voice* in 1984 and reprinted in *Gay Comix* 10 (Spring 1987), broadly targets the television news media for their coverage of gay issues. Primarily, Cruse critiques the way in which television news tries to reduce complicated issues to a sound bite, and so Howard hijacks the reporter to go off on a long tirade, though the reporter plans to cut it all down to three seconds anyway. Also at work here is the way in which television news makes one person represent an entire diverse culture or group. As "the gay in the street," Howard is being asked to speak for all members of the queer community, as if that group could be reduced to a single, monolithic opinion. This is an issue Cruse resisted in the first issue of *Gay Comix* as well: "Each artist speaks for himself or herself. No one speaks for any mythical 'average' homosexual. No one speaks for the Gay Movement." Even more specifically, though, this comic may also draw on Cruse's own experience with outlets like the *Village Voice,* which called him to serve as that mythical voice.

Howard's commentary on "future prospects for gay people" has a stream of consciousness quality as one topic flows into another. This loose structure allows Cruse to draw a bead on various other targets, like conservative fear of homosexual indoctrination, infighting between gay men and lesbians, and so on. Notably, Howard also covers the inevitability of gay marriage early in the strip, though it would be another twenty years before that happened.

In *From Headrack to Claude,* Cruse explains the last panel of this story, which may be lost on contemporary readers. The George Segal referenced here is an artist who created realistic sculptures by covering people in plaster of Paris. Specifically relevant to this story, he made statues to commemorate the gay liberation movement.

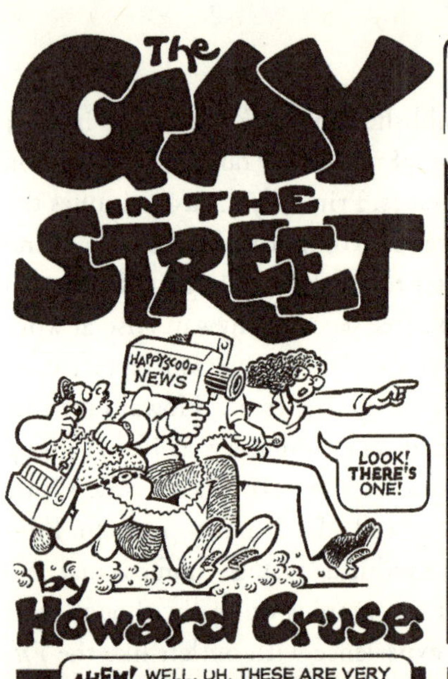

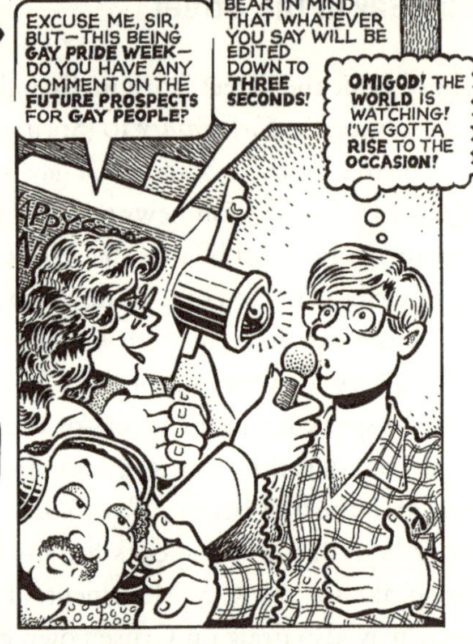

AHEM! WELL, UH, THESE ARE VERY COMPLICATED TIMES! WE'VE GOT THE FAR RIGHT AND THE 'MORAL MAJORITY' EXPLOITING THE AIDS CRISIS... MUMBLE MUMBLE... SYSTEMIC HOMOPHOBIA... MUMBLE... APATHY AND POLITICAL ALIENATION AMONG CONSUMPTION-ORIENTED GAYS... MUMBLE... BICKERING GAY LEADERSHIP... MUMBLE... WHO KNOWS WHAT LIES AHEAD?.. COULD BE BAD, COULD BE GOOD... IT'S HARD TO PULL TOGETHER IN A FEW WORDS... REALITY IS INEVITABLY DISTORTED!...

UH... COULD YOU PERHAPS BOIL SOME OF THAT DOWN?

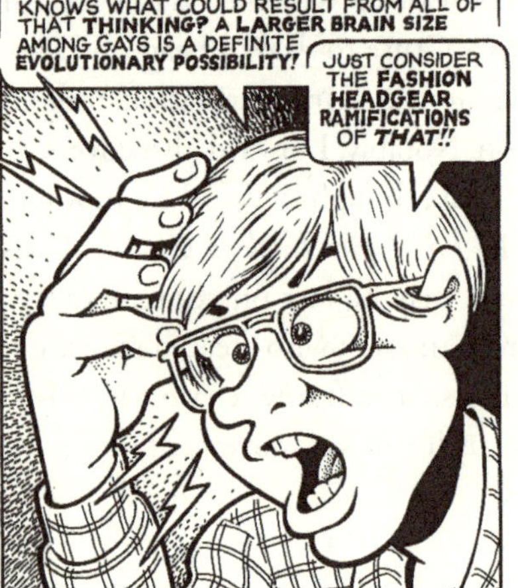

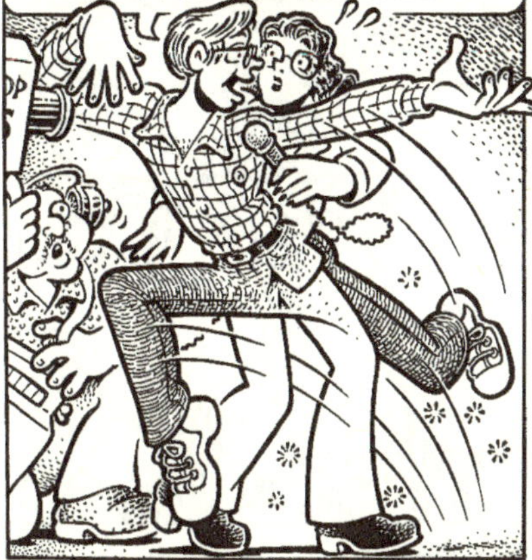
AND SPEAKING OF EVOLUTION, THE COMING DECADES MAY CAST NEW LIGHT ON THE ORIGINS OF GAYNESS! FAR FROM CURRENTLY HELD THEORIES THAT WE SPRANG FROM SPORES PLANTED BY ANCIENT EXTRA-TERRESTRIALS, IT WILL EMERGE THAT WE ARE MYSTICAL APPARITIONS SENT BY GOD TO COMPLETE THE MISSION OF SPREADING JOY AND LIGHT WHICH THE LATE JUDY GARLAND LEFT TRAGICALLY UNFINISHED!

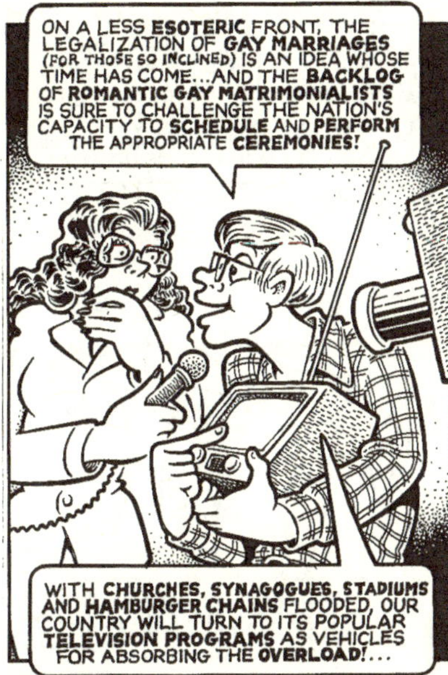
ON A LESS ESOTERIC FRONT, THE LEGALIZATION OF GAY MARRIAGES (FOR THOSE SO INCLINED) IS AN IDEA WHOSE TIME HAS COME...AND THE BACKLOG OF ROMANTIC GAY MATRIMONIALISTS IS SURE TO CHALLENGE THE NATION'S CAPACITY TO SCHEDULE AND PERFORM THE APPROPRIATE CEREMONIES!
WITH CHURCHES, SYNAGOGUES, STADIUMS AND HAMBURGER CHAINS FLOODED, OUR COUNTRY WILL TURN TO ITS POPULAR TELEVISION PROGRAMS AS VEHICLES FOR ABSORBING THE OVERLOAD!...

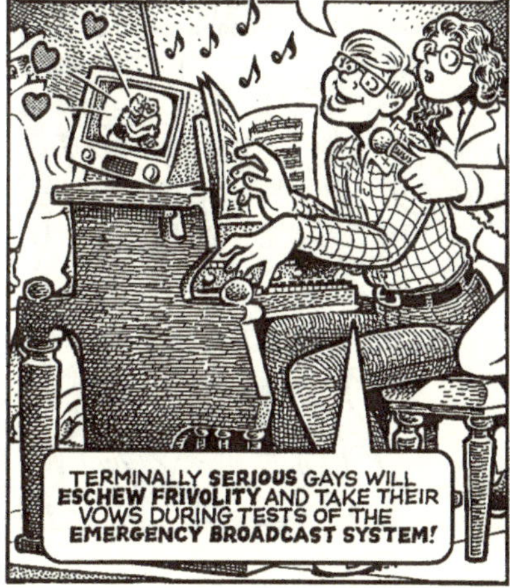
LESBIAN NUPTUALS WILL BE INCORPORATED SUBTLY INTO CAGNEY & LACEY PLOTS! GAY MALE COUPLES MAY GRAVITATE TOWARD THE CHEERY OPTIMISM OF THE RICHARD SIMMONS SHOW...OR, IF THEY'D RATHER GO FOR BUTCH, THEY CAN BE WED DURING THE COMMERCIAL BREAKS OF STARSKY & HUTCH RERUNS!
TERMINALLY SERIOUS GAYS WILL ESCHEW FRIVOLITY AND TAKE THEIR VOWS DURING TESTS OF THE EMERGENCY BROADCAST SYSTEM!

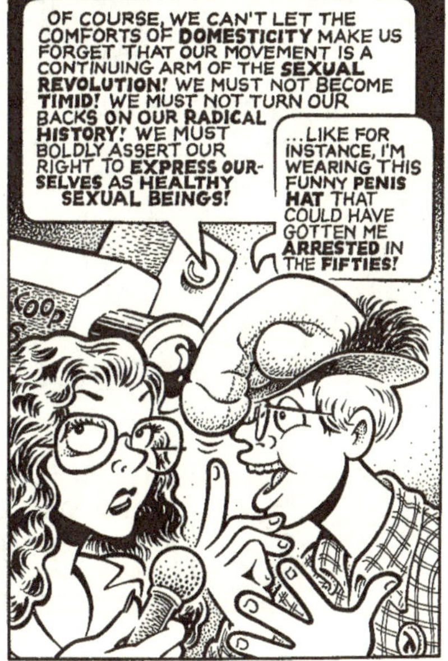
OF COURSE, WE CAN'T LET THE COMFORTS OF DOMESTICITY MAKE US FORGET THAT OUR MOVEMENT IS A CONTINUING ARM OF THE SEXUAL REVOLUTION! WE MUST NOT BECOME TIMID! WE MUST NOT TURN OUR BACKS ON OUR RADICAL HISTORY! WE MUST BOLDLY ASSERT OUR RIGHT TO EXPRESS OURSELVES AS HEALTHY SEXUAL BEINGS!
...LIKE FOR INSTANCE, I'M WEARING THIS FUNNY PENIS HAT THAT COULD HAVE GOTTEN ME ARRESTED IN THE FIFTIES!

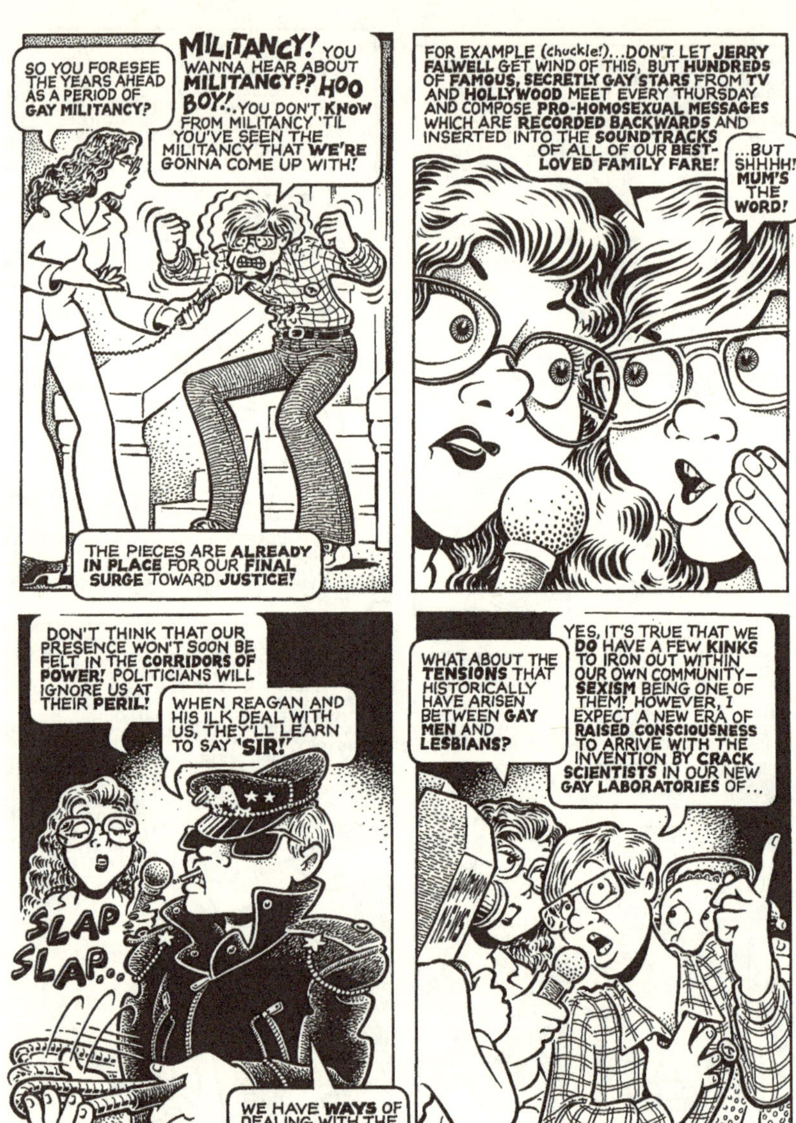
SO YOU FORESEE THE YEARS AHEAD AS A PERIOD OF GAY MILITANCY?
MILITANCY! YOU WANNA HEAR ABOUT MILITANCY?? HOO BOY!..YOU DON'T KNOW FROM MILITANCY 'TIL YOU'VE SEEN THE MILITANCY THAT WE'RE GONNA COME UP WITH!
THE PIECES ARE ALREADY IN PLACE FOR OUR FINAL SURGE TOWARD JUSTICE!
FOR EXAMPLE (chuckle!)...DON'T LET JERRY FALWELL GET WIND OF THIS, BUT HUNDREDS OF FAMOUS, SECRETLY GAY STARS FROM TV AND HOLLYWOOD MEET EVERY THURSDAY AND COMPOSE PRO-HOMOSEXUAL MESSAGES WHICH ARE RECORDED BACKWARDS AND INSERTED INTO THE SOUNDTRACKS OF ALL OF OUR BEST-LOVED FAMILY FARE!
...BUT SHHHH! MUM'S THE WORD!
DON'T THINK THAT OUR PRESENCE WON'T SOON BE FELT IN THE CORRIDORS OF POWER! POLITICIANS WILL IGNORE US AT THEIR PERIL!
WHEN REAGAN AND HIS ILK DEAL WITH US, THEY'LL LEARN TO SAY 'SIR!'
SLAP SLAP...
WE HAVE WAYS OF DEALING WITH THE RECALCITRANT!...
WHAT ABOUT THE TENSIONS THAT HISTORICALLY HAVE ARISEN BETWEEN GAY MEN AND LESBIANS?
YES, IT'S TRUE THAT WE DO HAVE A FEW KINKS TO IRON OUT WITHIN OUR OWN COMMUNITY— SEXISM BEING ONE OF THEM! HOWEVER, I EXPECT A NEW ERA OF RAISED CONSCIOUSNESS TO ARRIVE WITH THE INVENTION BY CRACK SCIENTISTS IN OUR NEW GAY LABORATORIES OF...

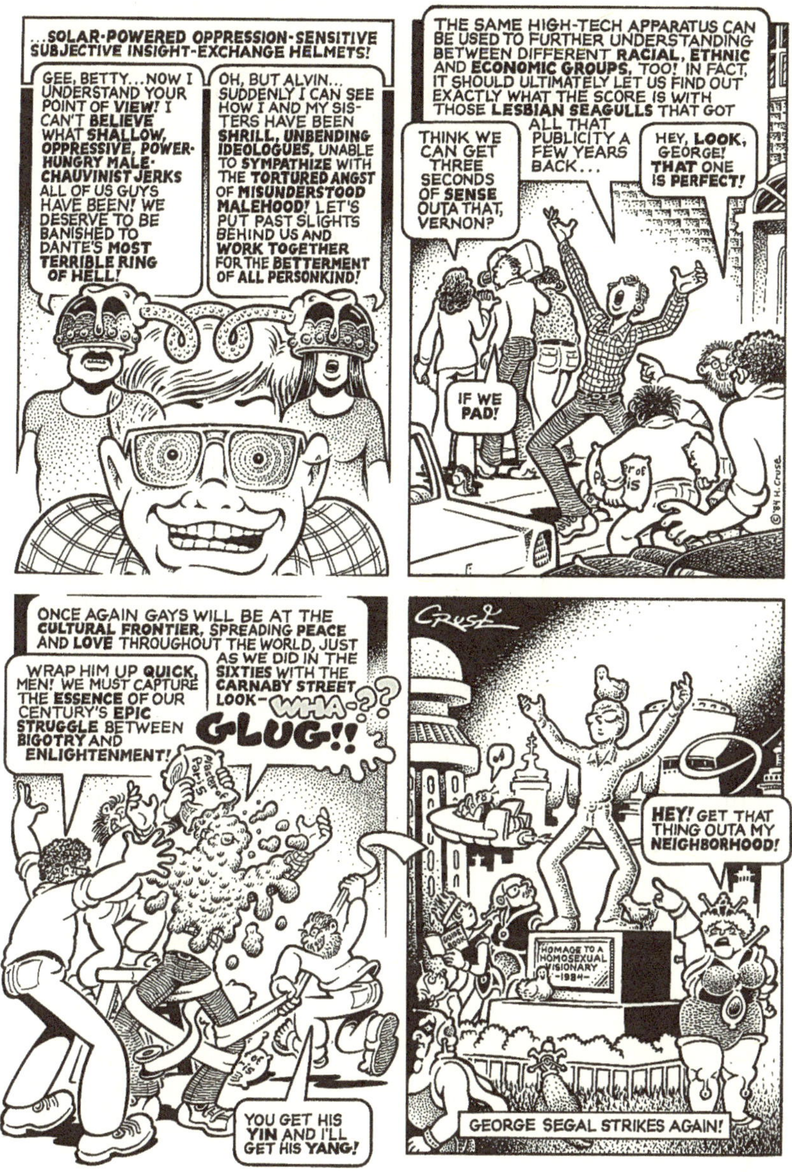

"The Gay in the Street" copyright the estate of Howard Cruse. Used by permission.

"My Life as a TV Pundit"

"My Life as a TV Pundit" can serve as a companion piece to "The Gay in the Street," even though it doesn't address issues of queer politics. Both feature the Howard avatar (though here he is fifteen years older) and take shots at the television news media. Basically, this story questions the level of expertise required to be a TV pundit, especially as demands for such positions increased due to the twenty-four-hour news cycle. This piece is set in the backdrop of the scandal over the White House affair between President Bill Clinton and intern Monica Lewinsky and features contemporary news media figures like Larry King, Charlie Rose, and pundits from *The McLaughlin Group*. The story is also framed by self-parody of Cruse's current status as a cartoonist, four years after the publication of *Stuck Rubber Baby*. As he insists in his commentary on this story in *The Other Sides of Howard Cruse*, he had not been called upon to serve as a TV pundit, but he would have embraced the opportunity nonetheless (210).

This comic first appeared in the short-lived humor magazine *Harpoon: A Serious Journal of Humor*, edited by Tom Toldrain and Jacqueline Jouret, which ran for three issues in 1999 (not to be confused with several other humor magazines that have also been called *Harpoon*). The magazine aimed at topical humor, and Cruse was a regular contributor during its short run. For another issue, he contributed an expanded version of "Why Are We Losing the War on Art?"—a response to conservative attacks on the National Endowment for the Arts—which had originally appeared as a shorter strip in the *Village Voice*.

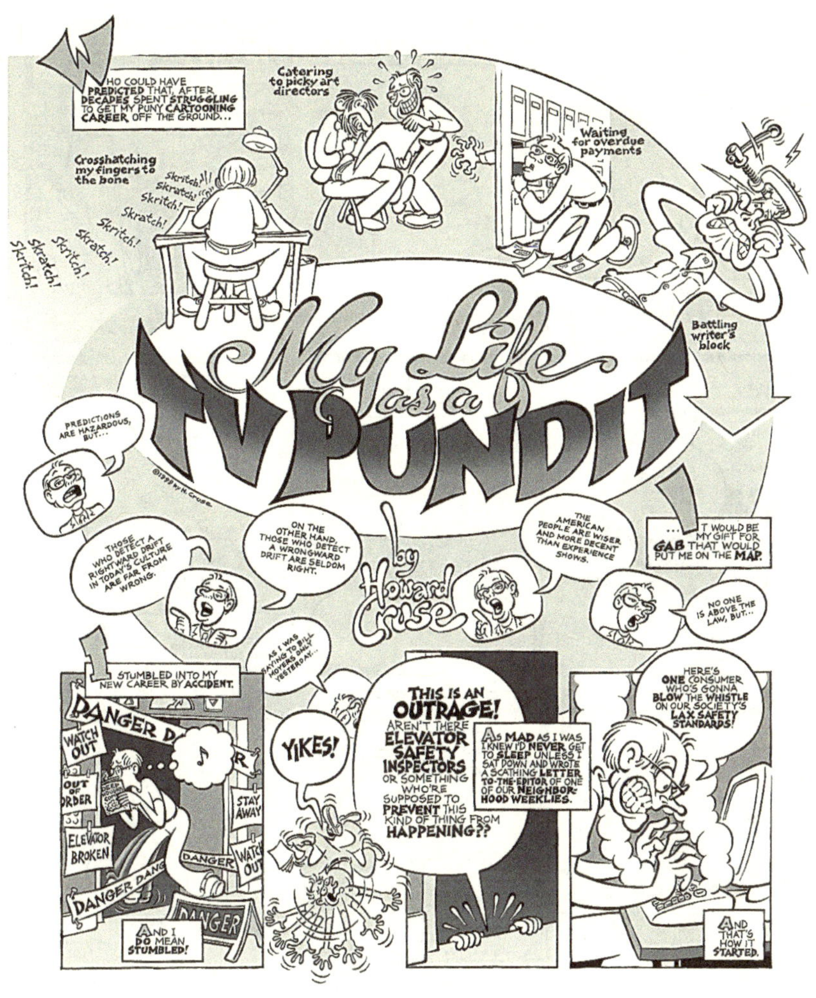

WHO COULD HAVE PREDICTED THAT, AFTER DECADES SPENT STRUGGLING TO GET MY PUNY CARTOONING CAREER OFF THE GROUND...
Crosshatching my fingers to the bone
Skritch! Skratch! Skritch! Skratch! Skritch! Skratch! Skritch! Skratch! Skritch!
Catering to picky art directors
Waiting for overdue payments
Battling writer's block
My Life as a TV PUNDIT
©1999 by H. Cruse
by Howard Cruse
...IT WOULD BE MY GIFT FOR GAB THAT WOULD PUT ME ON THE MAP.
PREDICTIONS ARE HAZARDOUS, BUT...
THOSE WHO DETECT A RIGHTWARD DRIFT IN TODAY'S CULTURE ARE FAR FROM WRONG.
ON THE OTHER HAND, THOSE WHO DETECT A WRONGWARD DRIFT ARE SELDOM RIGHT.
THE AMERICAN PEOPLE ARE WISER AND MORE DECENT THAN EXPERIENCE SHOWS.
NO ONE IS ABOVE THE LAW, BUT...
I STUMBLED INTO MY NEW CAREER BY ACCIDENT.
DANGER
WATCH OUT
OUT OF ORDER
ELEVATOR BROKEN
STAY AWAY
DANGER
WATCH OUT
DANGER DANG
DANGER
AND I DO MEAN STUMBLED!
AS I WAS SAYING TO BILL MOYERS ONLY YESTERDAY...
YIKES!
THIS IS AN OUTRAGE! AREN'T THERE ELEVATOR SAFETY INSPECTORS OR SOMETHING WHO'RE SUPPOSED TO PREVENT THIS KIND OF THING FROM HAPPENING??
AS MAD AS I WAS I KNEW I'D NEVER GET TO SLEEP UNLESS I SAT DOWN AND WROTE A SCATHING LETTER TO THE EDITOR OF ONE OF OUR NEIGHBORHOOD WEEKLIES.
HERE'S ONE CONSUMER WHO'S GONNA BLOW THE WHISTLE ON OUR SOCIETY'S LAX SAFETY STANDARDS!
AND THAT'S HOW IT STARTED.

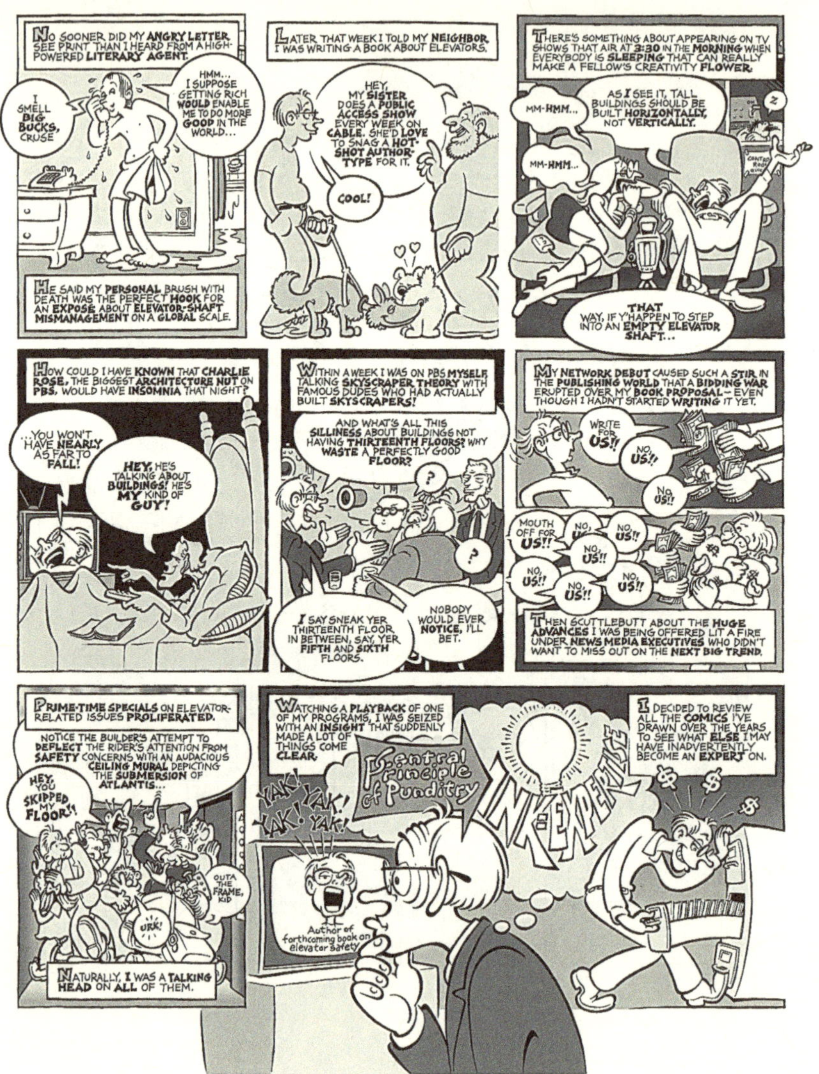

NO SOONER DID MY ANGRY LETTER SEE PRINT THAN I HEARD FROM A HIGH-POWERED LITERARY AGENT.
I SMELL BIG BUCKS, CRUSE
HMM... I SUPPOSE GETTING RICH WOULD ENABLE ME TO DO MORE GOOD IN THE WORLD...
HE SAID MY PERSONAL BRUSH WITH DEATH WAS THE PERFECT HOOK FOR AN EXPOSÉ ABOUT ELEVATOR-SHAFT MISMANAGEMENT ON A GLOBAL SCALE.
LATER THAT WEEK I TOLD MY NEIGHBOR I WAS WRITING A BOOK ABOUT ELEVATORS.
HEY, MY SISTER DOES A PUBLIC ACCESS SHOW EVERY WEEK ON CABLE. SHE'D LOVE TO SNAG A HOT-SHOT AUTHOR-TYPE FOR IT.
COOL!
THERE'S SOMETHING ABOUT APPEARING ON TV SHOWS THAT AIR AT 3:30 IN THE MORNING WHEN EVERYBODY IS SLEEPING THAT CAN REALLY MAKE A FELLOW'S CREATIVITY FLOWER.
MM-HMM...
AS I SEE IT, TALL BUILDINGS SHOULD BE BUILT HORIZONTALLY, NOT VERTICALLY.
MM-HMM...
Z
THAT WAY, IF Y'HAPPEN TO STEP INTO AN EMPTY ELEVATOR SHAFT...
HOW COULD I HAVE KNOWN THAT CHARLIE ROSE, THE BIGGEST ARCHITECTURE NUT ON PBS, WOULD HAVE INSOMNIA THAT NIGHT?
...YOU WON'T HAVE NEARLY AS FAR TO FALL!
HEY, HE'S TALKING ABOUT BUILDINGS! HE'S MY KIND OF GUY!
WITHIN A WEEK I WAS ON PBS MYSELF, TALKING SKYSCRAPER THEORY WITH FAMOUS DUDES WHO HAD ACTUALLY BUILT SKYSCRAPERS!
AND WHAT'S ALL THIS SILLINESS ABOUT BUILDINGS NOT HAVING THIRTEENTH FLOORS? WHY WASTE A PERFECTLY GOOD FLOOR?
?
?
I SAY SNEAK YER THIRTEENTH FLOOR IN BETWEEN, SAY, YER FIFTH AND SIXTH FLOORS.
NOBODY WOULD EVER NOTICE, I'LL BET.
MY NETWORK DEBUT CAUSED SUCH A STIR IN THE PUBLISHING WORLD THAT A BIDDING WAR ERUPTED OVER MY BOOK PROPOSAL — EVEN THOUGH I HADN'T STARTED WRITING IT YET.
WRITE FOR US!!
NO, US!!
NO, US!!
MOUTH OFF FOR US!!
NO, US!!
NO, US!!
NO, US!!
NO, US!!
NO, US!!
NO, US!!
THEN SCUTTLEBUTT ABOUT THE HUGE ADVANCES I WAS BEING OFFERED LIT A FIRE UNDER NEWS MEDIA EXECUTIVES WHO DIDN'T WANT TO MISS OUT ON THE NEXT BIG TREND.
PRIME-TIME SPECIALS ON ELEVATOR-RELATED ISSUES PROLIFERATED.
NOTICE THE BUILDER'S ATTEMPT TO DEFLECT THE RIDER'S ATTENTION FROM SAFETY CONCERNS WITH AN AUDACIOUS CEILING MURAL DEPICTING THE SUBMERSION OF ATLANTIS...
HEY, YOU SKIPPED MY FLOOR!!
OUTA THE FRAME, KID
URK!
NATURALLY, I WAS A TALKING HEAD ON ALL OF THEM.
WATCHING A PLAYBACK OF ONE OF MY PROGRAMS, I WAS SEIZED WITH AN INSIGHT THAT SUDDENLY MADE A LOT OF THINGS COME CLEAR.
YAK! YAK! YAK! YAK!
Central Principle of Punditry
INK=EXPERTISE
Author of forthcoming book on elevator safety
I DECIDED TO REVIEW ALL THE COMICS I'VE DRAWN OVER THE YEARS TO SEE WHAT ELSE I MAY HAVE INADVERTENTLY BECOME AN EXPERT ON.
$
$
$

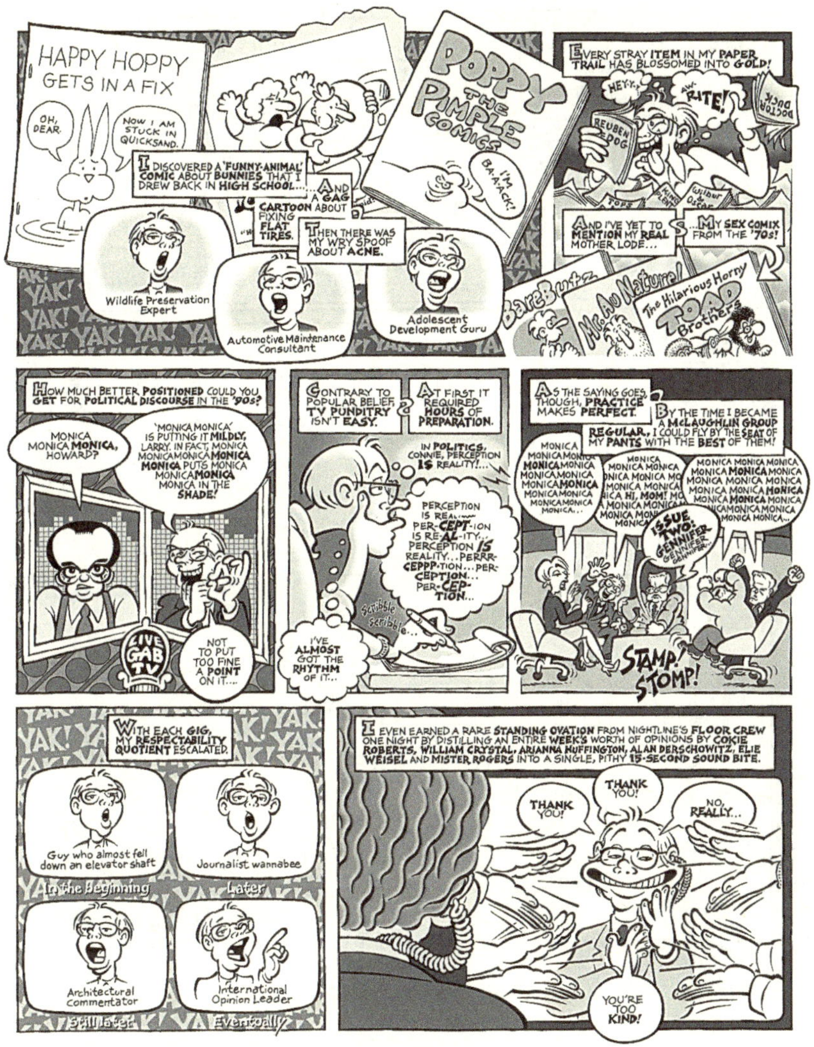
HAPPY HOPPY GETS IN A FIX
OH, DEAR.
NOW I AM STUCK IN QUICKSAND.
I DISCOVERED A 'FUNNY-ANIMAL' COMIC ABOUT BUNNIES THAT I DREW BACK IN HIGH SCHOOL...
...AND A GAG CARTOON ABOUT FIXING FLAT TIRES.
THEN THERE WAS MY WRY SPOOF ABOUT ACNE.
POPPY THE PIMPLE COMICS
I'M BA-A-ACK!
Wildlife Preservation Expert
Automotive Maintenance Consultant
Adolescent Development Guru
YAK! YAK! YAK! YAK!
EVERY STRAY ITEM IN MY PAPER TRAIL HAS BLOSSOMED INTO GOLD!
HEY-Y-Y...
AW-RITE!
REUBEN DOG
DOCTOR DUCK
KING PLENT
Wilbur & Oscar
AND I'VE YET TO MENTION MY REAL MOTHER LODE...
...MY SEX COMIX FROM THE '70s!
BareButz
Mr. Au Nature!
The Hilarious Horny TOAD Brothers
HOW MUCH BETTER POSITIONED COULD YOU GET FOR POLITICAL DISCOURSE IN THE '90s?
MONICA MONICA MONICA, HOWARD?
'MONICA MONICA' IS PUTTING IT MILDLY, LARRY. IN FACT, MONICA MONICAMONICAMONICA MONICA PUTS MONICA MONICAMONICA MONICA IN THE SHADE!
LIVE GAB TV
NOT TO PUT TOO FINE A POINT ON IT....
CONTRARY TO POPULAR BELIEF, TV PUNDITRY ISN'T EASY.
&
AT FIRST IT REQUIRED HOURS OF PREPARATION.
IN POLITICS, CONNIE, PERCEPTION IS REALITY!...
PERCEPTION IS REAL... PER-CEPT-ION IS RE-AL-ITY... PERCEPTION IS REALITY... PERRR-CEPPP-TION... PER-CEPTION... PER-CEP-TION...
Scribble scribble...
I'VE ALMOST GOT THE RHYTHM OF IT...
AS THE SAYING GOES, THOUGH, PRACTICE MAKES PERFECT.
BY THE TIME I BECAME A McLAUGHLIN GROUP REGULAR, I COULD FLY BY THE SEAT OF MY PANTS WITH THE BEST OF THEM!
MONICA MONICAMONICA MONICAMONICA MONICAMONICA MONICAMONICA MONICAMONICA MONICAMONICA MONICA...
MONICA MONICA MONICA ... HI, MOM! ...
MONICA MONICA MONICA MONICA MONICA MONICA MONICA MONICA MONICA MONICA MONICA MONICA MONICA MONICA MONICA MONICA MONICA MONICA...
ISSUE TWO: GENNIFER GENNIFER GENNIFER...
STAMP! STOMP!
WITH EACH GIG, MY RESPECTABILITY QUOTIENT ESCALATED.
Guy who almost fell down an elevator shaft
In the Beginning
Journalist wannabee
Later
Architectural Commentator
Still later
International Opinion Leader
Eventually
I EVEN EARNED A RARE STANDING OVATION FROM NIGHTLINE'S FLOOR CREW ONE NIGHT BY DISTILLING AN ENTIRE WEEK'S WORTH OF OPINIONS BY COKIE ROBERTS, WILLIAM CRYSTAL, ARIANNA HUFFINGTON, ALAN DERSCHOWITZ, ELIE WEISEL AND MISTER ROGERS INTO A SINGLE, PITHY 15-SECOND SOUND BITE.
THANK YOU!
THANK YOU!
NO, REALLY...
YOU'RE TOO KIND!

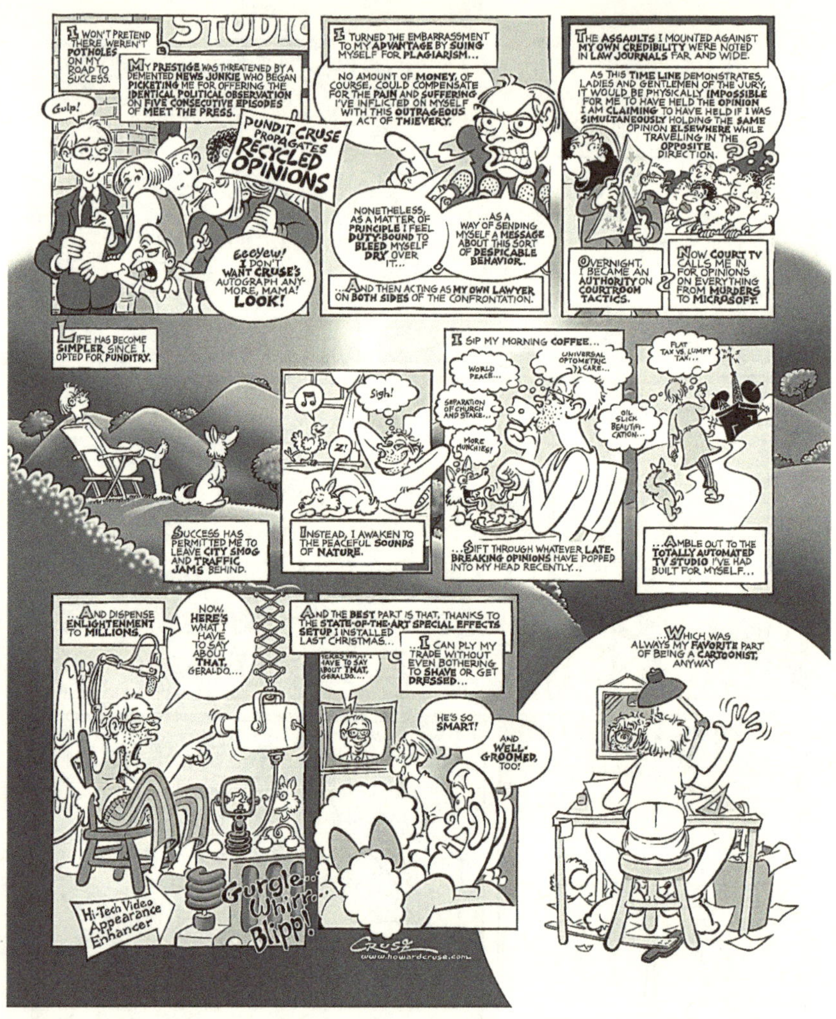

"My Life as a TV Pundit" copyright the estate of Howard Cruse. Used by permission.

"Some Words from the Guys in Charge"

"Some Words from the Guys in Charge" was a part of the anthology *Choices: A Pro-Choice Benefit Comic,* edited by Trina Robbins and published by Angry Isis Press in 1990. Proceeds from the collection benefited the National Organization for Women. Contributors included an array of underground, alternative, and mainstream comics creators, including Cathy Guisewite, Nicole Hollander, Garry Trudeau, Bill Griffith, Diane Noomin, Sharon Rudahl, Ramona Fradon, Jules Feiffer, Jennifer Camper, Phoebe Gloeckner, Roberta Gregory, and Alison Bechdel, among many others. The story is one of several examples where Cruse donated his work to comics anthologies that benefited worthy causes, including also "The Woeful World of Winnie and Walt" for *Strip AIDS U.S.A.* (1988).

This two-page strip came out soon after the end of *Wendel* and as Cruse was beginning work on *Stuck Rubber Baby.* Though the caricatured figures and Zip-a-Tone–style background are reminiscent of Cruse's 1980s work, elements of his *Stuck Rubber Baby* style are also evident in the crosshatching and heavy ink lines. It is a deceptively simple comic, with a static, repetitive point of view that runs through eight identically sized and shaped panels. But that apparent simplicity underlies a complex and effective visual argument about the limitations on choice and bodily autonomy imposed by an oppressive white male hegemony.

Note that Cruse does not rely on copying and pasting with any of the figures. Each is a unique drawing with changing facial expressions throughout. By recognizing the differences between figures in these panels, readers are invited to pause and carefully compare each panel. This, in turn, offers a dense and complex reading experience, where the reader can study each panel intensively or move backward and forward to study the visual differences in each grouping.

At whom are these men looking? Or, to think of it another way, whose point of view, or eyes, are we seeing through? First-person focalization like this is not often used in comics, and it's used to particularly good effect here in making the reader a part of the story. These men are speaking to the readers about regulating, controlling, and threatening their bodies, and the readers are silenced and helpless to respond.

Other formal elements impact the readers' sense of helplessness and oppression. This story is an example of Cruse's skills with lettering, especially taking advantage of the visual qualities of lettering and word balloons to enhance the story's overall effect. This can especially be seen in panel two.

This single word balloon dominates the panel space, and yet the words are densely packed into it. Lettering also varies in size, with some lines cramped into the space available while other words in bold dominate. We don't even have to read the words in order to feel the impact of this balloon. But the words are complemented by their visual qualities: the excessively complex vocabulary and syntax (careful observation shows that the balloon contains only one sentence) intentionally obfuscates meaning and contributes to the overwhelming oppression. These are way more than "some words." Finally, Cruse draws the balloon as if it appears behind the men's heads, creating a sense of depth that runs through every panel. Then panel three has word balloons that reach into the foreground and exceed the limits of the panel border.

The final panel demonstrates the subtle use of another common Cruse technique: treating the panel border as diegetic, where two of the men wrap their fingers around the edges and into the gutter. This further reinforces the first-person focalization—these men are going to reach through the page and come for *you*.

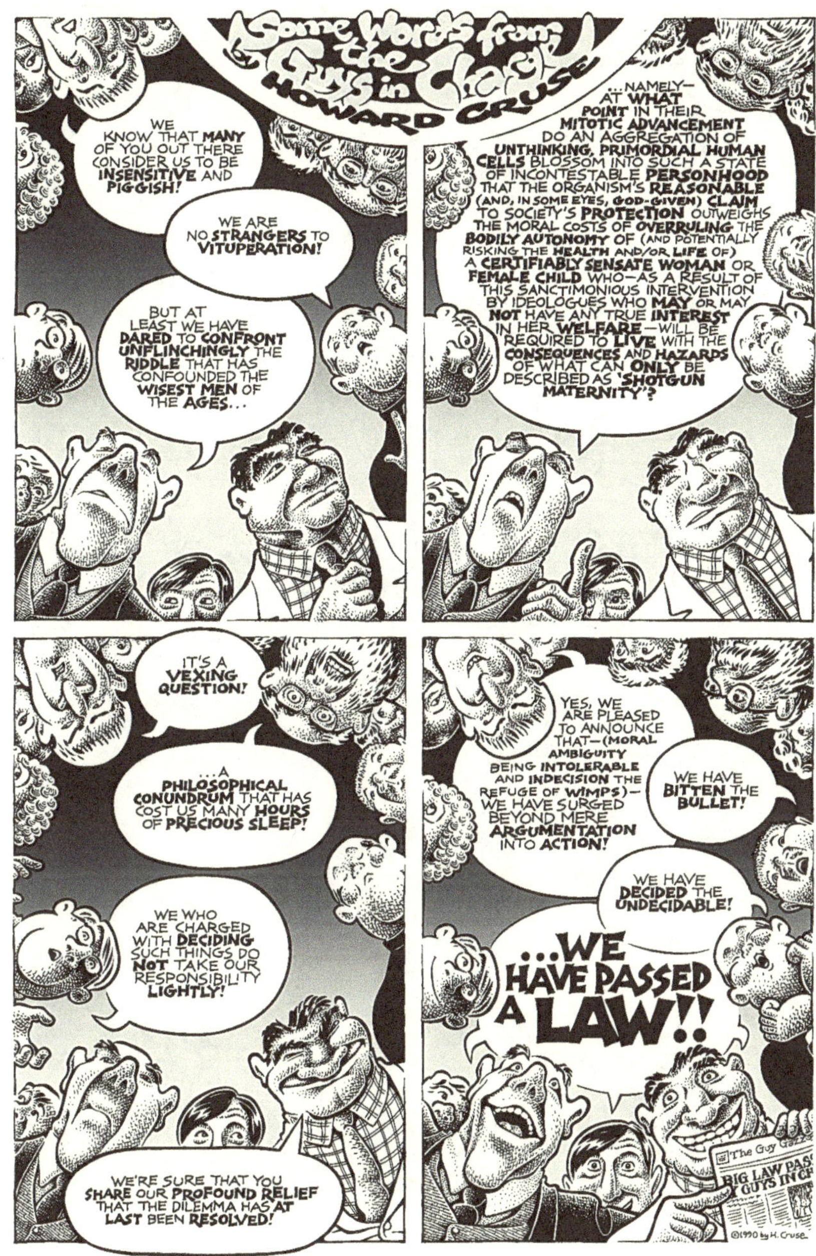
Some Words from the Guys in Charge
by HOWARD CRUSE
WE KNOW THAT MANY OF YOU OUT THERE CONSIDER US TO BE INSENSITIVE AND PIGGISH!
WE ARE NO STRANGERS TO VITUPERATION!
BUT AT LEAST WE HAVE DARED TO CONFRONT UNFLINCHINGLY THE RIDDLE THAT HAS CONFOUNDED THE WISEST MEN OF THE AGES...
...NAMELY— AT WHAT POINT IN THEIR MITOTIC ADVANCEMENT DO AN AGGREGATION OF UNTHINKING, PRIMORDIAL HUMAN CELLS BLOSSOM INTO SUCH A STATE OF INCONTESTABLE PERSONHOOD THAT THE ORGANISM'S REASONABLE (AND, IN SOME EYES, GOD-GIVEN) CLAIM TO SOCIETY'S PROTECTION OUTWEIGHS THE MORAL COSTS OF OVERRULING THE BODILY AUTONOMY OF (AND POTENTIALLY RISKING THE HEALTH AND/OR LIFE OF) A CERTIFIABLY SENSATE WOMAN OR FEMALE CHILD WHO—AS A RESULT OF THIS SANCTIMONIOUS INTERVENTION BY IDEOLOGUES WHO MAY OR MAY NOT HAVE ANY TRUE INTEREST IN HER WELFARE—WILL BE REQUIRED TO LIVE WITH THE CONSEQUENCES AND HAZARDS OF WHAT CAN ONLY BE DESCRIBED AS 'SHOTGUN MATERNITY'?
IT'S A VEXING QUESTION!
...A PHILOSOPHICAL CONUNDRUM THAT HAS COST US MANY HOURS OF PRECIOUS SLEEP!
WE WHO ARE CHARGED WITH DECIDING SUCH THINGS DO NOT TAKE OUR RESPONSIBILITY LIGHTLY!
WE'RE SURE THAT YOU SHARE OUR PROFOUND RELIEF THAT THE DILEMMA HAS AT LAST BEEN RESOLVED!
YES, WE ARE PLEASED TO ANNOUNCE THAT—(MORAL AMBIGUITY BEING INTOLERABLE AND INDECISION THE REFUGE OF WIMPS)—WE HAVE SURGED BEYOND MERE ARGUMENTATION INTO ACTION!
WE HAVE BITTEN THE BULLET!
WE HAVE DECIDED THE UNDECIDABLE!
...WE HAVE PASSED A LAW!!
The Guy
BIG LAW
GUYS IN
©1990 by H. Cruse

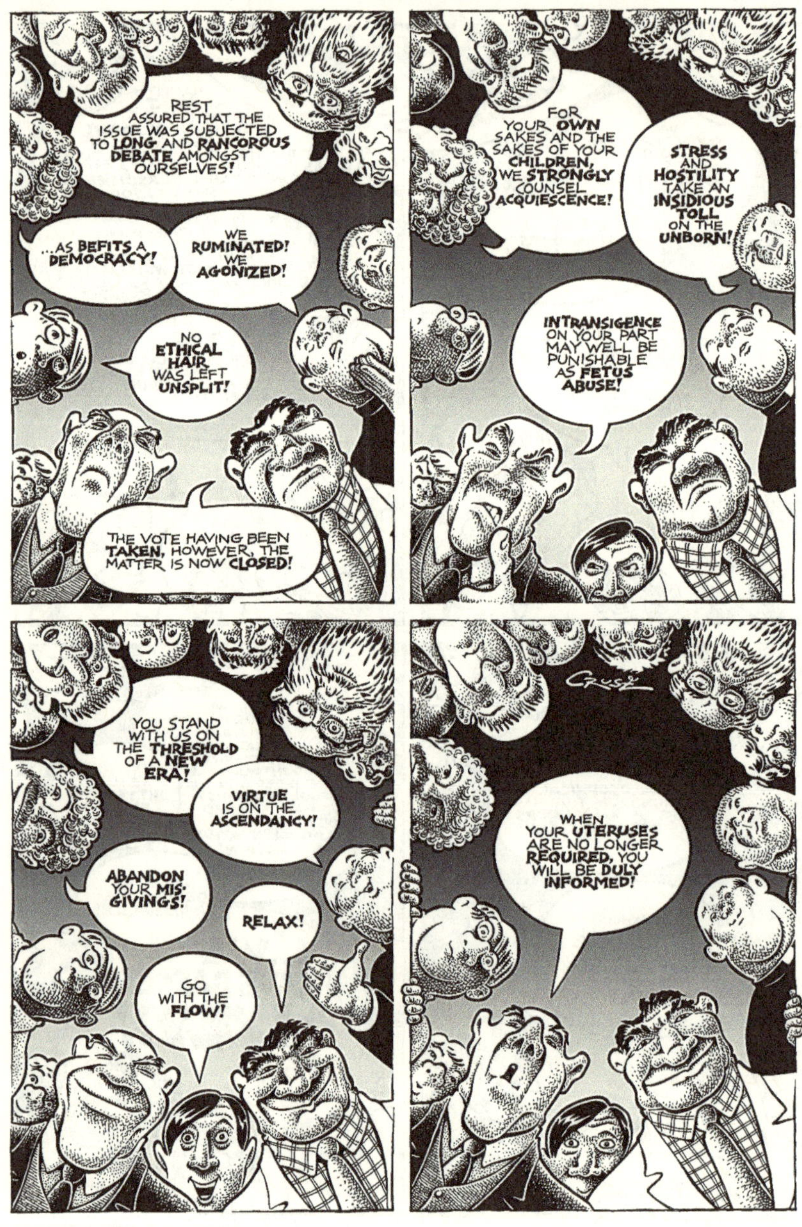

"Some Words from the Guys in Charge" copyright the estate of Howard Cruse. Used by permission.

"Death"

Cruse produced two short comic stories for the first two issues Jan and Dean Mullaney's fledgling *Eclipse* magazine when the publisher started in 1981: "Death" and the grotesque two-page story, "Quick Trim." Eclipse Comics famously paid a significantly higher page rate than other publishers, including Kitchen Sink. Along with Pacific Comics and later First Comics, Eclipse was a major player in the independent comics boom of the 1980s. The two stories for *Eclipse* ended up being rare forays outside of Kitchen Sink at the time. Eclipse had toyed with publishing a *Barefootz* collection at the same time, but nothing came about from that.

Like his other comics essays, "Death" has an autobiographical element, including the Howard avatar as narrator. The improvisationally structured story moves from general ideas about death to a contemplation of the artist's own death at the end. "Death" is yet another example of Cruse's dark humor. His avatar moves cheerfully through each depressing scene, even directly contributing to the trauma of a young boy by making him contemplate his parents' death as well as his own. As Cruse described the purpose of the essay in the commentary from *The Other Sides of Howard Cruse*: "I was meditating with dry eyes and a smile on the fact that, however much pleasure we take individually in being alive, we also spend our days on Earth as mannequins-in-waiting" (164). The phrase the Howard narrator uses to envision his own death—"dancin' nekkid with the angels"—became the title of Cruse's 1987 collection of short comics.

Forcing the child to contemplate death connects to Cruse's own fascination with death, as he explained: "I have always been fascinated by the physicality of death. One moment you have a conscious being with active brain waves and warm blood pulsing through its veins; the next you have an inert, swiftly stiffening slab of matter. Some might view this fascination as morbid, but for me it feels like awe, a respectful appreciation of one of the universe's great mysteries" (164). In that same commentary, he also revealed how he was exposed to death at an early age through the southern practice of open-casket funerals.

Though this story precedes the publication of Scott McCloud's *Understanding Comics* by twelve years, there are qualities of tone and direct address that are reminiscent of McCloud's avatar narrator. Both are humorous and good-natured in the way they engage with the reader, and both are aware that they exist within a comic. At one point, when the contemplation of death hits a bit too close to home, Howard asks the reader to "move on to the next panel."

When Howard Cruse passed away on November 26, 2019, this story was widely circulated on social media by fans, friends, and fellow cartoonists as a celebration of his humor, talent, and personality. He seems to anticipate that this comic would be used to such a purpose, as he says to the reader, "I might be dead by the time you read this." In that case, he has a modest request for his readers: "I like to think somebody might pick up my comic books and have a chuckle!" though he humbly dismisses the possibility. However, if this book has any function in the world, it can be to honor that wish.

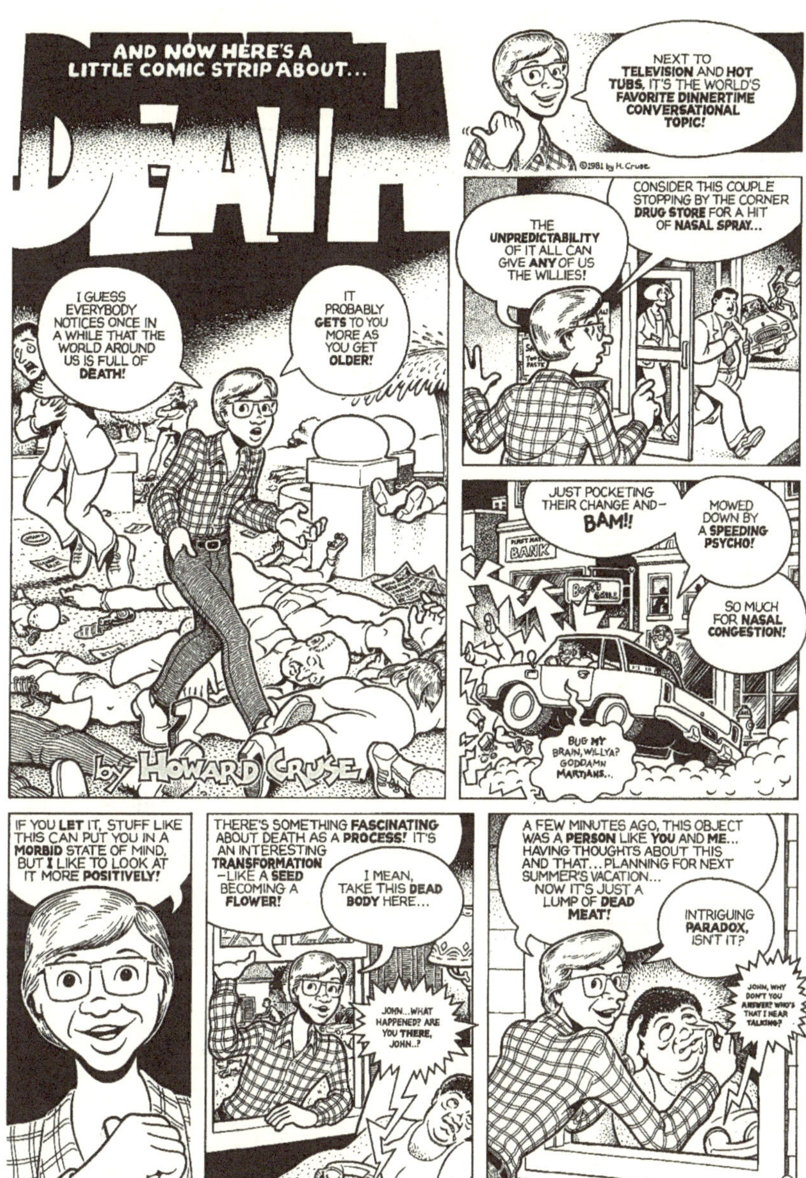
AND NOW HERE'S A LITTLE COMIC STRIP ABOUT...
DEATH
NEXT TO TELEVISION AND HOT TUBS, IT'S THE WORLD'S FAVORITE DINNERTIME CONVERSATIONAL TOPIC!
©1981 by H. Cruse
I GUESS EVERYBODY NOTICES ONCE IN A WHILE THAT THE WORLD AROUND US IS FULL OF DEATH!
IT PROBABLY GETS TO YOU MORE AS YOU GET OLDER!
by HOWARD CRUSE
CONSIDER THIS COUPLE STOPPING BY THE CORNER DRUG STORE FOR A HIT OF NASAL SPRAY...
THE UNPREDICTABILITY OF IT ALL CAN GIVE ANY OF US THE WILLIES!
JUST POCKETING THEIR CHANGE AND— BAM!!
MOWED DOWN BY A SPEEDING PSYCHO!
SO MUCH FOR NASAL CONGESTION!
BANK
BUG MY BRAIN, WILLYA? GODDAMN MARTIANS..
IF YOU LET IT, STUFF LIKE THIS CAN PUT YOU IN A MORBID STATE OF MIND, BUT I LIKE TO LOOK AT IT MORE POSITIVELY!
THERE'S SOMETHING FASCINATING ABOUT DEATH AS A PROCESS! IT'S AN INTERESTING TRANSFORMATION —LIKE A SEED BECOMING A FLOWER!
I MEAN, TAKE THIS DEAD BODY HERE...
JOHN...WHAT HAPPENED? ARE YOU THERE, JOHN..?
A FEW MINUTES AGO, THIS OBJECT WAS A PERSON LIKE YOU AND ME... HAVING THOUGHTS ABOUT THIS AND THAT... PLANNING FOR NEXT SUMMER'S VACATION... NOW IT'S JUST A LUMP OF DEAD MEAT!
INTRIGUING PARADOX, ISN'T IT?
JOHN, WHY DON'T YOU ANSWER? WHO'S THAT I HEAR TALKING?
1

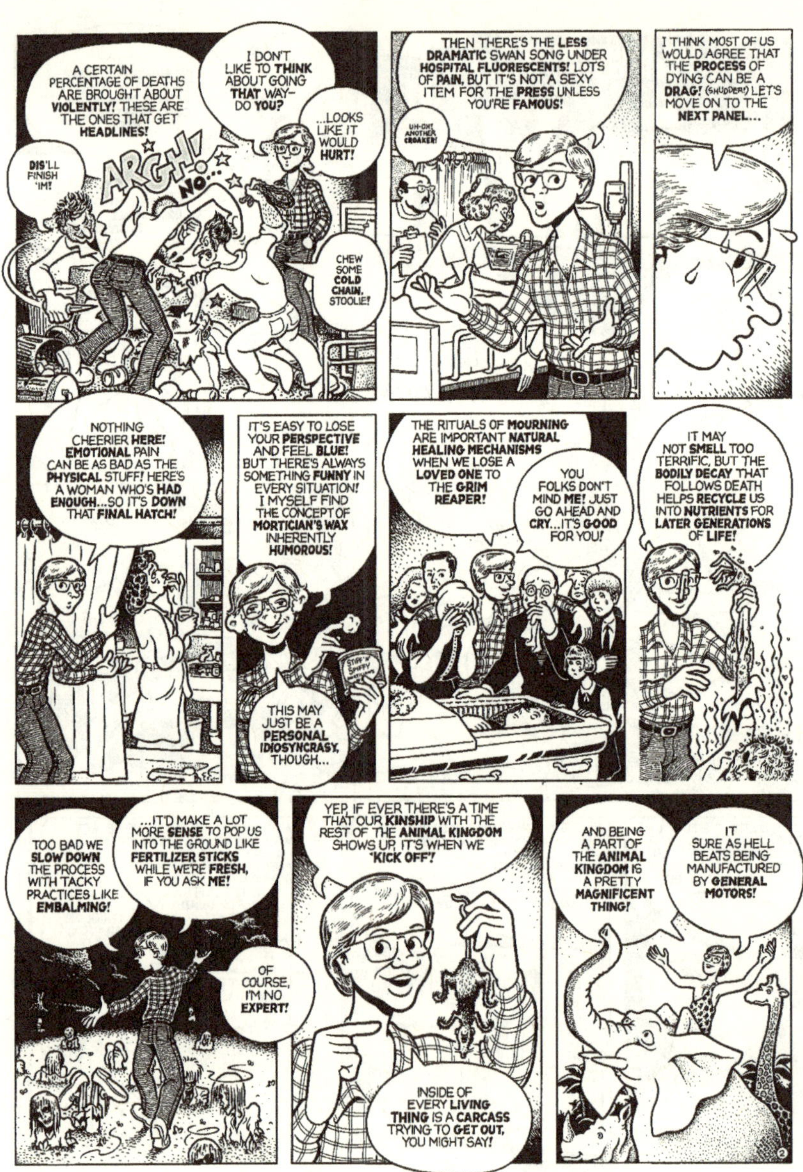
A CERTAIN PERCENTAGE OF DEATHS ARE BROUGHT ABOUT VIOLENTLY! THESE ARE THE ONES THAT GET HEADLINES!
I DON'T LIKE TO THINK ABOUT GOING THAT WAY— DO YOU?
...LOOKS LIKE IT WOULD HURT!
DIS'LL FINISH 'IM!
ARGH!
NO...
CHEW SOME COLD CHAIN, STOOLIE!
THEN THERE'S THE LESS DRAMATIC SWAN SONG UNDER HOSPITAL FLUORESCENTS! LOTS OF PAIN, BUT IT'S NOT A SEXY ITEM FOR THE PRESS UNLESS YOU'RE FAMOUS!
UH-OH! ANOTHER CROAKER!
I THINK MOST OF US WOULD AGREE THAT THE PROCESS OF DYING CAN BE A DRAG! (SHUDDER!) LET'S MOVE ON TO THE NEXT PANEL...
NOTHING CHEERIER HERE! EMOTIONAL PAIN CAN BE AS BAD AS THE PHYSICAL STUFF! HERE'S A WOMAN WHO'S HAD ENOUGH...SO IT'S DOWN THAT FINAL HATCH!
IT'S EASY TO LOSE YOUR PERSPECTIVE AND FEEL BLUE! BUT THERE'S ALWAYS SOMETHING FUNNY IN EVERY SITUATION! I MYSELF FIND THE CONCEPT OF MORTICIAN'S WAX INHERENTLY HUMOROUS!
THIS MAY JUST BE A PERSONAL IDIOSYNCRASY, THOUGH...
THE RITUALS OF MOURNING ARE IMPORTANT NATURAL HEALING MECHANISMS WHEN WE LOSE A LOVED ONE TO THE GRIM REAPER!
YOU FOLKS DON'T MIND ME! JUST GO AHEAD AND CRY...IT'S GOOD FOR YOU!
IT MAY NOT SMELL TOO TERRIFIC, BUT THE BODILY DECAY THAT FOLLOWS DEATH HELPS RECYCLE US INTO NUTRIENTS FOR LATER GENERATIONS OF LIFE!
TOO BAD WE SLOW DOWN THE PROCESS WITH TACKY PRACTICES LIKE EMBALMING!
...IT'D MAKE A LOT MORE SENSE TO POP US INTO THE GROUND LIKE FERTILIZER STICKS WHILE WE'RE FRESH, IF YOU ASK ME!
OF COURSE, I'M NO EXPERT!
YEP, IF EVER THERE'S A TIME THAT OUR KINSHIP WITH THE REST OF THE ANIMAL KINGDOM SHOWS UP, IT'S WHEN WE 'KICK OFF'!
INSIDE OF EVERY LIVING THING IS A CARCASS TRYING TO GET OUT, YOU MIGHT SAY!
AND BEING A PART OF THE ANIMAL KINGDOM IS A PRETTY MAGNIFICENT THING!
IT SURE AS HELL BEATS BEING MANUFACTURED BY GENERAL MOTORS!
2

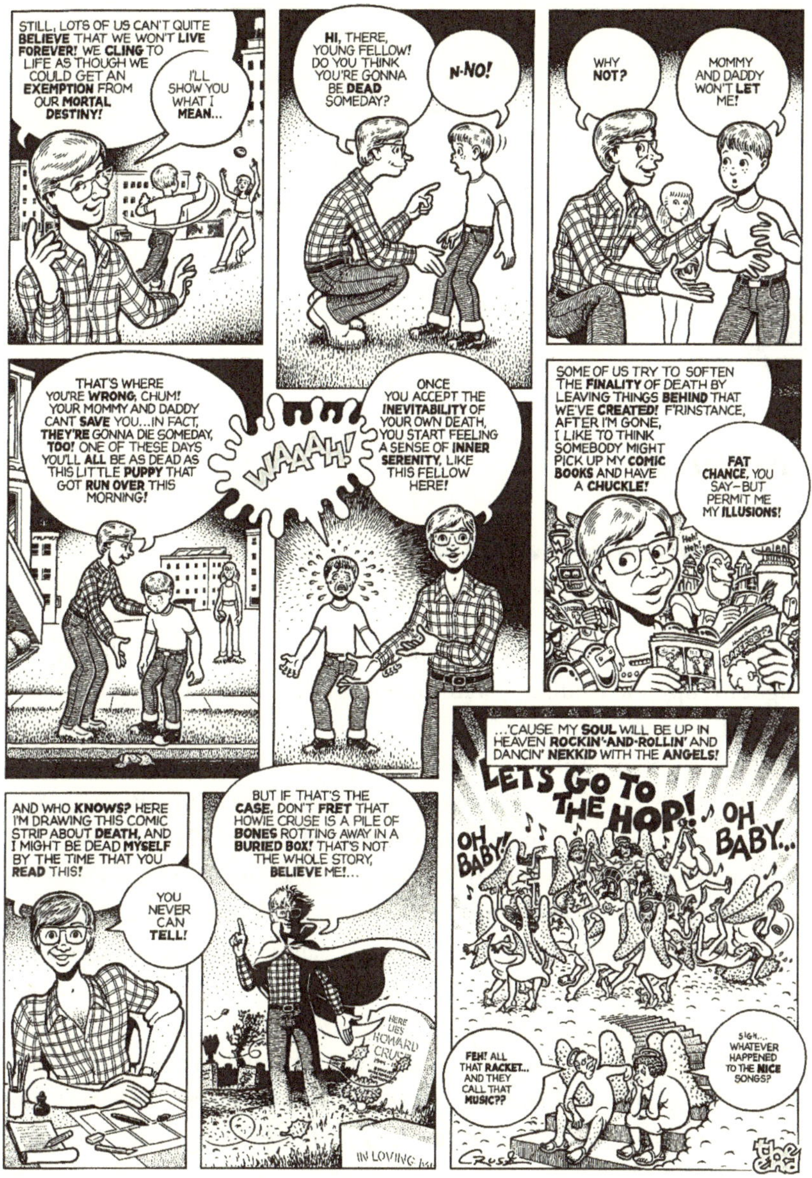

"Death" copyright the estate of Howard Cruse. Used by permission.

4

Parodies

Howard Cruse's earliest comic book influences—the comics that he first sought to copy and emulate—were humor comics, mainly those published by Dell and aimed at young readers. Dell's most successful comics featured the popular anthropomorphic animals owned by Walt Disney and Warner Bros., like Mickey Mouse, Donald Duck, Uncle Scrooge, Bugs Bunny, Porky Pig, and so on. In addition, Dell also published *Little Lulu* and *Nancy* comics, both of which had a strong influence on Cruse. In the 1950s, Dell escaped the moral scrutiny that plagued other comic book publishers, notably EC Comics with its crime and horror lines, because it mainly produced such tame, child-friendly fare. When testifying before the 1954 Senate Committee on Juvenile Delinquency, Dell's then vice president, Helen Meyer, stressed that their comics did not require censorship and oversight since Dell avoided the troubling and controversial crime and horror genres.[1] It seems quite ironic, then, that Dell's comics like *Donald Duck*, *Little Lulu*, and *Nancy* would form the basis for some of Cruse's most irreverent and explicit underground comics. Though these parodies occasionally explore themes and topics relevant to the focus of earlier chapters, they also collectively reveal Cruse's influences, stylistic choices, and reverence for the sources that inspired him to be a cartoonist.

Howard Cruse's visual style is disarmingly cute, and that style is notably on display when he borrows tropes and even characters from children's comics for darkly humorous purposes. Cruse was a master at mimicking other cartoonists' styles, as can be seen in his dead-on imitations of John Stanley and Irving Tripp's *Little Lulu* and Ernie Bushmiller's *Nancy*. This skill also helped Cruse get a job at *Playboy* magazine, when fellow underground cartoonist Skip Williamson recommended Cruse for the new "Playboy Funnies" section, edited by Michelle Urry. After looking through Cruse's portfolio, Urry zeroed in on the *Little Lulu* parody, and this led Cruse to produce comic strip parodies for the magazine. Strips he parodied included *Blondie*, *B.C.*, *Momma*, *Tumbleweeds*, *Miss Peach*, and *Doonesbury*, among others, though not all were published. (Cruse discusses how *Playboy* succumbed to threats of lawsuits over copyright infringement with these strips in his essay on parody, reprinted below.) Cruse would also later mimic the style of Matt Groening's *Life in Hell* in the one-page strip "Gay Dorks in Fezzes" for *Gay Comix* 14, where he parodies the sexually ambiguous duo Akbar and Jeff. One of his last works, "Coming Out with the Bunksteads," appeared in Rob Kirby's 2014 *QU33R* anthology. This parody of *Blondie* has the Bumsteads' son, Alexander, come out to his father, only Dagwood is, as usual, napping at the time.

The concept of parody has been much debated, especially the role that parody plays in postmodern literary theory as a key practice of postmodernism. Simon Dentith, in his study of parody, offers this definition: "Parody includes any cultural practice which provides a relatively polemical allusive imitation of another cultural production or practice" (9). This expansive definition that includes "any cultural practice" can thus be applied to the type of comics parody that Cruse engages in. The qualification of the "relatively polemical" aspect of the imitation seems to work for Cruse as well. While the satires of the previous chapter are much more polemical than the parodies in this chapter, there are some milder polemical qualities to them. The criticism of Cold War American culture in "The Nightmares of Little L*l*" and of consumer culture in "Raising Nancies" sits at a higher satirical level than the shots Cruse takes at cartoon ghosts and funny animals in the other parodies. In the essay "The Other Side of the Coin," Cruse works from an even narrower definition where he deals with comics parodies that imitate other comics. The functions of parody that he identifies as important—encouraging skepticism and offering social commentary—fit with the polemical element Dentith emphasizes.

Dentith's distinction between "specific" and "general" parodies also illuminates some of Cruse's practices (7). Specific parodies imitate specific sources, as when Cruse mimics the style of Irving Tripp's *Little Lulu* or Ernie Bushmiller's *Nancy*, while general parodies imitate larger groups of sources, like Cruse's parodies of the funny animal and humorous ghost subgenres. Therefore, in this chapter, we can see Cruse engaging in a continuum of parodic practices from the specific to the more general, though still narrow, targets within comic genres.

Much of Cruse's humor comes from the distance between the source material—comics aimed at children—and the things that Cruse has them do. This approach was common in underground comix, as so much of the movement's iconoclasm was in resistance to conservative mainstream culture, where comics were prominent. The underground was also influenced by *Mad* and its approach to parody, especially during the comic book and magazine era under Harvey Kurtzman's editorship. What separates Cruse from many of his contemporaries, though not exclusive to him, is the affection that he has for his sources, which are, after all, the comic books he grew up with.

From 1982 to 1983, Howard Cruse wrote the regular "Loose Cruse" column for *Comics Scene* magazine, which was published by Starlog Press, where Cruse had worked as art director. "The Other Side of the Coin," published in issue 8 (March 1983), is the third part of an essay series Cruse wrote about parody in comics. The first two parts focused on the Air Pirates case, where Walt Disney Productions sued a group of underground cartoonists (Dan O'Neill, Gary Hallgren, Bobby London, and Ted Richards)[2] for copyright and trademark infringement over the publication of *Air Pirates Funnies*, an underground comic featuring parodies of Disney cartoon characters like Mickey Mouse and Minnie Mouse having graphic sexual intercourse and taking drugs. The series ran for two issues in 1971, published by Last Gasp.

The collective took its name from a group of villains that had appeared in early Mickey Mouse stories. O'Neill's ability to mimic the Disney style, especially that of Mickey Mouse comic strip artist Floyd Gottfredson, was dead on. When the first issue was published, Disney almost immediately launched their lawsuit, which went through multiple appeals and decisions—all of which went against O'Neill and the Pirates—until 1980. The Pirates lost the initial court decision in 1972, but O'Neill pursued an appeal to the Ninth Circuit Court. That case dragged on until 1978, where O'Neill lost again on the grounds of copyright, but not trademark, infringement.[3] It was the Ninth Circuit Court decision that raised particular concerns for Cruse.

Cruse was affected by the Air Pirates case in a variety of ways. The decision against the cartoonists created a chilling effect on cartoon parodies. At the time of the Ninth Circuit Court of Appeals decision in 1978, Cruse was creating his comic strip parodies for *Playboy* magazine. Cruse's ability to mimic the drawing style of these various cartoonists made him particularly suited for this kind of work. However, *Playboy* editorial became concerned that the parodies were too close to the originals, and Cruse received some submissions back for revision. Even with significant changes, though, *Playboy* ended up not publishing the strips, for fear of legal repercussions similar to those experienced by the Air Pirates. The court's decision forbade "verbatim copying": the parody could only draw enough from the original to allow the audience to recognize the source. Perfect mimicry of the type that Cruse was doing in the *Playboy* strip parodies fell within this otherwise vague concept.[4]

Just before the Air Pirates decision came down, Cruse had submitted "The Nightmares of Little L*l*," a parody of *Little Lulu* comics, to Denis Kitchen for *Snarf* 8. While Lulu, Tubby, and the rest of the gang engage in activities that obviously would not have been acceptable under Dell Comics' editorial restrictions for the comic, Cruse covers himself by clearly establishing that this is a parody. In the essay below, he explains some of the decision making that went into the parody: for example, framing the story with scenes of Lulu and Tubby ("L*l*" and "Chubby") as adults to establish a difference from the original, and then within that frame using a near-perfect imitation of Irving Tripp's style. Nonetheless, as this essay indicates, the Air Pirates ruling caused him to second-guess the choices he made to create such an accurate duplication of the original source.

But most of all, Cruse is concerned about the negative effect this court decision has on an art form that he argues has important social value. He makes the case for the necessity of parody in developing a healthy skepticism: one that he developed from his earliest exposure to *Mad*, and one that continued to inform his work throughout much of his career. Therefore, this essay provides a window into Cruse's theory and practice of parody while also revealing a specific moment in comics history where artists and publishers were feeling under threat by this vague and restrictive court decision. The ruling was another blow to what remained of the underground movement: if these counterculture iconoclasts couldn't parody such a powerful and dominant cultural force as Disney, then underground comix would lose much of what was left of its ability to serve as an alternative voice against the mainstream.

This essay is included here also to show Cruse's skill as a prose essayist. In his "Loose Cruse" columns, he revealed himself to be a skilled, engaging opinion columnist. One point to note is his sense of balance in the argument. Though he obviously falls on the side of the parodists in the debate between parody and copyright, he also effectively addresses and accommodates the opposing argument by defining and advocating for limits on parody.[5]

"The Other Side of the Coin"

The first parody I ever saw was in the first *Mad* I ever saw, back in the days when weird little people cavorted inside that magazine's logo. The feature, drawn by Wally Wood, was titled "If Comic Strip Characters Answered Those Little Ads."[6]

Quibblers will note that it technically wasn't a parody; however, it did contain parodic elements. My jaw dropped in amazement at drawings of Nancy answering an ad for hair straightener and Dagwood responding to a body building pitch. There were before-and-after pictures of Henry, Popeye, Alley Oop and The Phantom wherein each was transformed by having clipped out a tacky back-of-the-book magazine ad.

What amazed me was seeing these diverse characters mingling in a single feature drawn by a single artist's hand. I'd naively assumed that such liberties weren't *allowed*, that no one could publish a drawing of Nancy other than Ernie Bushmiller himself. Couldn't these people get sued?

But what a thrill for me, like stepping without warning into the unstructured surrealism of the dream state! Suddenly, cartooning was invested with new and giddy potentials. Batman might patrol the night alongside Casper the Friendly Ghost. Pinocchio could share puppet gossip with Howdy Doody.

At that point, literary criticism and social commentary were far from my mind. I liked parody simply because it could break the normal rules.

Breaking rules made parody fun, but criticism and commentary are what make it an art form of substance. Just as most of us are initially drawn to movies which dazzle, tickle or scare us without providing any interesting insights about the human condition, most of us have cut our teeth on parodies which were designed to amuse us without making us think. (Nancy's hair looks like a Brillo pad—*so what*? A parodist points that out and we laugh, but we're not broadened by the experience.) The philosophically unthreatening themes of most parodies in today's *Mad* have encouraged us to view parody itself as an inherently trivial diversion.

But a thoughtful parodist can use the form to substantial effect. Harvey Kurtzman, editor of the formative *Mad*, used parody and other forms of satire to short-circuit our habitual responses to familiar images, enticing us with broad comedy into more skeptical frames of mind. He reminded us that Mickey Mouse was a mouse, one of those unsanitary rodents that make us feel queasy if they scamper across our bare feet in a dark kitchen.[7]

Skepticism is crucial in a society flooded with deceptive packaging. It's all too easy to let the "willing suspension of disbelief," which permits us to believe that Christopher Reeve can fly, carry over to the calculated images prepared by ad agencies who want to sell us a Ronald Reagan or a Jimmy Carter.

Parody reminds us that we are capable of stepping back from the machinations of busy manipulators and laughing at—or rebelling against—that which insults our intelligence. If the manipulation is benign, we can always reenter the illusion. No one's ability to enjoy a Mickey Mouse cartoon is permanently sabotaged by a Kurtzman parody. But by being reminded that appealing images are not the same as reality, we are less the prisoners of the gears and pistons of illusion which propel our art, shape our opinions, and potentially regiment our lives.

The Air Pirates . . . did not consider the manipulations of Walt Disney Productions benign. They chose parody (mixed with bawdiness and burlesque) to make their point. They weren't laughing at Mickey Mouse because his ears were round: they were satirizing the idea behind the Mouse. While opinions on their point of view are divided, most of us were forced to give fresh thought to some real issues. Art forms that stimulate fresh thought are not to be taken lightly.

In a modest way I had social commentary in mind when I drew "The Nightmares of Little L*l*," a *Little Lulu* parody which ran in a 1978 underground comic book called *Snarf* #8. On one level, I poked silly fun at a favorite old character, but I was also reflecting on how troubled childhood can be beneath a carefree surface. Maybe yours wasn't; mine was.

Drawing that parody, I had a vague sense of rules which should be followed. I assumed my piece should be easily distinguishable from its Dell / Gold Key model. No problem! My piece opened with Lulu as an adult, which no real *Lulu* story would ever do. My piece was in black & white, located inside a comic book targeted specifically at adults. All of the characters' names were altered. In my visual depictions of the characters, however, I tried to duplicate the prototypes exactly. I assumed that was allowed; I'd seen *Mad* do it a hundred times.

Snarf #8 was in production when I first got word of the 1978 ruling by the Ninth Circuit Court of Appeals. Soon the Supreme Court, by refusing to hear the Air Pirates' appeal, had left that ruling as the most authoritative precedent relating to comic strip parody. It wasn't the final word; courts in other geographical areas could hold a different opinion. But there was no way to know how the blade would cut until the parodist's head was already in the guillotine.

Take the matter of "verbatim copying"—exactly what I had done in my *Lulu* parody. That was a no-no, the Ninth Circuit now was telling me. *Mad* had led me down the primrose path. Suddenly, I was hearing a new (to me) principle: that no more of an original could be copied "than is necessary to 'recall or conjure up' the object of [a] satire."

That restriction pulled the rug out from under the kind of parody I had grown up enjoying, parody that looks like that which is being parodied, without saying how much original images had to be modified. This left individual artists like me completely at sea if we wished to obey the law—unless we declined to attempt parody at all.

In his "Communique #1 from the MLF Front" (*CoEvolution Quarterly*, Spring 1979),[8] Dan O'Neill puzzled over the same ambiguities that had me scratching my head. How much must a parody of Mickey Mouse alter the Mouse's image? Is changing a four-fingered hand to a five-fingered one enough? Will transplanting Mickey's head onto a furry rodent's body leave the parodist secure? I reflected on my own work: how might I have changed my *Lulu* parody had I anticipated the court's decision? Should I have given her extra ringlets, squared off her hairballs or beveled her pointed nose?

I had a chance to practice such games in the real marketplace. When the Ninth Circuit handed down its ruling, by coincidence, I was regularly creating short parodies of syndicated comic strips for *Playboy*. Lawyers for the syndicates were responding to the parodies (my own and those of other artists) with surly letters, and *Playboy*'s lawyers were getting uneasy, what with the turn things were taking for the Air Pirates. Several of my previously accepted strips were returned to me and I was instructed to do them over, changing the look of the characters so that they *differed from* but still *conjured up* the originals. So I set to work. If a nose hooked down, I bent it upward. I fiddled with hairdos, supplied new wardrobes. The revised versions bounced around *Playboy*'s bowels for a while but were ultimately returned to me, paid for but never published. The legal waters were just too murky for *Playboy*'s lawyers, so syndicate pressure carried the day. Comic strip parodies disappeared from *Playboy Funnies*.

Not an earthshaking cultural loss in itself, but an example of how vague laws result in self-censorship. And it's the controversial, challenging ideas, the ones that go beyond *Playboy*'s sexual silliness, the ones that parody is particularly well-equipped to communicate, that get killed. Individual artists cannot be blamed for taking note when wealthy *Playboy* knuckles under. The message is clear: keep your parodies to yourself if the ideas they express challenge the interests of the powerful.

Which leaves us with mediocre parody that threatens nobody. This consequence is of scant concern to Judge [Walter J.] Cummings, who wrote the

Ninth Circuit decision. He explicitly says that we'll just have to make do with less than the "best parody" in order to protect the rights of copyright holders.

It's nothing new to assert that certain conditions may justify limitations on free speech. We can't have someone yelling "Fire!" in a crowded theater, we're repeatedly reminded. Laws banning libel and slander limit the written and verbal options of those inclined to irresponsibly destroy the reputations of others, recognizing that person's ability to earn a living or exist without harassment in society can hinge on an honorable reputation.

But I don't think the effect of parody on a copyright holder's commercial viability can be compared to the effect of slander on a reputation. Otherwise, Edgar Allan Poe's *The Raven* would long ago have been drummed from the textbooks by the mob of jesters who have parodied it. Parody doesn't destroy its target; it merely invites the reader to view skeptically. No one suggests that we restrain professional criticism which pursues the same goal via expository prose. Having one's art ridiculed is one of the classic risks of performing in the public arena. The fact that criticism can be all the more incisive when cast in the mold of parody is reason for cheering, not scrambling to shave off portions of the Bill of Rights.

Parody is the literary equivalent of political cartoons. Instead of caricaturing public figures, the parodist caricatures other works of art. Because of the clear-cut impact that politicians have on our daily lives, the need for a skeptical citizenry is obvious, and the law guarantees great leeway for the Herblocks, Oliphants, and Trudeaus who keep us on guard against political tomfoolery.[9]

Dishonesty or shallowness in the arts may not appear as important as they are in politics. After all, nobody's cutting back aid to handicapped children because of Mickey Mouse's grin—right? Or *are* they? Much in our culture hinges on what our values truly are, as opposed to what values we give lip service to. The arts both reflect and shape the values we live by, work by and make critical national decisions by. Paying attention to the arts means paying attention to the kind of world we are in the process of building.

A judge who ruled that we must abandon aiming for the best political cartoons possible would provoke gasps of alarm. As a matter of fact, the First Amendment is there to make sure that we permit the best novels, plays, songs and essays possible. Parody is an art form with peculiar limitations that guarantee it will never play the large role in our culture that the novel does. But there are certain kinds of ideas for which parody is the best possible vehicle. Shall we demand that these ideas be expressed in softer, less trenchant, less persuasive terms?

And to use the form, one needs the tools of the form. In his 1972 deposition in the Air Pirates' defense, Gary Hallgren wrote, "Walt Disney has presented me and the public with a coin that has been 'heads up' for more than 40 years. I am aware that there are at least two sides to every coin . . . and in order to see what is on the 'tail' side, I must pick up *that very coin* and turn it over." Exploring the hidden facets of the Mickey Mouse myth is not accomplished with comics about a mouse who is vaguely similar. It is the use of the *exact image* that gives parody its special emotional power.

Fairness dictates that when parody is sold commercially, the consumer should know that he is buying a satirical alternative instead of the original. One needn't outlaw the use of the exact image to accomplish this. The traditional practice of altering titles and characters' names serves that end quite well; indeed, to mandate that a piece carry the word "parody" as a prominent label would not be a major intrusion on the work's integrity. I'm specifically talking about comic strip parody in this article, and in a comic strip the picture is the first to hit the eye. A label may be read, understood and left behind as the main artistic experience moves ahead.

It's also fair to expect that a parody of a particular work (as opposed to a genre) be a one-shot affair. To proceed with a continuing series suggests that commercial exploitation has supplanted the initial impulse toward satiric criticism.

It seems clear to me that fairness to both the parodist and the copyright holder can be assured without defanging the parodist's medium or intimidating the artist into self-censorship. As things stand now, unfortunately, the powerful copyright holder who can afford to sustain expensive lawsuits holds most of the cards. Let a lawyer tell you about it:

"There are no direct guidelines that one can compare one's drawings to and say, 'I'm on *this* side of the line, I'm fine,' or 'I'm on *that* side of the line, I'm definitely going to be considered a copyright infringer!'" Timothy Jensen is speaking; he's a staff attorney for New York's Volunteer Lawyers for the Arts. "If somebody wants to sue, they can sue. If you do something that we would consider a legitimate parody of Walt Disney and Walt Disney is offended, then Disney can absolutely sue you—even if they have a terrible case. Very often, even if they *have* a terrible case, they'll have big enough guns and a large enough law firm and enough money to spend, and they'll simply beat you down.

"It's a disturbing situation, because you really have justice being available to those who can afford it and not to those who can't."

So what about you fledgling parodists out there who want to know what's allowable at present? Well, you can't be entirely safe, but there are ways of improving your odds of survival.

Don't Copy Exactly. I bite my tongue as I say it. So while I'm biting, I'll let Henry Beard, formerly of the *National Lampoon*,[10] speak:

"I'm not a lawyer, but every step you take away from an exact reproduction is a further strengthening of your case. Often they use sort of a 'reasonable man' rule. A reasonable person passing a newsstand sees a magazine that says *T*me* instead of *Time.* You could argue that the person should have some serious doubts as to whether that's *Time* magazine. Maybe you obscure part of the *E* with a little banner that says *Parody Issue.* Maybe you choose something as subject matter that is immediately and obviously funny. There's no place where you're absolutely safe; where you're absolutely unsafe is when you just use their logo."

Now for some suggestions from William Gaines, publisher of *Mad*,[11] who cautions, "There are no legal rules on this. I made up this set of rules for myself, from which I didn't seem to get into any trouble."

One time use only. Mad, of course, may hit *Peanuts* a hundred times, but each time it's from a distinct parodic angle, and the magazine isn't sold on the basis of any continuing *Peanuts* satire. "I don't think it's fair to take something and use it constantly. If you hit 'em once, it's more accurately portrayed as some kind of criticism."

Don't put it on the cover. That's a rule which Gaines admits he has violated, but he still says that keeping the parody inside the book is "just more proof that you're not trying to commercialize on it." Henry Beard enlarges on this point: "If you use someone's characteristic style or logo, if you use their character or one very much like it on the cover of a magazine, book or other product, you run a very grave risk. Because then the person whose license or logo has been used can claim that all the sales that accrued from that publication are due to your theft of their item. If they win, they're able to seize all the profits of the enterprise."

Now back to Gaines:

Establish a parody premise that sets the parody clearly apart from the original. This is the famous and oft-copied *Mad* approach. "If Comic Strip Characters Answered Those Little Ads," etc. Many parodists choose to do this more obliquely than does *Mad*, but an artist is merely stealing unless a significant thematic distinction exists between the parody and the original.

These few cautionary points are frail reassurances to those of us who'd like to create parodies. Like it or not, the status quo isn't *fair* to us and works against the free exchange of ideas.

Which is why I'm on my soapbox here yelling. A few historic notables like Aristophanes, Cervantes, and Henry Fielding might yell along with me, were they alive. Parodists all, they would probably lampoon the hell out of judges or opinion makers who suggest that we water down an art form unnecessarily in the interest of commerce.

But they aren't here; you and I are. I've put forward my ideas; now you bounce back with yours.

But if you're tempted to express them in the form of a parody, heed the bottom-line advice of Tim Jensen of the VLA:

Consult a lawyer! Before you publish!

And be wary playing with guillotines.

"The Nightmares of Little L*l*"

"The Nightmares of Little L*l*" was sent to Denis Kitchen in April 1978 and published in *Snarf* 8 (October 1978). Cruse later described it as "one of the most enjoyable projects [he] ever did" (Ringgenberg 84).The story demonstrates Howard Cruse's skill at parody and imitation. Also evident in this story is the strong influence of *Mad* magazine on Cruse, though Cruse's irreverent treatment of the source material goes much further than any *Mad* parody dared. The narration in the opening splash panel especially resembles the prose introductions to *Mad*'s parodies. That narration also clearly establishes the target of this parody: "Was her simple world—like the Fifties themselves—a façade? Did the sunny suburban games mask a turbulent reality whose pain would ultimately erupt to the surface?" The target, then, is the white, middle-class, suburban myth of the 1950s, popularized across all entertainment media, including movies, television, and, most important for this example, comics.

As Cruse points out in "The Other Side of the Coin," he makes several choices to identify this work as a parody, like the framing device that shows us a contemporary, adult Lulu and Tubby still dealing with the traumas of their childhoods. Cruse also changes all of the relevant names: Lulu becomes "L*l*," Tubby is "Chubby,"[12] truant officer Mr. McNabbem changes to "Mr. McNabber," and even the favorite medicine of Lulu's parents, Tiny Tot's Syrup, is now "Tiny Tyke's Tonic." Yet these changes don't impact the overall effect of the parody to offer serious criticism and social commentary, as Cruse wrote in his essay: "On one level, I poked silly fun at a favorite old character, but I was also reflecting on how troubled childhood can be beneath a carefree surface." The reflection on childhood trauma is just one element of the critique Cruse offers, however.

Though "The Nightmares of Little L*l*" appears in *The Other Sides of Howard Cruse*—ostensibly an anthology of his comics that are not focused on LGBTQ issues or themes—it presents a kind of "queering" of comics that early twenty-first-century scholarship on queer comics has explored. In their 2018 essay "Queer about Comics," Darieck Scott and Ramzi Fawaz identify several ways in which the comics medium is always already queer in terms of its formal properties and socially marginalized status (200–203). One of these ways involves the formal gaps and repetitions at the heart of comics: "The unpredictability of serial narrative and narration and the visual structure of comics as a set of sequential panels that repeat, but always with a difference, suggest that comics are *formally* queer" (202). This concept can also be applied to comics parodies, where the gaps and repetitions not only function on the page, but also exist between the parody and the source material. The parody repeats the source while also establishing its difference, yet the parody can also fill a gap between the source and the cultural reality where the source resided. Scott and Fawaz's conception of queering comics through repetition with a difference relates to Cruse's point that one purpose of parody is "to short-circuit our habitual responses to familiar images, enticing us with broad comedy into more skeptical frames of mind." In this case, Cruse brings forward the dark side of fifties America that exists just beneath the surface of *Little Lulu*. There was always something odd about Lulu's parents pushing Tiny Tot's Syrup on Lulu or about Mr. McNabbem's obsession with catching truant schoolchildren. It should not be surprising that Alvin's constant demands for stories from Lulu serve as masturbation fantasies. And the frequent identity changes Tubby underwent for his detective Spider persona could belie a closeted queerness as well, not to mention the homoerotic world of the "fellers" and their "No Girls Allowed" clubhouse.

But *Little Lulu* was already a queer comic even before Cruse parodied it. Take, for example, one of the more famous stories, "Five Little Babies," first published in *Little Lulu* 38 (August 1951) and reprinted in Michael Barrier and Martin Williams's *A Smithsonian Book of Comic-Book Comics*. Rich kid Wilbur van Snobbe bets the fellers that he can make Lulu follow him on her hands and knees. He then tricks Lulu into wearing a dog collar and leash, while also holding a rubber ball in her mouth, as a way to help find his lost dog. When Lulu figures out that she has been tricked, she vows revenge. She tracks the fellers to their swimming pond, where they are all skinny-dipping, and she hides their clothes. When they discover that their clothes are missing, Lulu offers them diapers to wear instead. She then has them pile on each other in a wagon and covers them with a large blanket so no one can see them while she takes them home. During the wagon trip, the boys constantly complain about being poked by each other. Instead of going home, though, Lulu pushes the wagon down a hill, where a crowd forms to see what is happening. A police officer removes the blanket, revealing the pile of boys in diapers to the entire community.

The nonnormative sexual practices of Lulu's world—part of the hidden realm of Cold War America—are right at the surface in a story that involves a leash, a ball gag, and a diapered-boy pile. The trip from a story like this to Cruse's parody is short.[13]

Despite the story's irreverence, though, Cruse was quite fond of the original *Little Lulu* comics, especially those written and laid out by John Stanley and drawn by Irving Tripp (like "Five Little Babies"), which he considered his favorite comic book while growing up: "She wasn't funny because she was making a fool of herself; she was quite a clever person. She could always surprise the boys with her cleverness, because everyone assumed that girls were not as smart as boys. But she and the girls knew better" (Ringgenberg 84). What Cruse recognizes here is the way in which Lulu always challenged conventional gender expectations (in a way similar to what Jessica Q. Stark sees in *Nancy* [see note 13]). He also considered *Little Lulu* an important influence on his work: "Some of the rhythms of dialogue . . . the way characters gain shading. And I liked that Lulu was a smart central character" (Ringgenberg 84). As a kid, Cruse spent time trying to duplicate Irving Tripp's style, making the influence of the series even more profound. This early practice also accounts for the accuracy of Cruse's parody.

We can see a connection here between the subtly transgressive qualities of *Little Lulu* and Cruse's philosophy behind *Barefootz*. *Little Lulu* is cute while simultaneously challenging the status quo. *Barefootz* looks cute, too (much to the chagrin of some other underground cartoonists and readers), but that cuteness masks profound commentaries on gender, sexuality, and the relation of humanity to the larger universe. Therefore, a line of influence runs from Cruse's childhood love of *Little Lulu* as an early comics reader to his earliest underground comix and beyond.

Cruse was not the only underground cartoonist to parody Little Lulu. In the groundbreaking anthology of female underground cartoonists, *It Aint Me Babe Comix* (1970, edited by Trina Robbins), the collective behind the anthology targeted a variety of classic female comic characters, including Little Lulu, Juliet Jones (from the comic strip *The Heart of Juliet Jones*), Betty and Veronica, Supergirl, and Petunia Pig. In the story "Breaking Out," Lulu asks the fellers if she can join in their parade. When they reject her with the usual "no girls allowed," Lulu rebelliously responds "fuck this shit" (20). The female comic characters all have similar epiphanies and gather together to claim their independence. Lulu does so by making her own "No Boys Allowed" clubhouse, much to the chagrin of the fellers, along with Archie and Jughead (23).[14]

In her prime during the Fifties, she was one of the funniest and most distinctive comic book characters ever created—this rosy-cheeked little girl with the bell-shaped dress, the light-bulb-shaped head, and the hair concocted of meatballs and bedsprings. She was tough; she was tender; she got spanked; she cried; she fought; she splurged. Like her readers, she was a real kid. Not a **child**...a **kid!**

But was she really **happy?** Was her simple world—like the Fifties themselves—a facade? Did the sunny suburban games mask a turbulent reality whose pain would ultimately erupt to the surface? In short, while we thought we were laughing at the adventures of carefree innocents, were we really sharing...

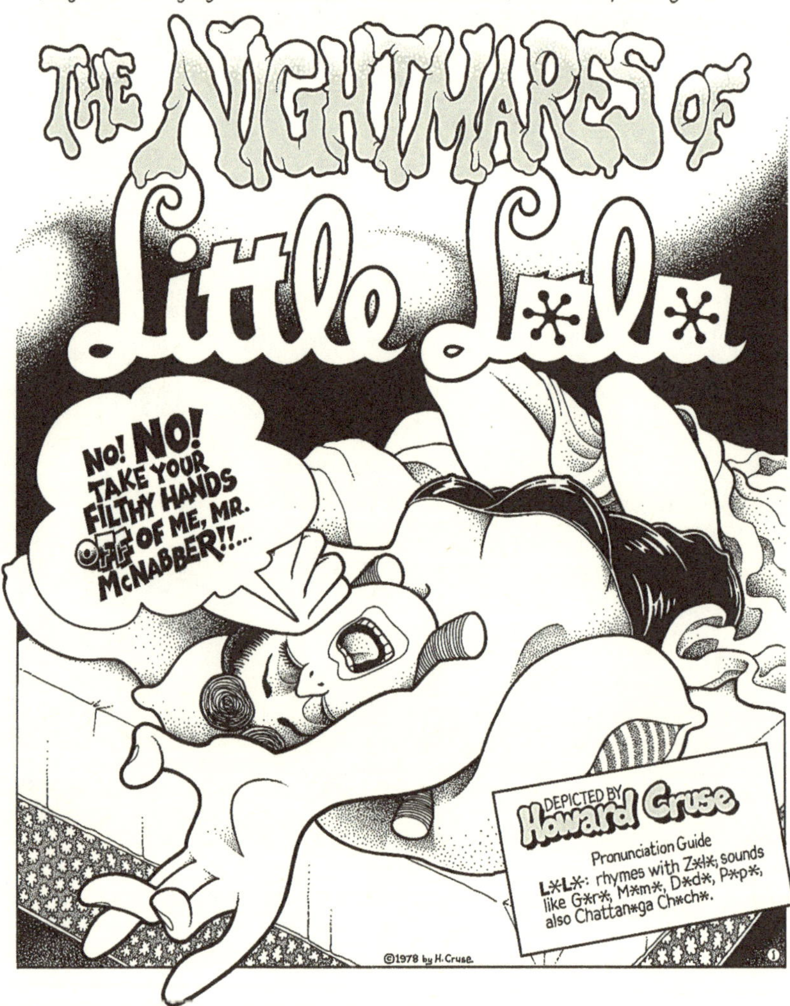

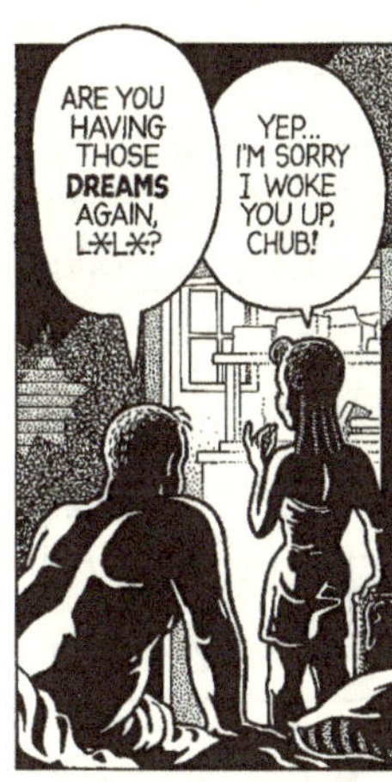

ARE YOU HAVING THOSE **DREAMS** AGAIN, L✻L✻?
YEP... I'M SORRY I WOKE YOU UP, CHUB!

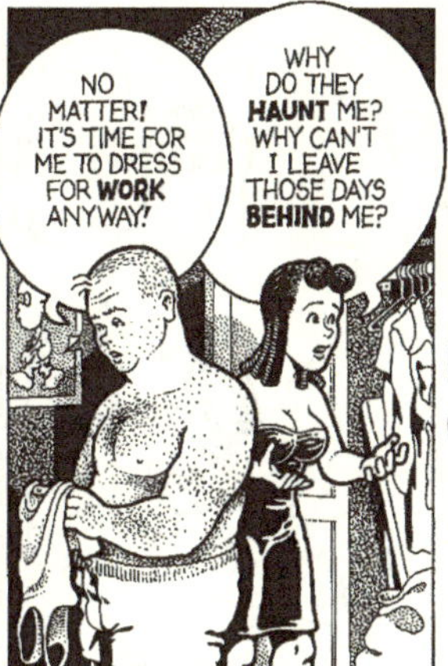

NO MATTER! IT'S TIME FOR ME TO DRESS FOR **WORK** ANYWAY!
WHY DO THEY **HAUNT** ME? WHY CAN'T I LEAVE THOSE DAYS **BEHIND** ME?

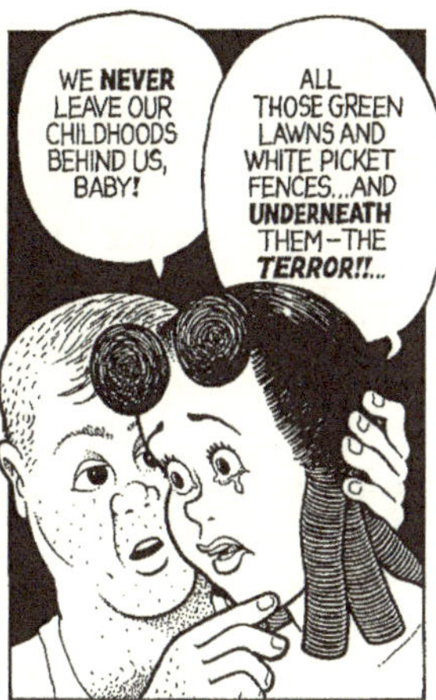

WE **NEVER** LEAVE OUR CHILDHOODS BEHIND US, BABY!
ALL THOSE GREEN LAWNS AND WHITE PICKET FENCES...AND **UNDERNEATH** THEM—THE ***TERROR!!***...

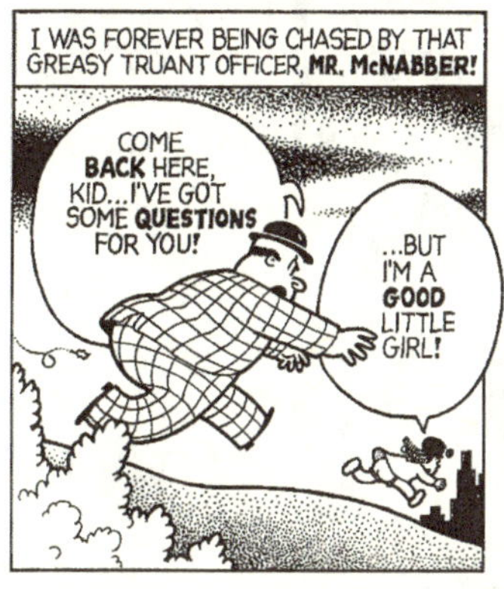

I WAS FOREVER BEING CHASED BY THAT GREASY TRUANT OFFICER, **MR. McNABBER!**
COME **BACK** HERE, KID...I'VE GOT SOME **QUESTIONS** FOR YOU!
...BUT I'M A **GOOD** LITTLE GIRL!

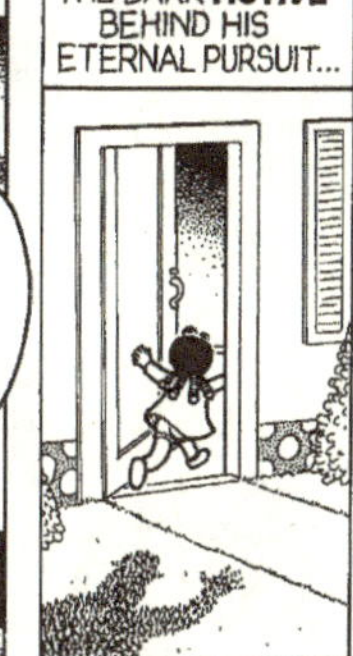

LITTLE DID I KNOW THE DARK **MOTIVE** BEHIND HIS ETERNAL PURSUIT...

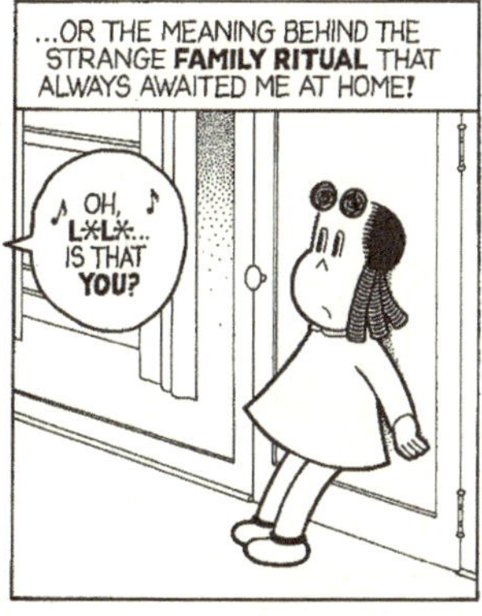

...OR THE MEANING BEHIND THE STRANGE **FAMILY RITUAL** THAT ALWAYS AWAITED ME AT HOME!
♪ OH, **L✻L✻**... IS THAT **YOU?** ♪

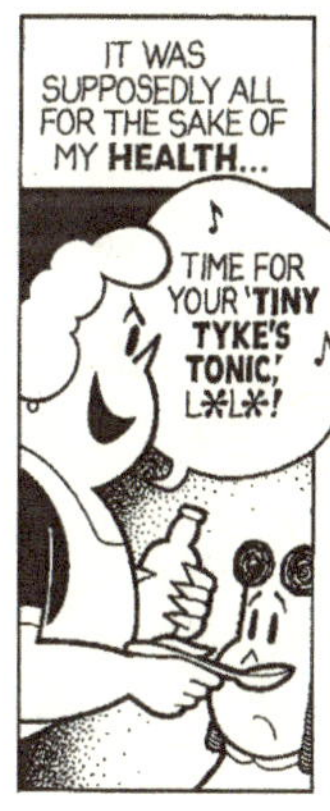

IT WAS SUPPOSEDLY ALL FOR THE SAKE OF MY **HEALTH...**
♪ TIME FOR YOUR **'TINY TYKE'S TONIC,'** L✻L✻! ♪

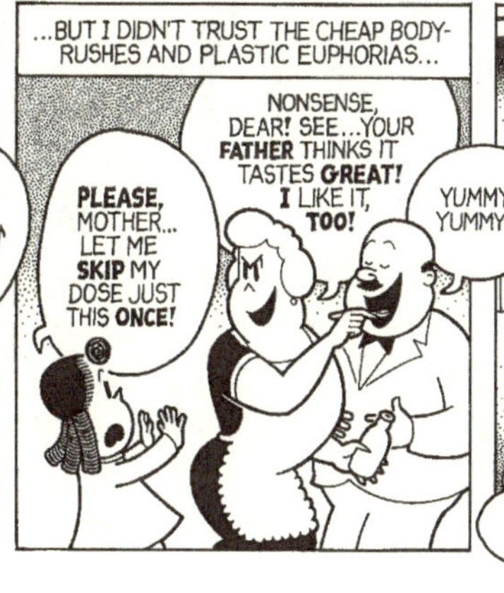

...BUT I DIDN'T TRUST THE CHEAP BODY-RUSHES AND PLASTIC EUPHORIAS...
PLEASE, MOTHER... LET ME **SKIP** MY DOSE JUST THIS **ONCE!**
NONSENSE, DEAR! SEE...YOUR **FATHER** THINKS IT TASTES **GREAT!** **I** LIKE IT, **TOO!**
YUMMY, YUMMY!

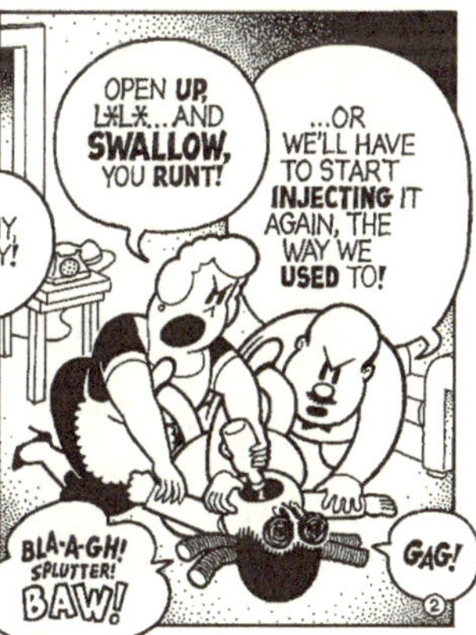

OPEN **UP,** L✻L✻...AND **SWALLOW,** YOU **RUNT!**
...OR WE'LL HAVE TO START **INJECTING** IT AGAIN, THE WAY WE **USED** TO!
BLA-A-GH! SPLUTTER! BAW!
GAG!
2

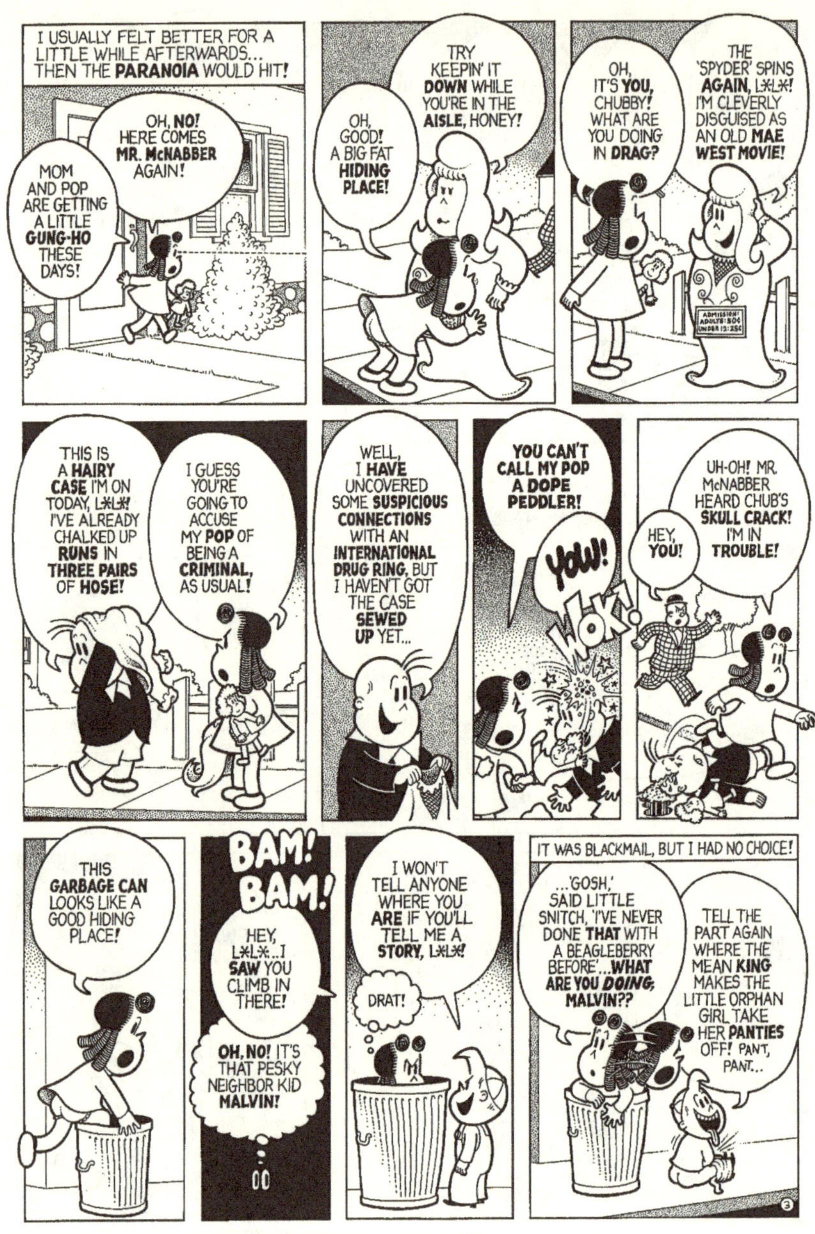
I USUALLY FELT BETTER FOR A LITTLE WHILE AFTERWARDS... THEN THE **PARANOIA** WOULD HIT!
OH, **NO!** HERE COMES **MR. McNABBER** AGAIN!
MOM AND POP ARE GETTING A LITTLE **GUNG-HO** THESE DAYS!
TRY KEEPIN' IT **DOWN** WHILE YOU'RE IN THE **AISLE,** HONEY!
OH, GOOD! A BIG FAT **HIDING PLACE!**
OH, IT'S **YOU,** CHUBBY! WHAT ARE YOU DOING IN **DRAG?**
THE 'SPYDER' SPINS **AGAIN,** L✱L✱! I'M CLEVERLY DISGUISED AS AN OLD **MAE WEST MOVIE!**
THIS IS A **HAIRY CASE** I'M ON TODAY, L✱L✱! I'VE ALREADY CHALKED UP **RUNS** IN **THREE PAIRS** OF **HOSE!**
I GUESS YOU'RE GOING TO ACCUSE MY **POP** OF BEING A **CRIMINAL,** AS USUAL!
WELL, I **HAVE** UNCOVERED SOME **SUSPICIOUS CONNECTIONS** WITH AN **INTERNATIONAL DRUG RING,** BUT I HAVEN'T GOT THE CASE **SEWED UP** YET...
YOU CAN'T CALL MY POP A DOPE PEDDLER!
YOW!
WOK!
UH-OH! MR. McNABBER HEARD CHUB'S **SKULL CRACK!** I'M IN **TROUBLE!**
HEY, **YOU!**
THIS **GARBAGE CAN** LOOKS LIKE A GOOD HIDING PLACE!
BAM! BAM!
HEY, L✱L✱...I **SAW** YOU CLIMB IN THERE!
OH, NO! IT'S THAT PESKY NEIGHBOR KID **MALVIN!**
I WON'T TELL ANYONE WHERE YOU **ARE** IF YOU'LL TELL ME A **STORY, L✱L✱!**
DRAT!
IT WAS BLACKMAIL, BUT I HAD NO CHOICE!
...'GOSH,' SAID LITTLE SNITCH, 'I'VE NEVER DONE **THAT** WITH A BEAGLEBERRY BEFORE'...**WHAT ARE YOU *DOING*, MALVIN??**
TELL THE PART AGAIN WHERE THE MEAN **KING** MAKES THE LITTLE ORPHAN GIRL TAKE HER **PANTIES** OFF! PANT, PANT...
3

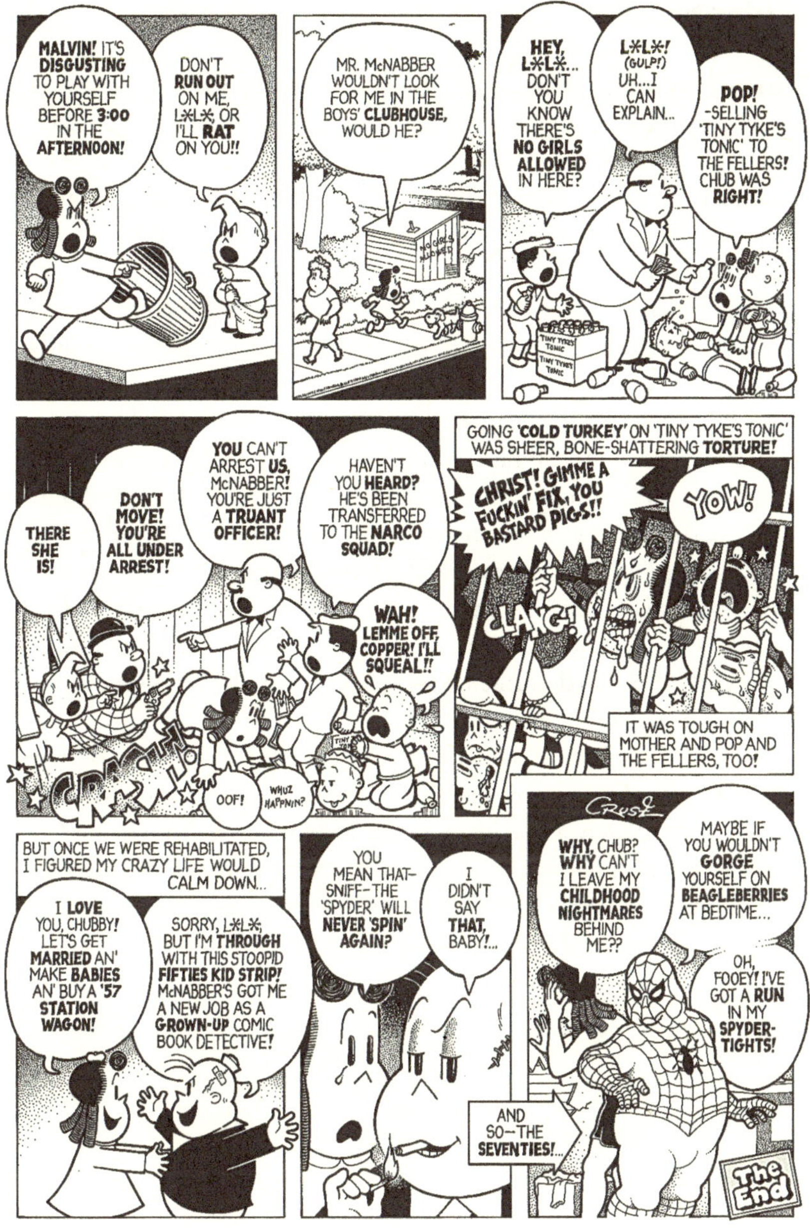
MALVIN! IT'S DISGUSTING TO PLAY WITH YOURSELF BEFORE 3:00 IN THE AFTERNOON!
DON'T RUN OUT ON ME, L*L*, OR I'LL RAT ON YOU!!
MR. McNABBER WOULDN'T LOOK FOR ME IN THE BOYS' CLUBHOUSE, WOULD HE?
HEY, L*L*... DON'T YOU KNOW THERE'S NO GIRLS ALLOWED IN HERE?
L*L*! (GULP!) UH...I CAN EXPLAIN...
POP! -SELLING 'TINY TYKE'S TONIC' TO THE FELLERS! CHUB WAS RIGHT!
TINY TYKE'S TONIC
THERE SHE IS!
DON'T MOVE! YOU'RE ALL UNDER ARREST!
YOU CAN'T ARREST US, McNABBER! YOU'RE JUST A TRUANT OFFICER!
HAVEN'T YOU HEARD? HE'S BEEN TRANSFERRED TO THE NARCO SQUAD!
WAH! LEMME OFF, COPPER! I'LL SQUEAL!!
CRASH!
OOF!
WHUZ HAPPNIN?
GOING 'COLD TURKEY' ON 'TINY TYKE'S TONIC' WAS SHEER, BONE-SHATTERING TORTURE!
CHRIST! GIMME A FUCKIN' FIX, YOU BASTARD PIGS!!
YOW!
CLANG!
IT WAS TOUGH ON MOTHER AND POP AND THE FELLERS, TOO!
CRUSE
BUT ONCE WE WERE REHABILITATED, I FIGURED MY CRAZY LIFE WOULD CALM DOWN...
I LOVE YOU, CHUBBY! LET'S GET MARRIED AN' MAKE BABIES AN' BUY A '57 STATION WAGON!
SORRY, L*L*, BUT I'M THROUGH WITH THIS STOOPID FIFTIES KID STRIP! McNABBER'S GOT ME A NEW JOB AS A GROWN-UP COMIC BOOK DETECTIVE!
YOU MEAN THAT—SNIFF—THE 'SPYDER' WILL NEVER 'SPIN' AGAIN?
I DIDN'T SAY THAT, BABY!...
AND SO—THE SEVENTIES!...
WHY, CHUB? WHY CAN'T I LEAVE MY CHILDHOOD NIGHTMARES BEHIND ME??
MAYBE IF YOU WOULDN'T GORGE YOURSELF ON BEAGLEBERRIES AT BEDTIME...
OH, FOOEY! I'VE GOT A RUN IN MY SPYDER-TIGHTS!
The End

"Raising Nancies"

"Raising Nancies," from *Snarf* 12 (1989), casts a wide parodic net. The title, with its play on a homophobic slur, might make a reader think that this could be another Cruse comic about gay themes, but the story doesn't carry through with that idea. Instead, it is primarily a parody of the infamous "Sea Monkey" ads that appeared on the back covers of comics for decades. While the ads promised kids the opportunity to raise cute families of sea monkeys, what they really got when they ordered were tiny, freeze-dried brine shrimp that would allegedly return to life when immersed in water. One had to squint to see anything that might resemble the cavorting shown in the ads. Cruse extends that disappointment into the realm of horror, as the seemingly cute Nancies that kids can raise become annoying, smelly creatures. In the end, the story evolves into a broader satire of consumer culture and human cruelty, with unwanted Nancies sent to factory farms / concentration camps, where they are neglected and abused before being slaughtered for their valuable pelts—that is, Nancy's signature spiky hair. Most of all, this story serves as one of the more extreme examples of Cruse's dark humor—the image of a horribly deformed Nancy riddled with bullets as she attempts to escape the farm is not easy to forget.

This story doesn't challenge the reader's conception of Ernie Bushmiller's *Nancy* in the way that, say, Joe Brainerd's 1960s *Nancy* parodies do, where Brainerd draws Nancy as having male genitalia under her skirt and depicts her having sex with fellow comic strip character, Henry (see Stark for more on Brainerd's *Nancy*). But Cruse's story still has a sharp polemical component aimed at the dark side of consumer culture.

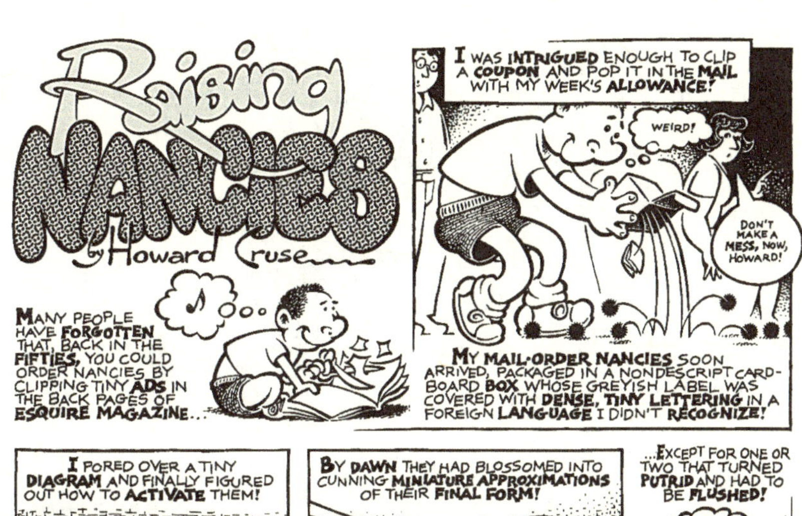
Raising Nancies
by Howard Cruse
Many people have forgotten that, back in the fifties, you could order Nancies by clipping tiny ads in the back pages of Esquire Magazine...
I was intrigued enough to clip a coupon and pop it in the mail with my week's allowance!
WEIRD!
DON'T MAKE A MESS, NOW, HOWARD!
My mail-order Nancies soon arrived, packaged in a nondescript card-board box whose greyish label was covered with dense, tiny lettering in a foreign language I didn't recognize!

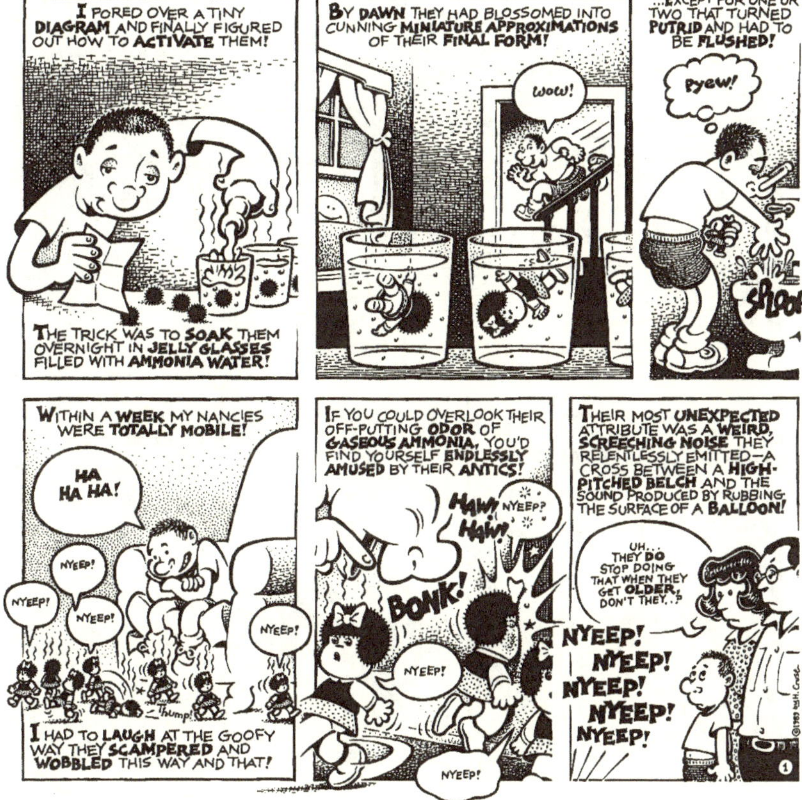
I pored over a tiny diagram and finally figured out how to activate them!
The trick was to soak them overnight in jelly glasses filled with ammonia water!
By dawn they had blossomed into cunning miniature approximations of their final form!
WOW!
...Except for one or two that turned putrid and had to be flushed!
PYEW!
SPLOOP!
Within a week my Nancies were totally mobile!
HA HA HA!
NYEEP!
NYEEP!
NYEEP!
NYEEP!
Thump!
I had to laugh at the goofy way they scampered and wobbled this way and that!
If you could overlook their off-putting odor of gaseous ammonia, you'd find yourself endlessly amused by their antics!
HAW! HAW!
NYEEP?
BONK!
NYEEP!
NYEEP!
Their most unexpected attribute was a weird, screeching noise they relentlessly emitted—a cross between a high-pitched belch and the sound produced by rubbing the surface of a balloon!
UH... THEY DO STOP DOING THAT WHEN THEY GET OLDER, DON'T THEY..?
NYEEP! NYEEP! NYEEP! NYEEP! NYEEP!
1

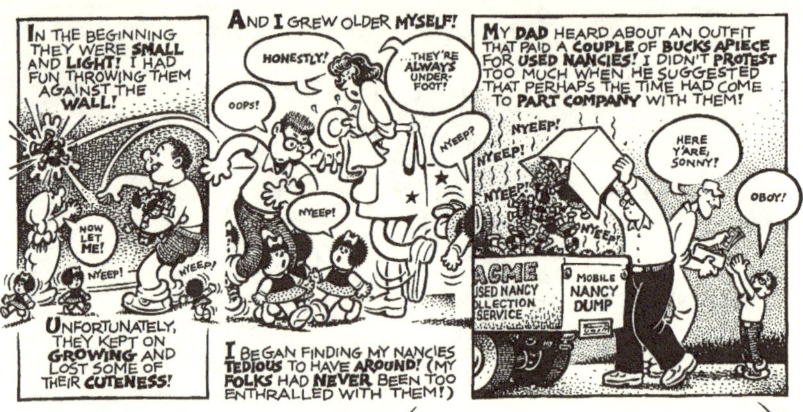
IN THE BEGINNING THEY WERE SMALL AND LIGHT! I HAD FUN THROWING THEM AGAINST THE WALL!
NOW LET ME!
NYEEP!
NYEEP!
UNFORTUNATELY, THEY KEPT ON GROWING AND LOST SOME OF THEIR CUTENESS!
AND I GREW OLDER MYSELF!
HONESTLY!
...THEY'RE ALWAYS UNDER-FOOT!
OOPS!
NYEEP?
NYEEP!
I BEGAN FINDING MY NANCIES TEDIOUS TO HAVE AROUND! (MY FOLKS HAD NEVER BEEN TOO ENTHRALLED WITH THEM!)
MY DAD HEARD ABOUT AN OUTFIT THAT PAID A COUPLE OF BUCKS APIECE FOR USED NANCIES! I DIDN'T PROTEST TOO MUCH WHEN HE SUGGESTED THAT PERHAPS THE TIME HAD COME TO PART COMPANY WITH THEM!
NYEEP!
NYEEP!
NYEEP!
NYEEP!
HERE Y'ARE, SONNY!
OBOY!
ACME
USED NANCY
LLECTION
SERVICE
MOBILE NANCY DUMP

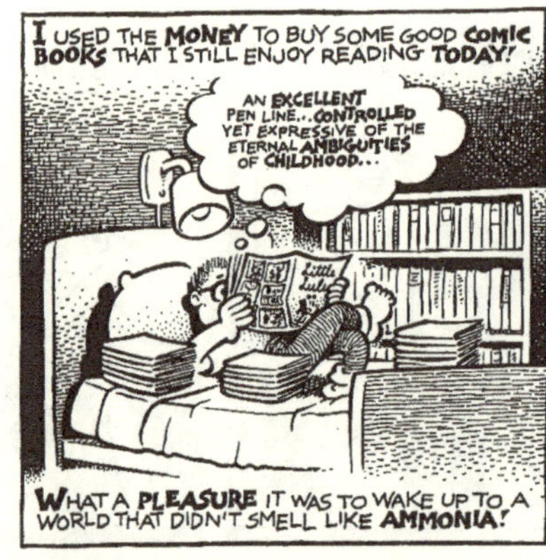
I USED THE MONEY TO BUY SOME GOOD COMIC BOOKS THAT I STILL ENJOY READING TODAY!
AN EXCELLENT PEN LINE...CONTROLLED YET EXPRESSIVE OF THE ETERNAL AMBIGUITIES OF CHILDHOOD...
WHAT A PLEASURE IT WAS TO WAKE UP TO A WORLD THAT DIDN'T SMELL LIKE AMMONIA!

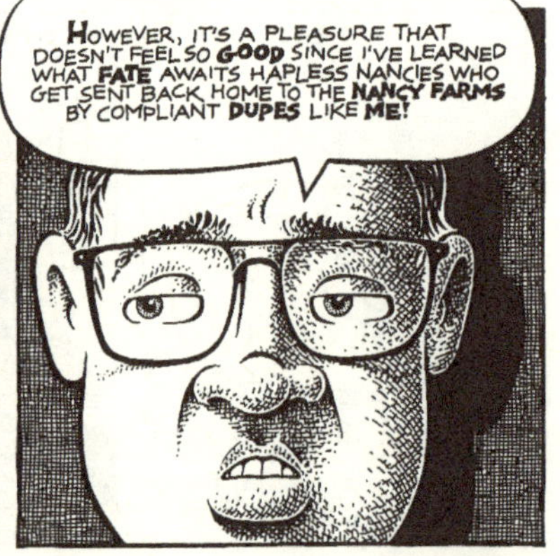
HOWEVER, IT'S A PLEASURE THAT DOESN'T FEEL SO GOOD SINCE I'VE LEARNED WHAT FATE AWAITS HAPLESS NANCIES WHO GET SENT BACK HOME TO THE NANCY FARMS BY COMPLIANT DUPES LIKE ME!

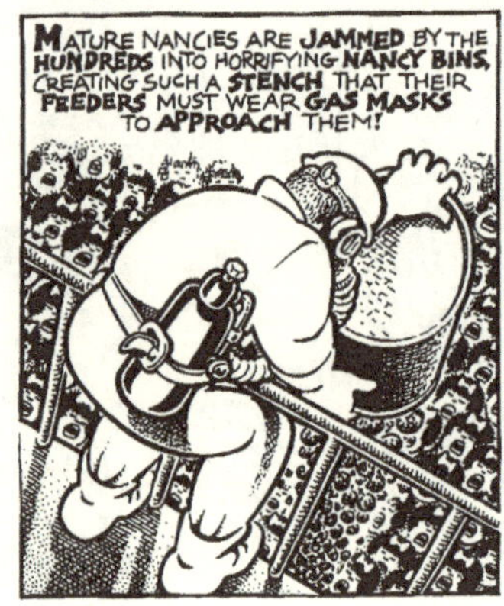
MATURE NANCIES ARE JAMMED BY THE HUNDREDS INTO HORRIFYING NANCY BINS, CREATING SUCH A STENCH THAT THEIR FEEDERS MUST WEAR GAS MASKS TO APPROACH THEM!

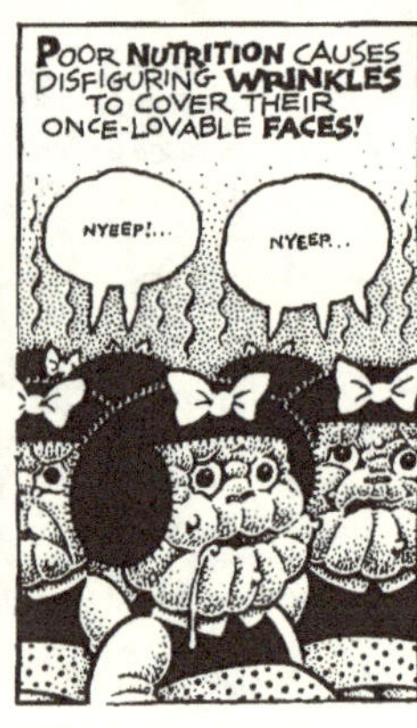
POOR NUTRITION CAUSES DISFIGURING WRINKLES TO COVER THEIR ONCE-LOVABLE FACES!
NYEEP!...
NYEEP...

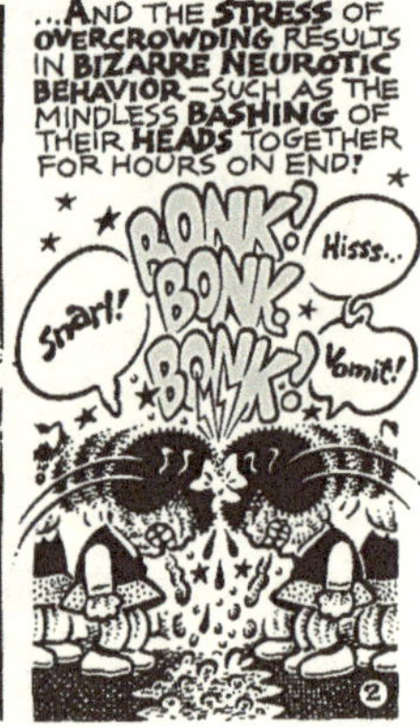
...AND THE STRESS OF OVERCROWDING RESULTS IN BIZARRE NEUROTIC BEHAVIOR—SUCH AS THE MINDLESS BASHING OF THEIR HEADS TOGETHER FOR HOURS ON END!
BONK!
BONK
BONK!
Hisss..
Snarl!
Vomit!
2

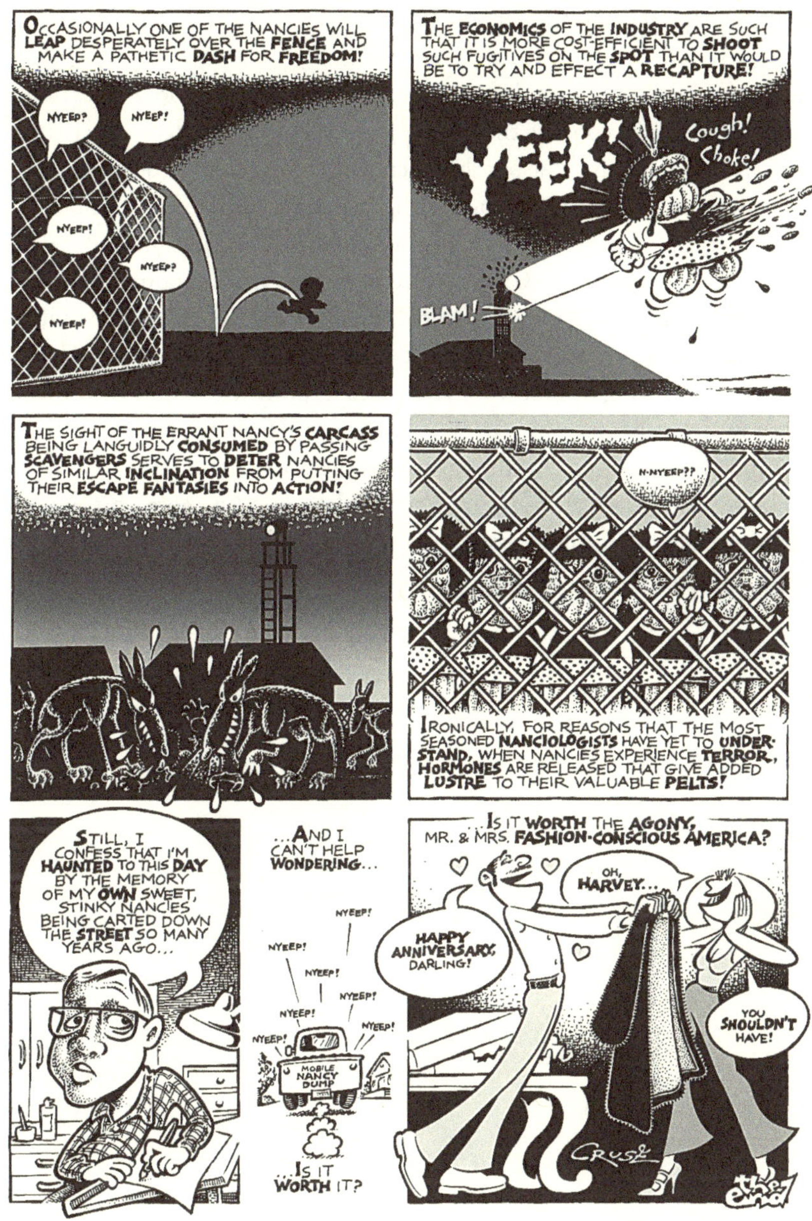

"Raising Nancies" copyright the estate of Howard Cruse. Used by permission.

"Hubert the Humorless Ghost"

This 1999 story takes the idea of the cartoon ghost to its logical extreme, building on the epiphany that many young comics readers experienced when they realized that Casper the Friendly Ghost was just a dead little boy. By keeping this strip to one page with six panels, Cruse does not belabor the joke. It capitalizes on the funny ghost subgenre of kids' humor comics, which includes not only Casper, but also his friend Spooky the Tuff Little Ghost, and many Casper knockoffs, like Homer the Happy Ghost from Timely/Atlas, Spencer Spook from American Comics Group, Spunky the Smiling Spook from Ajax, and Timmy the Timid Ghost from Charlton. So even late in his career, Cruse was still finding connections with the comic books of his childhood. It also presents a later style that Cruse developed after *Stuck Rubber Baby*, which has an even more abstract and fluid look than his earlier work. On his website, Cruse provides a color version of this story.

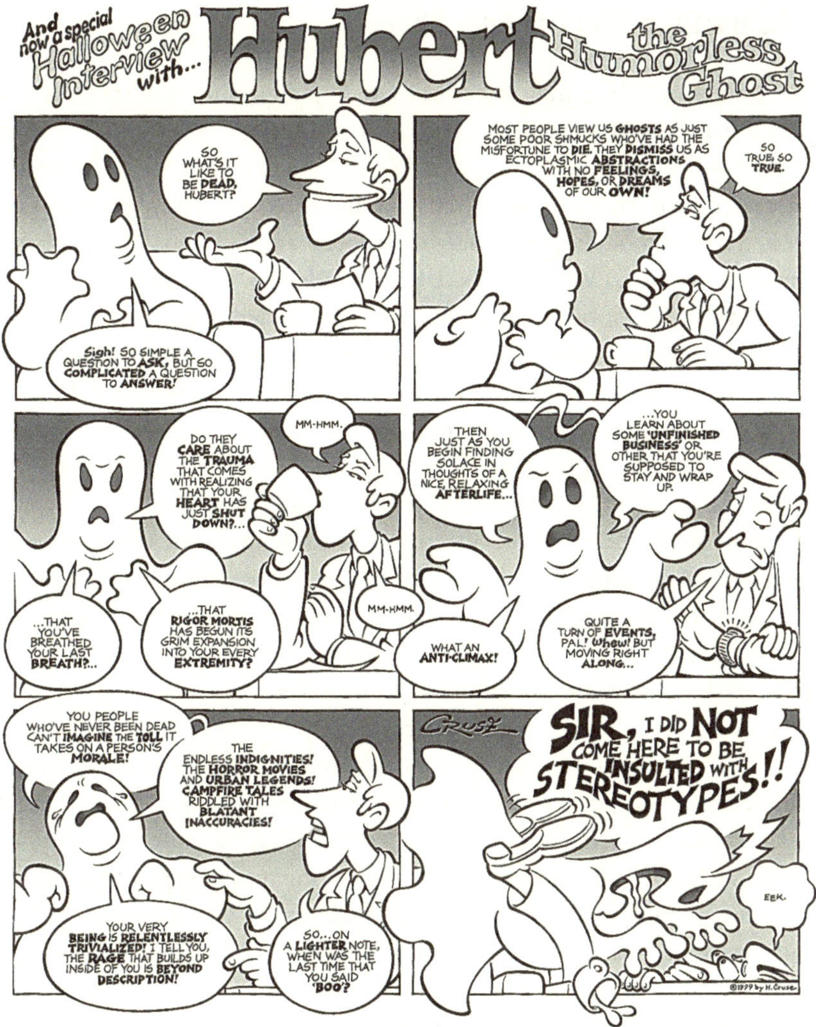

"Hubert the Humorless Ghost" copyright the estate of Howard Cruse. Used by permission.

"Shearwell in 'The Prodigal Sheep'"

This story took a long and circuitous route to publication. It started out as a story solicited by Mike Friedrich for *Quack*, the "ground-level" funny animal comic book series published by Star*Reach and featuring work by Frank Brunner, Sergio Aragones, Steve Leialoha, and Dave Sim. However, Friedrich rejected the story on the basis that Ms. Henpeck was "objectionably sexist and degrading" (Cruse, *Other Sides* 124). It later ended up with Scott Shaw for an anthology, *Wild Animals*, to be published by Kitchen Sink. That book languished in production with Shaw for years until Kitchen finally canceled it. That freed up Shearwell for inclusion in Kitchen Sink's *Bizarre Sex* 8. Though this was the first Shearwell story that Cruse produced, it was not the first to see print. That was "Li'l Nirvana Sees God," from *Dope Comix* 2 (June 1982).

The story resurrects two minor characters from Cruse's early *Tops & Button* comic strip: Shearwell the Sheep and Mrs. Henpeck the Chicken (now known as Ms.). Their innocent adventures in that narratively limited strip were no match for the paces that Cruse puts them through in this story.

"Prodigal Sheep" is also a prime example of the ironic relationship between style and content that infuses Cruse's work. Shearwell and his companions are easily recognizable as part of the funny animal genre that has been a part of the comics medium almost from its inception. And Cruse's rounded, cartoony style serves that genre well. However, readers disarmed by the cuteness of these characters get a series of increasingly shocking surprises as the story delves into content that is obviously unconventional for the genre. Nonetheless, the overall structure of this story still follows those genre conventions. Cruse was a fan of funny animal comics as a young reader, especially the legendary Carl Barks comics featuring Donald Duck, Uncle Scrooge, and assorted supporting characters. In a 1998 interview, Cruse identified the narrow influence that Barks had on his comics work: "I think the main thing that I got from Barks [was] that it was possible to be funny in a smart way. As well as to have a sense of a larger world in your comics rather than being restricted by these very narrow horizons. I liked the world-travelling aspect of Uncle Scrooge" (Gay League). However, the influence may be more significant than that, especially with Shearwell. Though Barks never published sexually explicit stories of interspecies romance, "Prodigal Sheep" has some Barksian elements in its structure and development. The protagonist is dissatisfied with his life and wishes to challenge some element of his current status (Donald Duck wants a new job; Uncle Scrooge needs to add to his tremendous wealth); the quest for change becomes increasingly more complicated and chaotic, leading the protagonist to regret his choice; and then a slapstick climax ensues where the status quo is ultimately restored. Also like a lot of Barks stories, this one involves the quick accumulation and loss of wealth.

The opening splash starts to establish a world not that far removed from the innocent Dell comics of Cruse's youth. The adult sheep invites the young lambs to get some exercise by "bounding cheerfully over the fence!" Three lambs are enthusiastic about the activity, but the fourth, Shearwell, asks, "What is this bullshit?," immediately undercutting the familiar funny animal story world.

Shearwell is a sheep with big dreams—to move to the big city and have sex with a chicken. When that chicken, the dominatrix Ms. Henpeck, turns out to be more than he bargained for, Shearwell goes back to the pasture to re-establish the status quo. However, the status quo doesn't completely return: Shearwell can now share his erotic adventures with the other impressionable young sheep, replacing their normal evening bible stories.

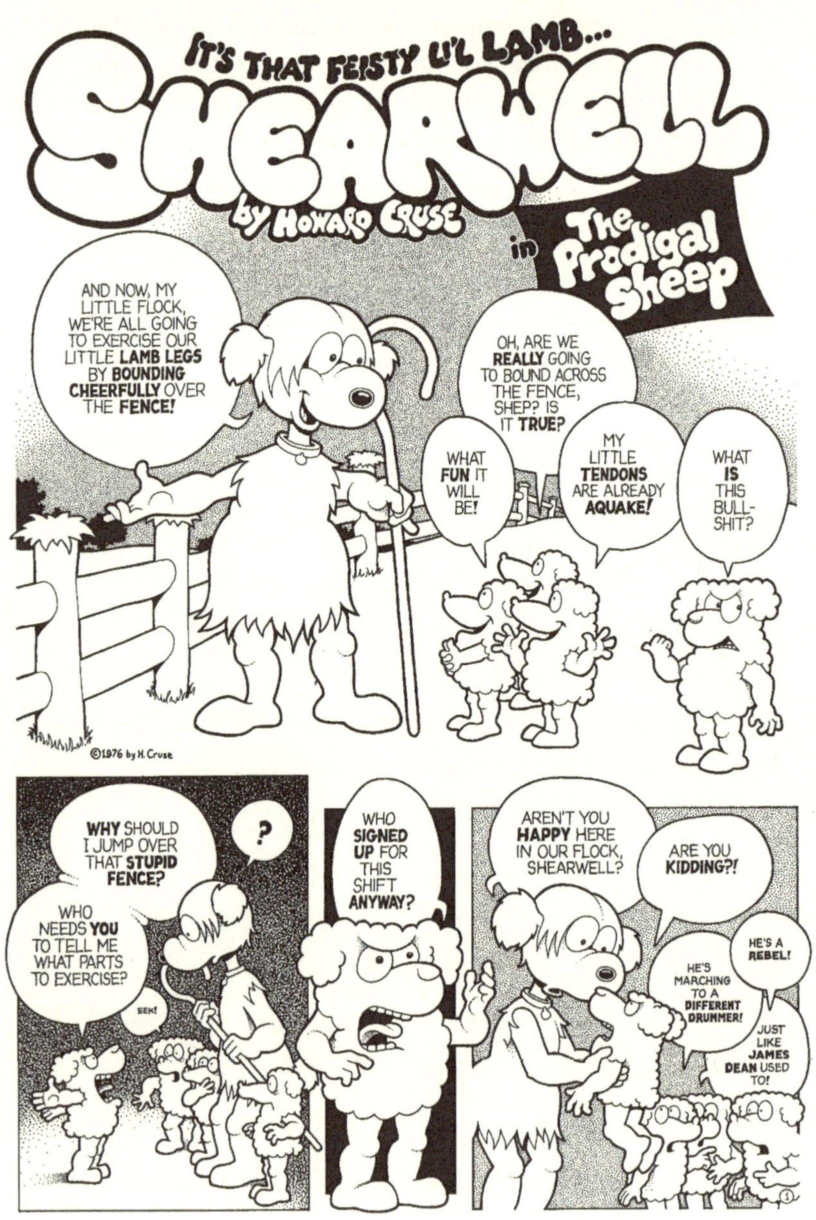
IT'S THAT FEISTY LI'L LAMB...
SHEARWELL
by HOWARD CRUSE
in The Prodigal Sheep
AND NOW, MY LITTLE FLOCK, WE'RE ALL GOING TO EXERCISE OUR LITTLE LAMB LEGS BY BOUNDING CHEERFULLY OVER THE FENCE!
OH, ARE WE REALLY GOING TO BOUND ACROSS THE FENCE, SHEP? IS IT TRUE?
WHAT FUN IT WILL BE!
MY LITTLE TENDONS ARE ALREADY AQUAKE!
WHAT IS THIS BULL-SHIT?
©1976 by H. Cruse
WHY SHOULD I JUMP OVER THAT STUPID FENCE?
?
WHO NEEDS YOU TO TELL ME WHAT PARTS TO EXERCISE?
EEK!
WHO SIGNED UP FOR THIS SHIFT ANYWAY?
AREN'T YOU HAPPY HERE IN OUR FLOCK, SHEARWELL?
ARE YOU KIDDING?!
HE'S A REBEL!
HE'S MARCHING TO A DIFFERENT DRUMMER!
JUST LIKE JAMES DEAN USED TO!
1

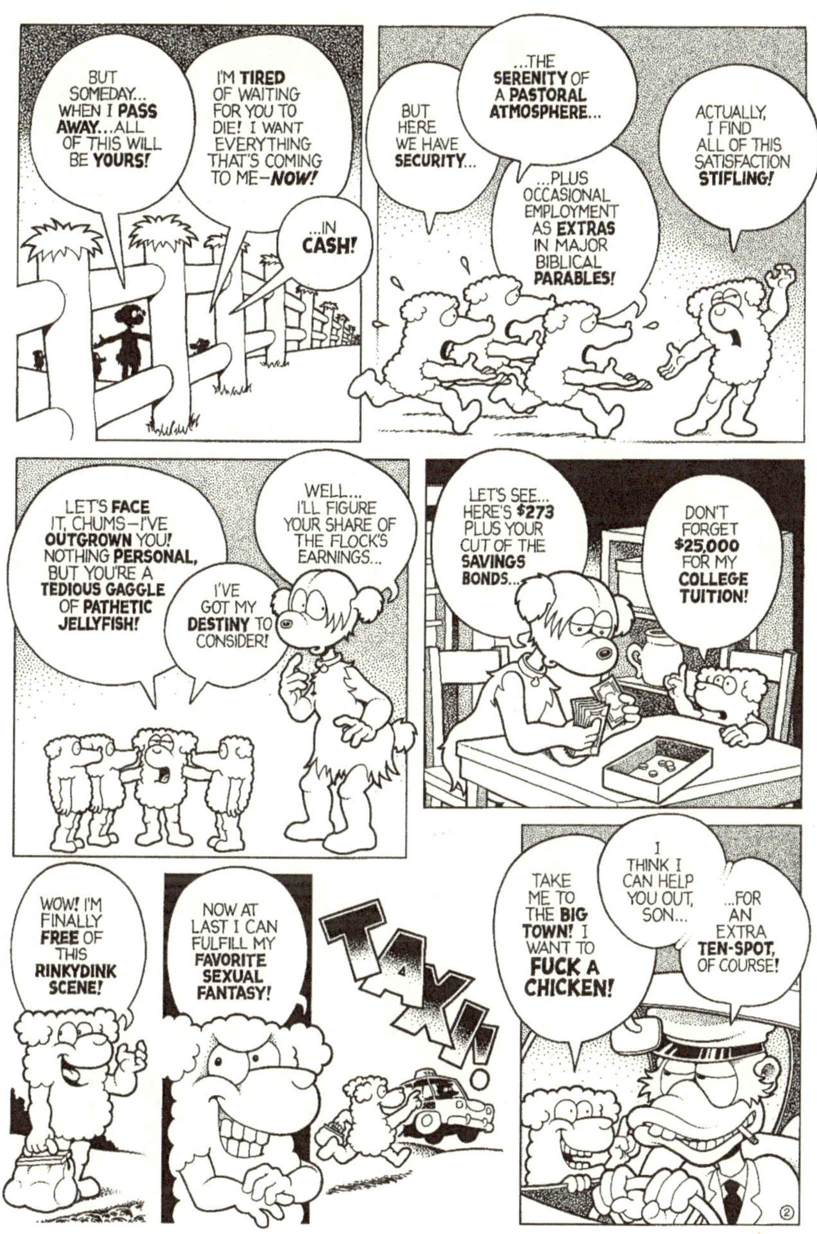
BUT SOMEDAY... WHEN I PASS AWAY...ALL OF THIS WILL BE YOURS!
I'M TIRED OF WAITING FOR YOU TO DIE! I WANT EVERYTHING THAT'S COMING TO ME—NOW!
...IN CASH!
BUT HERE WE HAVE SECURITY...
...THE SERENITY OF A PASTORAL ATMOSPHERE...
...PLUS OCCASIONAL EMPLOYMENT AS EXTRAS IN MAJOR BIBLICAL PARABLES!
ACTUALLY, I FIND ALL OF THIS SATISFACTION STIFLING!
LET'S FACE IT, CHUMS—I'VE OUTGROWN YOU! NOTHING PERSONAL, BUT YOU'RE A TEDIOUS GAGGLE OF PATHETIC JELLYFISH!
I'VE GOT MY DESTINY TO CONSIDER!
WELL... I'LL FIGURE YOUR SHARE OF THE FLOCK'S EARNINGS...
LET'S SEE... HERE'S $273 PLUS YOUR CUT OF THE SAVINGS BONDS...
DON'T FORGET $25,000 FOR MY COLLEGE TUITION!
WOW! I'M FINALLY FREE OF THIS RINKYDINK SCENE!
NOW AT LAST I CAN FULFILL MY FAVORITE SEXUAL FANTASY!
TAXI!
TAKE ME TO THE BIG TOWN! I WANT TO FUCK A CHICKEN!
I THINK I CAN HELP YOU OUT, SON...
...FOR AN EXTRA TEN-SPOT, OF COURSE!
2

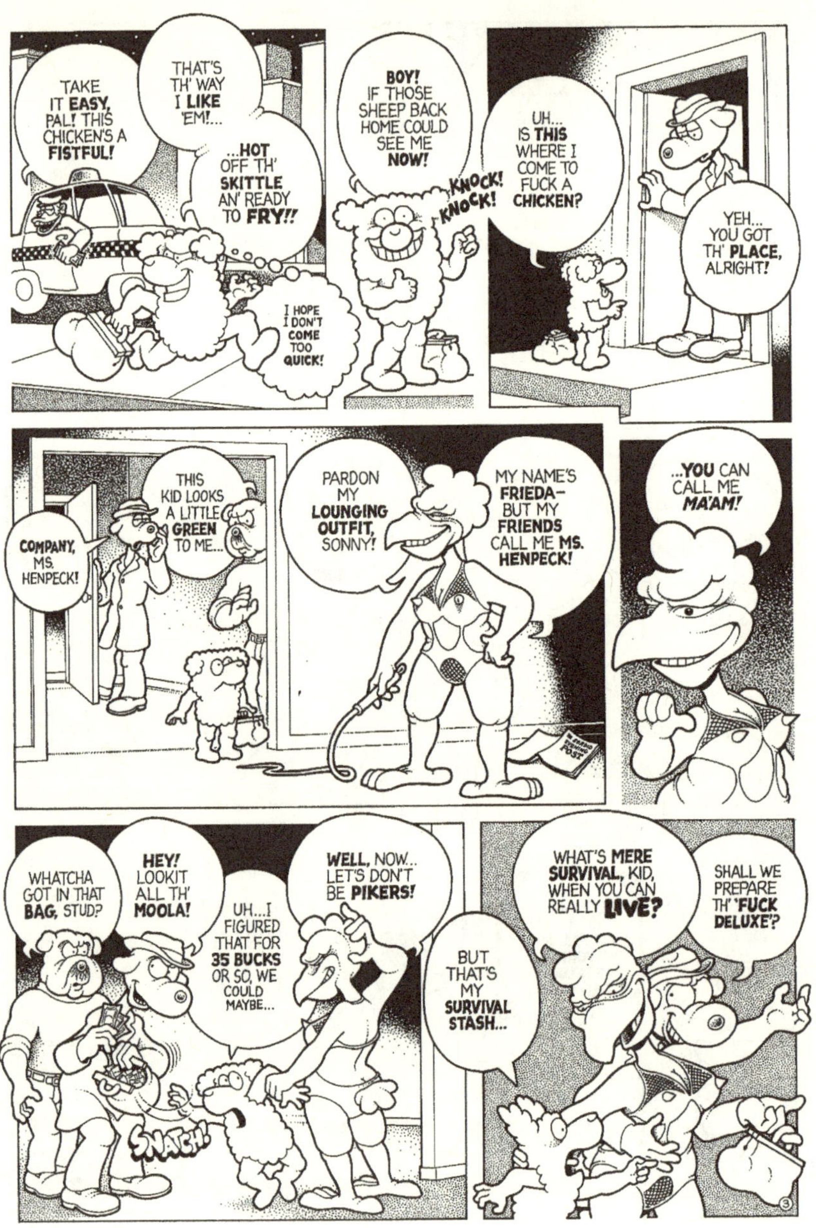
TAKE IT EASY, PAL! THIS CHICKEN'S A FISTFUL!
THAT'S TH' WAY I LIKE 'EM!...
...HOT OFF TH' SKITTLE AN' READY TO FRY!!
I HOPE I DON'T COME TOO QUICK!
BOY! IF THOSE SHEEP BACK HOME COULD SEE ME NOW!
KNOCK! KNOCK!
UH... IS THIS WHERE I COME TO FUCK A CHICKEN?
YEH... YOU GOT TH' PLACE, ALRIGHT!
COMPANY, MS. HENPECK!
THIS KID LOOKS A LITTLE GREEN TO ME...
PARDON MY LOUNGING OUTFIT, SONNY!
MY NAME'S FRIEDA– BUT MY FRIENDS CALL ME MS. HENPECK!
...YOU CAN CALL ME MA'AM!
WHATCHA GOT IN THAT BAG, STUD?
HEY! LOOKIT ALL TH' MOOLA!
UH...I FIGURED THAT FOR 35 BUCKS OR SO, WE COULD MAYBE...
WELL, NOW... LET'S DON'T BE PIKERS!
SNATCH!
BUT THAT'S MY SURVIVAL STASH...
WHAT'S MERE SURVIVAL, KID, WHEN YOU CAN REALLY LIVE?
SHALL WE PREPARE TH' 'FUCK DELUXE'?
3

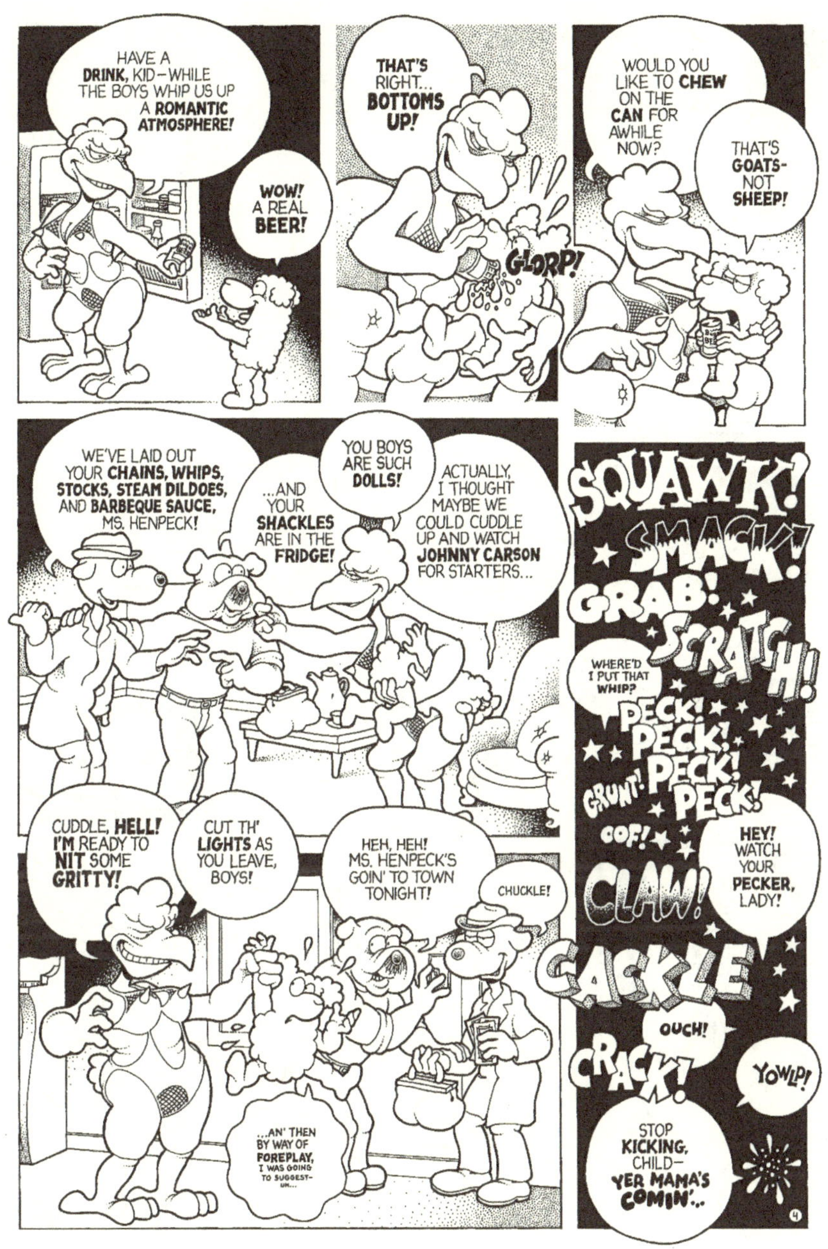

HAVE A DRINK, KID–WHILE THE BOYS WHIP US UP A ROMANTIC ATMOSPHERE!
WOW! A REAL BEER!
THAT'S RIGHT... BOTTOMS UP!
GLORP!
WOULD YOU LIKE TO CHEW ON THE CAN FOR AWHILE NOW?
THAT'S GOATS- NOT SHEEP!
WE'VE LAID OUT YOUR CHAINS, WHIPS, STOCKS, STEAM DILDOES, AND BARBEQUE SAUCE, MS. HENPECK!
...AND YOUR SHACKLES ARE IN THE FRIDGE!
YOU BOYS ARE SUCH DOLLS!
ACTUALLY, I THOUGHT MAYBE WE COULD CUDDLE UP AND WATCH JOHNNY CARSON FOR STARTERS...
CUDDLE, HELL! I'M READY TO NIT SOME GRITTY!
CUT TH' LIGHTS AS YOU LEAVE, BOYS!
HEH, HEH! MS. HENPECK'S GOIN' TO TOWN TONIGHT!
CHUCKLE!
...AN' THEN BY WAY OF FOREPLAY, I WAS GOING TO SUGGEST- UH...
SQUAWK!
SMACK!
GRAB!
SCRATCH!
WHERE'D I PUT THAT WHIP?
PECK! PECK! PECK! PECK!
GRUNT!
OOF!
CLAW!
HEY! WATCH YOUR PECKER, LADY!
CACKLE
OUCH!
CRACK!
YOWLP!
STOP KICKING, CHILD– YER MAMA'S COMIN'..
4

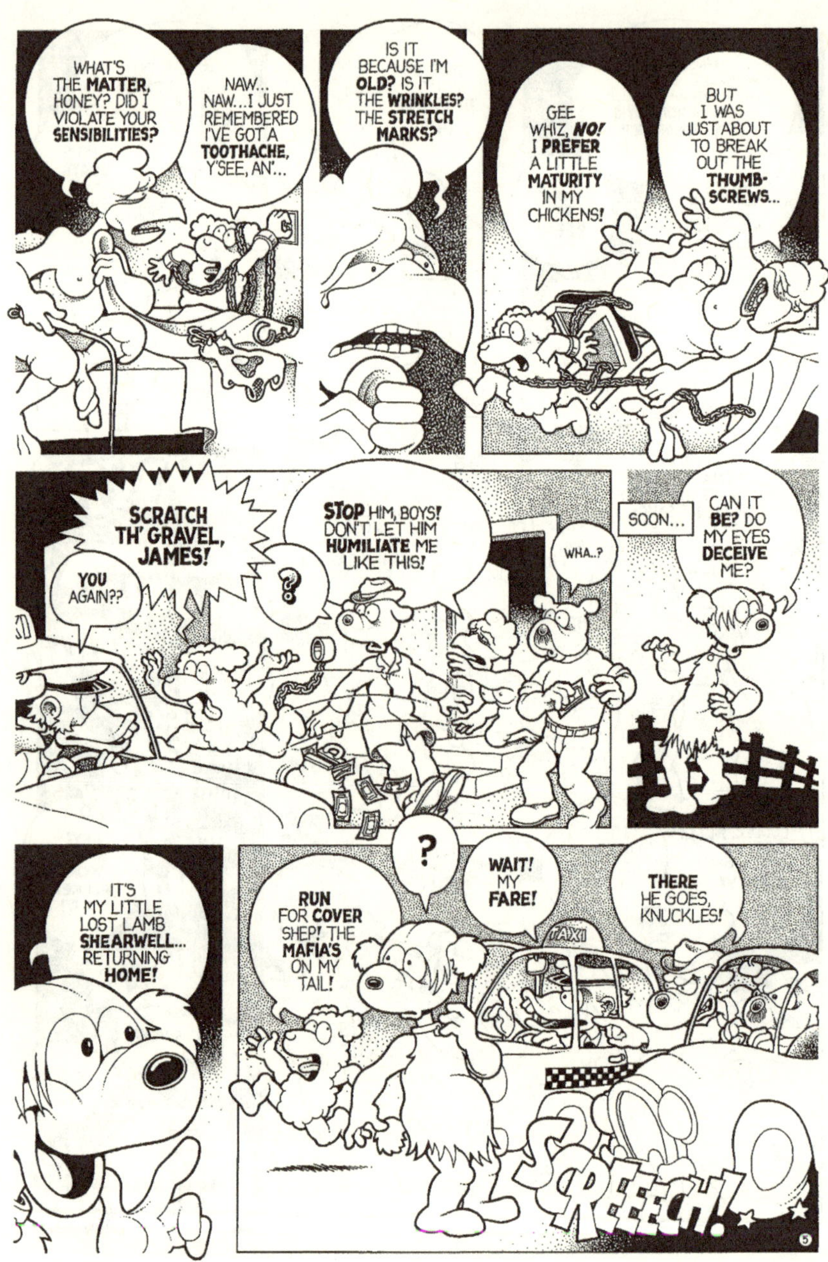
WHAT'S THE MATTER, HONEY? DID I VIOLATE YOUR SENSIBILITIES?
NAW... NAW...I JUST REMEMBERED I'VE GOT A TOOTHACHE, Y'SEE, AN'...
IS IT BECAUSE I'M OLD? IS IT THE WRINKLES? THE STRETCH MARKS?
GEE WHIZ, NO! I PREFER A LITTLE MATURITY IN MY CHICKENS!
BUT I WAS JUST ABOUT TO BREAK OUT THE THUMB-SCREWS...
YOU AGAIN??
SCRATCH TH' GRAVEL, JAMES!
?
STOP HIM, BOYS! DON'T LET HIM HUMILIATE ME LIKE THIS!
WHA..?
SOON...
CAN IT BE? DO MY EYES DECEIVE ME?
IT'S MY LITTLE LOST LAMB SHEARWELL... RETURNING HOME!
RUN FOR COVER SHEP! THE MAFIA'S ON MY TAIL!
?
WAIT! MY FARE!
THERE HE GOES, KNUCKLES!
TAXI
SCREEECH!
5

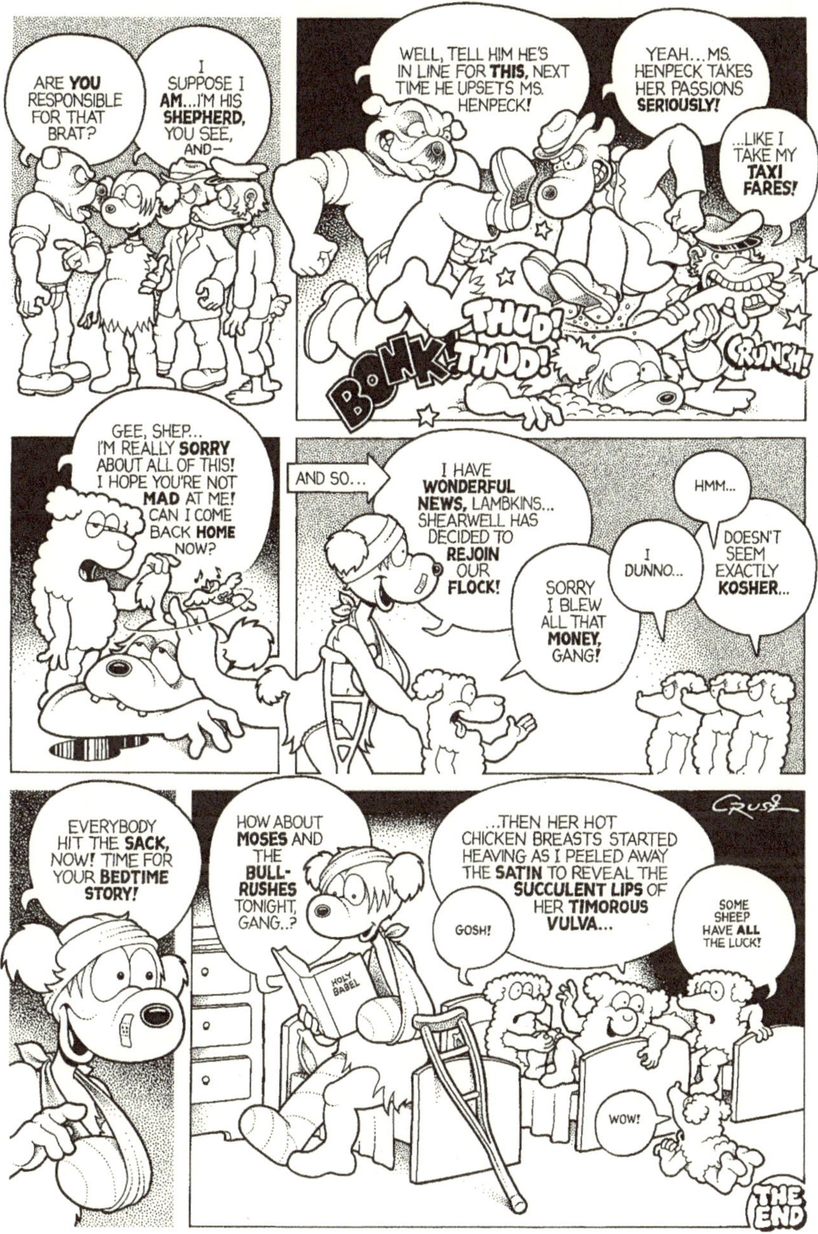

"Shearwell in 'The Prodigal Sheep'" copyright the estate of Howard Cruse. Used by permission.

Acknowledgments

This project started because Frederick Luis Aldama asked if I was interested in proposing a book for his new Critical Graphics series from Rutgers University Press. When he described his vision for the series, one of the first names that came to mind was Howard Cruse. I had recently finished the book *Autobiographical Comics* for Bloomsbury. One of the thoughts that occurred to me while working on that project was that so many important underground cartoonists did not have good collections of their short works that could be used in a classroom. So, I'm grateful to Frederick for reaching out in the first place and for being so positive and enthusiastic about the project from the beginning. This was not the first time Frederick asked me to be involved in one of his many scholarly enterprises, so my gratitude extends beyond just this one project. He is a model for the kindness, generosity, and mentorship we should all try to emulate.

This project received generous support from the University of South Carolina's Research Initiative for Summer Engagement (RISE) Program, which provided funding for a weeklong research trip to Columbia University's Rare Book and Manuscript Library in July 2019 to work in the Denis Kitchen and Howard Cruse archives. Thanks to Karen Green, Carolyn Smith, and the staff at the Rare Book and Manuscript Library for helping to make that research both productive and enjoyable. Thanks also to Karen for taking me out to lunch and for all of the support she has continued to give for this project since, including input on the title. In a late stage of this book's production, Karen provided some last-minute research help by tracking down a source that had eluded me.

I'm grateful for the community of comics scholars who have provided both moral and research support throughout this project. The many messages I received that said "I'm looking forward to this book!" gave me further motivation to get it done. Thanks go to Qiana Whitted, Brannon Costello, Brian Cremins, Zack Kruse, Justin Wigard, Julian Chambliss, Dale Jacobs, Rachel Miller, Osvaldo Oyola, Jeremy Carnes, Brittany Tullis, Johnathan Flowers, Marc Singer, José Alaniz, Carol Tilley, Nick Miller, Leah Misemer, Francesca Lyn, Adrienne Resha, Frederik Byrn Køhlert, Charles Hatfield, Sydney Heifler, Dale Jacobs, Biz Nijdam, Aaron Kashtan, and many other comics scholars who listened to me talk about this project (either face to face or virtually) or just hung out with me at conferences. Thanks also to Colin Beineke for the many Facebook Messenger exchanges about independent comics publishing in the 1980s and 1990s. And special thanks to Margaret Galvan for not only her encouragement and inspiring scholarship, but also for some clutch research help, even sending me some rare references unsolicited. Margaret also gave me some thorough and essential suggestions that helped to make this a better book, and she helped me work through some of the more difficult problems that came up as the book progressed. I'm truly grateful for her help.

Speaking of research help, thanks to Craig Yoe and Ger Apeldoorn for providing me with a scan of Cruse's humor piece in *Fooey* 3. I had despaired of the possibility of ever seeing that obscure work, but Ger and Craig came through. Its inclusion in this book allows me to cover an even wider range of Cruse's cartooning career than I had originally planned. Also, their book, *Behaving Madly*, about the many *Mad* knockoffs from the 1950s and later, is a blast.

I'm also lucky to work with a group of supportive colleagues at the University of South Carolina Sumter. Thanks to the faculty and administration there for the tangible and intangible ways that they helped with this project. Special thanks to the best administrative assistant, Rachel Webb, for helping with some of the details of this project, but also just listening as I talked through ideas and issues I was having with it.

Nicole Solano at Rutgers University Press was especially supportive during the course of this project, shepherding the proposal through the approval process, answering questions, and being generous when I needed more time. Thanks also go out to Alissa Zarro for her assistance, as well as Sherry Gerstein and Barbara Goodhouse, whose copyediting helped make this a better book.

During the process of researching and writing this book, I lost two close friends: Derek Parker Royal and Tom Spurgeon. I learned of Derek's death through a text message from a mutual friend—the text coming while I was disembarking from a plane on my return home from Columbia University to research this book. As editor of the Bloomsbury Comics Studies series, Derek invited me to do the *Autobiographical Comics* book, where I first got to write about Howard Cruse. And as founder and cohost of the *Comics Alternative* podcast, he helped introduce me to a wider world of underground and independent comics, as well as connecting me with a variety of creators through our interviews, including Denis Kitchen. Tom was also an important connector in my life—I can trace most of the people I know in comics and comics studies through Derek and Tom. Tom also gave me a much-needed break by letting me participate in the great Cartoon Crossroad Columbus festival in September 2019, which helped me get out of my head for a weekend, recharge, and remember why I love comics.

Thanks to Allan Cruse for his comments on parts of the manuscript.

In my copy of *The Best of Comix Book*, Denis Kitchen wrote, "To Andy, who knows way too much about comix!" He also once told me that he liked the cut of my jib. I consider those two of the best compliments I have ever received. When I reached out to Howard and Denis to get permissions for this project, they were both incredibly supportive, and Denis was generous with his time and advice from the start. He went out of his way to be helpful, even reading over the manuscript before I sent it in. I'm particularly thankful for the scan of a greeting card that Howard drew for Kitchen Sink. Stacey Kitchen and John Lind also provided some much-needed help with images for this book.

After Howard passed away, his husband, Ed Sedarbaum, stepped in to provide the high-resolution page scans that appear in this book. He generously read through the manuscript and provided essential corrections and additions. He also regularly encouraged and inspired me to make a book that would reflect Howard's legacy. Howard and Eddie's forty-year relationship is an inspiration to all of us. I'm grateful that Ed continued to trust me on this book, and for the invaluable input he provided.

When I first reached out to Howard about this project, I was incredibly nervous, and I stressed over the initial email message. His response, though, put me at ease, and his enthusiasm for the project carried me through, even posthumously. Of course, the project I proposed to him was different than this end result, primarily because I also asked if he would participate in a career-spanning interview that would anchor this book. He generously agreed, but that interview never happened, to my regret. In the meantime, though, he did email me with anecdotes and sources to help me along, and he was more than generous with his permissions to use his comics and letters. I appreciate that generosity and trust. And so, I want to thank Howard for his lifetime of inspiring work and for his support of this project.

Thanks to my parents for the support and encouragement in my lifelong comics habit. Even more specific, thanks for buying me that $12 subscription to *Comics Scene* magazine, where I was first exposed to Howard Cruse's work. That was a lot of money in 1983.

And to Jennifer, who is not only the best puppy and kitty mommy, but also the best partner. I am so lucky and grateful that you are in my life.

Notes

Chapter 1 Critical Biography

1 For more on the success of Dell Comics as the dominant comics publisher in the 1940s and 1950s, and its relationship with Western, see Gabilliet 40. In the early 1950s, Dell accounted for a third of all comic book sales, with eleven titles that sold between nearly one million and two million copies each month. Dell's best-selling title, *Walt Disney's Comics and Stories*, had as many as three million copies in print during the first half of the decade (Gabilliet 40).

2 Cruse describes his affection for the Barks Duck comics in his "Loose Cruse" column, "Ducks and a Legacy," from *Comics Scene* 5 (Sept. 1982). Fans figured out that there was a "good duck artist" whose work could be identified in comparison to that of other cartoonists, but it wasn't until 1960 that intrepid fans were able to figure out that the artist whose work they revered was Carl Barks. See Barrier 324–325.

3 For more on *Fooey*, *Sick*, and other *Mad* imitators, see Apeldoorn and Yoe, *Behaving Madly*.

4 On his website, Cruse provides an early paper that he wrote as a freshman at Indian Springs. The essay, "Slang & Profanity," shows just how quickly Cruse embraced the pedagogy of self-assessment and questioning beliefs that the school encouraged. In 2014, Cruse adapted the essay as a comic strip for the website.

5 According to Ed Sedarbaum, the Famous Artists Cartoon Course was an anonymous gift to Cruse. He later learned that the gift came from Doc Armstrong, the head of Indian Springs School (email to author, 8 Aug. 2020).

6 When Howard and Pam's daughter turned twenty-one, she sought out her birth parents. She and Howard continued to have a close relationship until his death.

7 The John Birch Society is an ultraconservative organization whose influence over right-wing politics was gaining traction during Cruse's college years. The society promoted a conspiracy theory that communists had infiltrated U.S. society up to the highest levels of government. Hence, Cruse's title "Commonest Conspiracy"

is a play on "Communist Conspiracy," and it also shows the kind of wordplay that Cruse would favor in later works.

8 Tiny Tim and LSD play important roles in another major event: it was following a Tiny Tim concert, while tripping on acid, that Cruse stumbled into the Stonewall Riots in late June 1969, as documented in "That Night at the Stonewall."

9 See Hatfield, *Alternative Comics* 3–31 for more on this transition.

10 Thanks to Karen Green for tracking down and sending to me a copy of Benson's hard-to-find article.

11 Underground comix publishing was quite different from mainstream comics publishing, so these sales figures may require some explanation. Kitchen Sink, like most other underground publishers, did not treat its comic books like periodicals in the way that mainstream comic book publishers did. That is, while mainstream comic books sold on newsstands, with each issue replaced by a new one on a regular basis (usually monthly, bimonthly, or quarterly), underground comix were more perennial. Publishers would keep their comic books in stock for reorder from dealers and would go through additional printings if the backstock ever ran out before demand was extinguished. Many underground comix would continue selling and generating royalty revenue for creators long after the initial publication, sometimes even years later. For example, *Barefootz Funnies* 1 continued to sell around 100–200 copies a quarter until the original 10,000-copy print run was nearly sold out in September 1980, more than five years after its first publication. Another way in which underground comix publication was different from the mainstream: undergrounds were usually not published on a regular schedule, and there could be months, if not years, between issues.

12 Though issue 2 did not sell well, Cruse and his investors still went forward with a third issue of *Barefootz Funnies* in December 1979, this time raising the price from 75 cents to $1.25, hoping that the extra 50 cents would make the book profitable even with lower sales. In 1986, Renegade Press, an alternative publisher run by Deni Loubert, released another *Barefootz* comic book—*Howard Cruse's Barefootz: The "Comix Book" Stories*—which reprinted all of the strips from the Kitchen-edited *Comix Book* magazine.

13 Though Cruse was done publishing new *Barefootz* comics 1979, with the release of *Barefootz Funnies* 3, he did make one more attempt to pitch the series as a syndicated comic strip in 1985. The samples he created for the strip have never been printed.

14 This description comes from the draft submission of the card located in Denis Kitchen's papers at Columbia University.

15 Larry Page "Deacon" Maccubbin is a pioneering figure in LGBTQ history as cofounder of the Lambda Rising bookstores, which started in Washington, D.C., in 1974, and as an organizer of the first Gay Pride Day in the nation's capital the following year. He also notably hosted the Lambda Literary Awards for achievement in queer literature.

16 At least part of that hesitance seems to come from Kitchen's disappointment with the sales of the greeting cards. While he had success with the adult holiday cards, the "all-season" cards flopped, with Cruse's gay-themed card one of the worst sellers, according to a December 23, 1977, letter from Kitchen.

17 More on Cruse's work for *Playboy* and his departure from the magazine can be found in chapter 4.

18 Though Rand Holmes's cover was generally well received, Mary Wings objected to it in a letter that Cruse published in *Gay Comix* 3. She specifically objected to two elements on the cover. First, she felt that the giant penis seen through the shorts of

the foreground figure violated Cruse's resistance to "genitally oriented" comics, as expressed in his solicitation material for contributors. Second, she criticized the depiction of a female figure in the background drawn with enormous breasts.

19 For more on Lee Marrs's and Roberta Gregory's early queer comics, see Galvan, "Feminism Underground."

20 Galvan relies on Michael Warner's concept of "counterpublics" as they apply to sexuality and gender. As Galvan explains, "A counterpublic exists at a distance from and in opposition to a larger public, often on the basis of an identity at odds with oppressive norms like patriarchy and White supremacy" ("Making Space" 375). In these terms, queer communities can create and define their worlds, which is evident in the communities' creative activity in general, and in anthologies like *Gay Comix* in particular.

21 Galvan summarizes, discusses, and analyzes the initial correspondence between Camper and Cruse in "Making Space" 377–378.

22 The brackets in this quote are found in the original.

23 Gay periodicals had a tradition of featuring regular comics, as Sina Shamsavari details. Shamsavari identifies the spy parody *Harry Chess: That Man from A.U.N.T.I.E.* appearing in *Drum* starting in 1964 as "the first ongoing gay comic strip." The *Advocate,* in its earliest incarnation as the *Los Angeles Advocate,* ran Joe Johnson's one-panel gag strip, *Miss Thing,* beginning in 1967, and later Johnson's *Big Dick.* Other comic strips published in the *Advocate* include Sean's *Gayer Than Strange,* Donelan's *It's a Gay Life,* Tim Barela's *Leonard & Larry,* and Alison Bechdel's *Servants to the Cause.*

24 Piranha Press was a short-lived imprint from DC Comics, running from 1989 to 1994, that tried to tap into the alternative comics market that had boomed earlier in the 1980s but had experienced its bust by 1986. Under the editorship of Mark Nevelow, Piranha released an eclectic mix of comics and illustrated books, like Kyle Baker's *Why I Hate Saturn,* Dave Louapre and Dan Sweetman's *Beautiful Stories for Ugly Children,* Gerard Jones and Mark Badger's *The Score,* Marc Hempel's *Gregory,* Alison Marek's *Desert Streams,* and William Messner-Loebs and Sam Keith's *Epicurus the Sage,* as well as comics starring musical legend Prince.

25 Exceptions include histories of queer comics, like those by Hall (2012) and Shamsavari (2017), where Cruse's work on *Gay Comix* is highlighted as a watershed moment in that history.

26 Some of the scholarship on *Stuck Rubber Baby* also focuses on Cruse's use of popular culture from the era depicted in the graphic novel, like magazines, newspapers, and books (Bordelon) and both contemporaneous and original music (Dickel).

27 Even when he didn't provide an original story for a queer comics project, he often offered visible support in other ways. For example, he provided an introduction to Don Melia's *Buddies* 1 (1991), the UK equivalent of *Gay Comix,* thus providing a transatlantic and transhistorical continuity between the two series. He also had a history of contributing to benefit anthologies for various causes, like "The Woeful World of Winnie and Walt" in *Strip AIDS U.S.A.*, edited by Trina Robbins, Bill Sienkiewicz, and Robert Triptow (1988); and "Some Words from the Guys in Charge" from *Choices: A Pro-Choice Benefit Comic,* edited by Trina Robbins (1990). For more on "Some Words," see chapter 3. Thanks to Margaret Galvan for providing me with a scan of Cruse's introduction to *Buddies* 1.

Chapter 2 Autobiographical Fiction / Fictional Autobiography

1 For more on the challenges that autobiographical comics present to Lejeune's "autobiographical pact," see Kunka 5–10; El Refaie 17, 51–52; and Hatfield 124–127.

2 The letter contains enough information, including Bill's last name and other family and occupational details, that he could be easily identified. However, I have left out this identifying information due to ethical concerns about outing someone without their permission or knowledge. The decision to come out should be left to the individual.

3 Whether or not one considers Nancy and Sluggo "totally sexless" is open to debate.

4 For more on acid trip comics in the early underground, see Gardner, *Projections* 119–124. As Gardner explains the ultimate weakness of these plots, "In the end, acid trips don't often make for the best comics precisely because they reinscribe conventional narrative structure and—perhaps most importantly—leave little if any room for readerly participation" (*Projections* 124). Gardner does not address "The Guide" in this discussion, however.

Chapter 4 Parodies

1 Meyer's testimony is discussed in Nyberg (77) and Beaty (160–161).

2 Shary Flenniken was also a member of the Air Pirates, but she was not included in the lawsuit because she did not participate in the Disney parodies. Disney also included Last Gasp publisher Ron Turner in the lawsuit.

3 The Air Pirates case is long and complicated, and this brief summary does not do it justice. For a more thorough account of the case and the history of the Air Pirates, see Bob Levin, *The Pirate and the Mouse: Disney's War against the Counterculture*.

4 At the time, Cruse wrote to Denis Kitchen about the situation: "PLAYBOY apparently will run one more of my cartoons, but they have sent back to me everything else they were holding, including three finished that they had bought and paid for. The syndicates have them running scared about parodies, and PLAYBOY plans to virtually abandon them. I am shocked that PLAYBOY has allowed itself to be bullied, but I guess I don't really know the ins and outs of it. I am just concerned . . . that the idea of parody as a valid and protected form is being wiped out" (25 Aug. 1979).

5 This essay was originally published in *Comics Scene* 8 (March 1983) as part of the "Loose Cruse" series of opinion columns that appeared regularly in the magazine from 1982 to 1983. Spelling and grammar errors from the original have been silently edited. Copyright the estate of Howard Cruse. Used by permission.

6 "If Comic Strip Characters Answered Those Little Ads," written by Paul Krassner and drawn by Wally Wood, first appeared in issue 35 of *Mad* magazine (Oct. 1957). The story includes parodies of *Little Orphan Annie*, *Nancy*, *Dick Tracy*, Mickey Mouse and Donald Duck, *Alley Oop*, *Henry*, *The Phantom*, *Blondie*, and *Popeye*.

7 Cruse is describing the story "Mickey Rodent!," which appeared in *Mad*, no. 19 (Jan. 1955), written by Harvey Kurtzman and drawn by Will Elder. The story includes Mickey Rodent (with an unshaven, stubbly face), Darnold Duck, Goony, Pluted Pup, Minny Rodent, and other parodies of Disney characters in the background.

8 The publication of "Communique #1 from the M.L.F." led Disney to request that O'Neill be charged with contempt of court, as he continued to produce Disney

parodies despite losing the lawsuit. "M.L.F." stands for "Mouse Liberation Front."

9 Herbert Lawrence "Herblock" Block was a popular and influential Pulitzer Prize–winning political cartoonist whose career covered most of the twentieth century. Pat Oliphant is another one of the major political cartoonists of the second half of the twentieth century. Garry Trudeau created the daily comic strip *Doonesbury*, known for its political satire.

10 Henry Beard was one of the founding editors of *National Lampoon*, along with Doug Kenney and Rob Hoffman. He worked on the magazine from its founding in 1969 to 1975.

11 William M. Gaines was the publisher of EC Comics, which included *Mad* first as a comic book, then, starting in 1955, as a magazine. Gaines served as publisher of *Mad* until his death in 1992.

12 In the *Little Lulu* comics, Tubby actually had a look-alike cousin named Chubby, which Cruse may be alluding to here.

13 Jessica Q. Stark's analysis of the queerness evident in Ernie Bushmiller's *Nancy* comic strip can also be applied to *Little Lulu*, since both comics share many similarities, especially parallels between the Nancy/Sluggo and Lulu/Tubby relationships. Both comics also challenge conventions of gender identity, sexuality, and heteronormative practices as part of their "cute" humor (Stark 320–326). Stark's essay focuses on Joe Brainerd's *Nancy* parodies, which began in the 1960s and which went to further extremes than Cruse's, especially in terms of sexuality (for example, Brainerd has a series of images in which Nancy has sex with bald, mute comic strip character Henry). However, what Stark says about Brainerd's parodies could equally apply to Cruse's: "Brainerd's appropriations [from Bushmiller] reveal the queerness as having been always already resident within the mainstream iterations of *Nancy*" (327).

14 The story "Breaking Out" in the anthology *It Aint Me Babe Comix* is attributed to the It Aint Me Babe Basement Collective, with art credited to "Carole." The collective included Meredith Kurtzman, Peggy White, Michele Brand, Willy Mendes, Trina Robbins, Lisa Lyons, and Nancy Kalish. According to Trina Robbins in *The Complete Wimmen's Comix*, the artist Carole's last name is unknown ("Babes & Women" vii).

Works Cited

Anderson, Ho Che. "Rings True." *Comics Journal*, no. 182 (Nov. 1995): 103–105.

Apeldoorn, Ger, and Craig Yoe. *Behaving Madly*. IDW, 2017.

Armstrong, Julie Buckner. "*Stuck Rubber Baby* and the Intersections of Civil Rights Historical Memory." *Redrawing the Historical Past: History, Memory, and Multiethnic Graphic Novels*. Ed. Martha J. Cutter and Cathy J. Schlund-Vials. University of Georgia Press, 2018, 106–128.

Barrier, Michael. *Funnybooks: The Improbable Glories of the Best American Comic Books*. University of California Press, 2015.

Barrier, Michael, and Martin Williams. *A Smithsonian Book of Comic-Book Comics*. Smithsonian Institution, 1981.

Beaty, Bart. *Fredric Wertham and the Critique of Mass Culture*. University Press of Mississippi, 2005.

Beauchamp, Monte, ed. "Notes from the Underground." *Blab!*, no. 1 (1986); reprint (Spring 1993): 17–75.

Bechdel, Alison. Introduction. *Stuck Rubber Baby*, by Howard Cruse. First Second, 2020.

Bell, Blake. *"I Have to Live with This Guy!"* TwoMorrows, 2002.

Benson, John. "Perversions, Subversions, and Twisted Truths: The Comix Revolution." *Alternative Media* 11.1 (1979): 19–23.

Bill. Undated Letter to Howard Cruse. Howard Cruse Archive, Rare Book and Manuscript Library, Columbia University Library, Box 2, Folder 8.

Bordelon, David. "Picturing Books: Southern Print Culture in Howard Cruse's *Stuck Rubber Baby*." *Crossing Boundaries in Graphic Narrative: Essays on Form, Series and Genre*. Ed. Jake Jakaitis and James E. Wurtz. McFarland, 2012, 107–122.

Chute, Hillary. *Why Comics? From Underground to Everywhere*. Harper, 2017.

Comic-Con International. "32nd Annual Will Eisner Comic Industry Awards / Comic-Con@Home 2020." *YouTube*, 24 July 2020.

Cruse, Allan B. "How Doc Did It?" http://fly.hiwaay.net/~mdsmith/iss-cruse-story1.htm.

———. Undated Letter to Bill. Howard Cruse Archive, Rare Book and Manuscript Library, Columbia University Library, Box 2, Folder 8.
Cruse, Howard. *The Complete Wendel*. Universe, 2011.
———. "The Dream of Democracy." http://www.iss-alums.net/democracy-dream-howardcruse.htm.
———. "Ducks and a Legacy." *Comics Scene*, no. 5 (Sept. 1982): 22–24.
———. *Early Barefootz*. Fantagraphics, 1990.
———. *From Headrack to Claude: Collected Gay Comix*. Northwest Press, 2012.
———. *Howard Cruse's Wendel Comix*. Kitchen Sink, 1990.
———. Introduction. *Gay Comix*, no. 1 (Sept. 1980).
———. Letter to Bill. 5 Jan. 1982. Howard Cruse Archive, Rare Book and Manuscript Library, Columbia University Library, Box 2, Folder 8.
———. Letter to Deacon (Larry Page Maccubbin). 31 Jan. 1977. Kitchen Sink Press Records, Rare Book and Manuscript Library, Columbia University Library, Correspondence, Primary Correspondence Box 2, Howard Cruse Folder 3.
———. Letter to Denis Kitchen. 23 May 1977. Kitchen Sink Press Records, Rare Book and Manuscript Library, Columbia University Library, Correspondence, Primary Correspondence Box 2, Howard Cruse Folder 3.
———. Letter to Denis Kitchen. 13 July 1973. Kitchen Sink Press Records, Rare Book and Manuscript Library, Columbia University Library, Correspondence, Primary Correspondence Box 2, Howard Cruse Folder 1.
———. Letter to Denis Kitchen. 9 Aug. 1976. Kitchen Sink Press Records, Rare Book and Manuscript Library, Columbia University Library, Correspondence, Primary Correspondence Box 2, Howard Cruse Folder 2.
———. Letter to Denis Kitchen. 29 Nov. 1976. Kitchen Sink Press Records, Rare Book and Manuscript Library, Columbia University Library, Correspondence, Primary Correspondence Box 2, Howard Cruse Folder 2.
———. Letter to Denis Kitchen. 25 Aug. 1979. Kitchen Sink Press Records, Rare Book and Manuscript Library, Columbia University Library, Correspondence, Primary Correspondence Box 2, Howard Cruse Folder 4.
———. Letter to Denis Kitchen. 29 Jan. 1984. Kitchen Sink Press Records, Rare Book and Manuscript Library, Columbia University Library, Correspondence, Primary Correspondence Box 2, Howard Cruse Folder 6.
———. Letter to Jackie Urbanovic. 24 Jan. 1983. Howard Cruse Archive, Rare Book and Manuscript Library, Columbia University Library, Box 2, Folder 11.
———. Letter to Jan Strnad. 18 Jan. 1984. Howard Cruse Archive, Rare Book and Manuscript Library, Columbia University Library, Box 3, Folder 2.
———. Letter to John Benson. 8 Sept. 1979. Howard Cruse Archive, Rare Book and Manuscript Library, Columbia University Library, Box 2, Folder 3.
———. Letter to Nancy and Jon. 31 Jan. 1981. Howard Cruse Archive, Rare Book and Manuscript Library, Columbia University Library, Box 2, Folder 5.
———. Letter to Richard Bruning. 13 Feb. 1982. Howard Cruse Archive, Rare Book and Manuscript Library, Columbia University Library, Box 2, Folder 8.
———. *The Other Sides of Howard Cruse*. Boom!, 2012.
———. "Slang & Profanity." *Howard Cruse's Occasional Comix*. 2014. http://www.howardcruse.com/cruseblog/occasionalcomix/slangandprofanity.html.
———. *Stuck Rubber Baby*. Paradox Press-DC Comics, 1995.
———. *Stuck Rubber Baby: 25th Anniversary Edition*. Introduction by Alison Bechdel. First Second, 2020.

———. Undated solicitation letter for *Gay Comix* 1. Kitchen Sink Press Records, Rare Book and Manuscript Library, Columbia University Library, Correspondence, Primary Correspondence Box 2, Howard Cruse Folder 4.

———. *Wendel All Together.* Olmstead Press, 2001.

———. *Wendel on the Rebound.* St. Martin's, 1989.

Dentith, Simon. *Parody.* Routledge, 2000.

Dickel, Simon. "'Can't Leave Me Behind': Racism, Gay Politics, and Coming of Age in Howard Cruse's *Stuck Rubber Baby.*" *American Comic Books and Graphic Novels.* Spec. issue of *Amerikastudien / American Studies* 56.4 (2011): 617–635.

El Refaie, Elisabeth. *Autobiographical Comics: Life Writing in Pictures.* University Press of Mississippi, 2012.

Gabilliet, Jean-Paul. *Of Comics and Men: A Cultural History of American Comic Books.* Trans. Bart Beaty and Nick Nguyen. University Press of Mississippi, 2010.

Galvan, Margaret. "Feminism Underground: The Comics Rhetoric of Lee Marrs and Roberta Gregory." *WSQ: Women's Studies Quarterly* 43.3–4 (2015): 203–222.

———. "Making Space: Jennifer Camper, LGBTQ Anthologies, and Queer Comics Communities." *Journal of Lesbian Studies* 22.4 (2018): 373–389.

Gardner, Jared. "Autography's Biography, 1972–2007." *Biography* 31.1 (2008): 1–26.

———. *Projections: Comics and the History of Twenty-First Century Storytelling.* Stanford University Press, 2012.

Gay League. "Gay League's First Howard Cruse Interview from 1998." Interview by Anton Kawasaki. 24 Mar. 2020. https://gayleague.com/gay-leagues-first-howard-cruse-interview-from-1998/.

Hall, Justin, ed. *No Straight Lines: Four Decades of Queer Comics.* Fantagraphics, 2012.

Hatfield, Charles. *Alternative Comics: An Emerging Literature.* University Press of Mississippi, 2005.

It Aint Me Babe Basement Collective and Carole. "Breaking Out." *It Aint Me Babe Comix,* 1970, reprinted in *The Complete Wimmen's Comix,* vol. 1, Fantagraphics, 2016, 20–23.

Kitchen, Denis. Letter to Howard Cruse. 8 Dec. 1972. Kitchen Sink Press Records, Rare Book and Manuscript Library, Columbia University Library, Correspondence, Primary Correspondence Box 2, Howard Cruse Folder 1.

———. Letter to Howard Cruse. 14 Mar. 1973. Kitchen Sink Press Records, Rare Book and Manuscript Library, Columbia University Library, Correspondence, Primary Correspondence Box 2, Howard Cruse Folder 1.

———. Letter to Howard Cruse. 10 July 1973. Kitchen Sink Press Records, Rare Book and Manuscript Library, Columbia University Library, Correspondence, Primary Correspondence Box 2, Howard Cruse Folder 1.

———. Letter to Howard Cruse. 28 Mar. 1974. Kitchen Sink Press Records, Rare Book and Manuscript Library, Columbia University Library, Correspondence, Primary Correspondence Box 2, Howard Cruse Folder 1.

———. Letter to Howard Cruse. 10 Dec. 1974. Kitchen Sink Press Records, Rare Book and Manuscript Library, Columbia University Library, Correspondence, Primary Correspondence Box 2, Howard Cruse Folder 1.

———. Letter to Howard Cruse. 4 Feb. 1975. Kitchen Sink Press Records, Rare Book and Manuscript Library, Columbia University Library, Correspondence, Primary Correspondence Box 2, Howard Cruse Folder 2.

———. Letter to Howard Cruse. 28 Jan. 1977. Kitchen Sink Press Records, Rare Book and Manuscript Library, Columbia University Library, Correspondence, Primary Correspondence Box 2, Howard Cruse Folder 3.

———. Letter to Howard Cruse. 23 Dec. 1977. Kitchen Sink Press Records, Rare Book and Manuscript Library, Columbia University Library, Correspondence, Primary Correspondence Box 2, Howard Cruse Folder 3.

———. Letter to Howard Cruse. 21 Aug. 1979. Kitchen Sink Press Records, Rare Book and Manuscript Library, Columbia University Library, Correspondence, Primary Correspondence Box 2, Howard Cruse Folder 4.

Krassner, Paul, and Wally Wood. "If Comic Strip Characters Answered Those Little Ads." *Mad*, no. 35 (Oct. 1957): 7–9.

Kunert-Graf, Rachel. "Lynching Iconography: Looking in Graphic Narrative." *Inks* 2.5 (2018): 312–333.

Kunka, Andrew. *Autobiographical Comics*. Bloomsbury Comics Studies. Bloomsbury, 2018.

Kurtzman, Harvey, and Will Elder. "Mickey Rodent!" *Mad*, no. 19 (Jan. 1955): 1–7.

Lejeune, Philip. *On Autobiography*. University of Minnesota Press, 1989.

Levin, Bob, *The Pirates and the Mouse: Disney's War against the Counterculture*. Fantagraphics, 2003.

LGBTCenterNYC. "Howard Cruse: The Stonewall Oral History Project." Interview by Steven Palmer. National Park Service: Stonewall Oral History Project. Recorded 22 June 2018. Posted 18 Nov. 2019. https://youtu.be/exAbi5mrGhM.

Maccubbin, Larry P. Letter to Howard Cruse. 3 Feb. 1977. Kitchen Sink Press Records, Rare Book and Manuscript Library, Columbia University Library, Correspondence, Primary Correspondence Box 2, Howard Cruse Folder 3.

Mangels, Andy. "Out of the Closet and into the Comics—Part I." *Amazing Heroes*, no. 143 (15 June 1988): 39–53.

———. "Out of the Closet and into the Comics—Part II." *Amazing Heroes*, no. 144 (1 July 1988): 47–66.

Mazur, Dan, and Alexander Danner. *Comics: A Global History, 1968 to the Present*. Thames and Hudson, 2014.

Mescallado, Ray. "Easy Comparisons." *Comics Journal*, no. 182 (Nov. 1995): 99–102.

Nyberg, Amy Kiste. *Seal of Approval: The History of the Comics Code*. University Press of Mississippi, 1998.

Puc, Samantha. "Interview: Howard Cruse Dives into Queer Comics History & His Own Career as a Cartoonist." Interview with Howard Cruse. *The Beat*, 13 June 2019. https://www.comicsbeat.com/howard-cruse-interview/.

Richards, Gary. "Everybody's Graphic Protest Novel: *Stuck Rubber Baby* and the Anxieties of Racial Difference." *Comics and the U.S. South*. Ed. Brannon Costello and Qiana J. Whitted. University Press of Mississippi, 2012, 161–183.

Ringgenberg, Steve. "Sexual Politics and Comic Art." Interview with Howard Cruse. *Comics Journal*, no. 111 (Sept. 1986): 64–96.

Robbins, Trina. "Babes & Women." *The Complete Wimmen's Comix,* vol. 1, Fantagraphics, 2016, vii–xv.

Rubenstein, Anne. "Matters of Conscience: A Howard Cruse Interview." *Comics Journal*, no. 182 (Nov. 1995): 106–118.

Santos, Jorge J., Jr. *Graphic Memories of the Civil Rights Movement: Reframing History in Comics*. University of Texas Press, 2019.

Scott, Darieck, and Ramzi Fawaz. "Introduction: Queer about Comics." *American Literature* 30.2 (2018): 197–219.

Sedarbaum, Ed. Email to the author. 8 Aug. 2020.

Shamsavari, Sina. "The History of Gay Male Comics in America from before Stonewall to the 21st Century." *International Journal of Comic Art* 19.2 (2017). https://ualresearchonline.arts.ac.uk/id/eprint/12212/.

Sherman, Bill. "In Praise of *Barefootz*." *Cascade Comix Monthly*, no. 21 (May 1980): 12–13.

Spurgeon, Tom. "Comics Reporter Sunday Interview: Howard Cruse." *Comics Reporter*, 18 Nov. 2012. https://www.comicsreporter.com/index.php/cr_sunday_interview_howard_cruse/.

Stanley, John, and Irving Tripp. "Five Little Babies." *Marge's Little Lulu*, no. 38 (Aug. 1951).

Stark, Jessica Q. "*Nancy* and the Queer Adorable in the Serial Comics Form." *American Literature* 90.2 (2018): 315–345.

Tilley, Carol L. "Comics: A Once-Missed Opportunity." *Journal of Research on Libraries and Young Adults* 4 (May 2014). http://www.yalsa.ala.org/jrlya/2014/05/comics-a-once-missed-opportunity/.

Vance, James. "The Birth, Death, and Afterlife of *Comix Book*." *The Best of Comix Book*. Ed. Denis Kitchen and John Lind. Dark Horse Comics, 2013, 12–32.

Willinet. "I Must Be Important, 'Cause I'm in a Documentary!!" Film by Sean Wheeler. *Vimeo*, 6 Aug. 2013.

Wings, Mary. Letter to the Editor. *Gay Comics*, no. 3 (Dec. 1982).

Witek, Joseph. *Comic Books as History: The Narrative Art of Jack Jackson, Art Spiegelman, and Harvey Pekar*. University Press of Mississippi, 1989.

Index

About the Author

ANDREW J. KUNKA is a professor of English at the University of South Carolina Sumter. He is the author of *Autobiographical Comics*. He has also published articles and book chapters on Will Eisner, Kyle Baker, Doug Moench, Jack Katz, and Dell Comics.